AF553359

Sustaining India's Growth Miracle

Sustaining India's Growth Miracle

EDITED BY

JAGDISH N. BHAGWATI AND
CHARLES W. CALOMIRIS

Published by Stanza, 2008

ISBN-10: 81-89632-16-7
ISBN-13: 978-81-89632-16-8

Copyright © 2008 Jerome A. Chazen Institute of International Business

This English-language reprint edition is specially authorized by the original publisher, Columbia University Press, for publication and sale only in South Asia.

All rights reserved. No part of this book may be reproduced or transmitted in any form or by any means, electronic or mechanical, including photocopying, recording or by any information storage and retrieval system, without permission in writing from the publisher.

This book is sold subject to the condition that it shall not, by way of trade or otherwise, be lent, re-sold, hired out, or otherwise circulated without the publisher's prior consent in any form of binding or cover other than that in which it is published and without a similar condition including this condition being imposed on the subsequent purchaser.

stanza

An imprint of RAVE MEDIA
22-C, Pocket-C
Siddhartha Extension
New Delhi - 110 014

Printed & Bound by: Gopsons Papers Ltd., Noida

CONTENTS

CONTENTS

ACRONYMS

AIG	American International Group
APDRP	Accelerated Power Development and Reform Programme
AT&C	average transmission and commercial
BGS	Basic Generation Supply
BIFR	Board of Industrial and Financial Rehabilitation
BJP	Bharatiya Janata Party
BLS	Bureau of Labor Statistics
BPO	business processing outsourcing
BPT	business, professional, and technical
CAC	capital account convertibility
CARE	California Alternative Rates for Energy
CBO	Congressional Budget Office
CERC	Central Electricity Regulatory Commission
CMC	Computer Maintenance Corporation
CMM	Capability Maturity Model
CPSU	Central Public Sector Undertaking
CPUC	California Public Utilities Commission
CRR	cash reserve ratio
DMK	Dravida Munnetra Kazhagam
EC	European Commission
ECSFM	Empowered Committee of State Finance Ministers
E&H	education and health
EIA	Energy Information Administration
EPO	engineering processing outsourcing
ERP	Enterprise Resource Planning
EU	European Union

FCAC	fuller capital account convertibility
FDI	foreign direct investment
FERA	Foreign Exchange Regulation Act
FERC	Federal Energy Regulatory Commission
FICCI	Federation of Indian Chambers of Commerce and Industry
FPC	Fifth Pay Commission
FPI	Fund for Public Investment
FPRC	Fiscal Policy Review Council
FRBMA	Fiscal Responsibility and Budget Management Act
FRC	Fiscal Review Council
GDP	Gross Domestic Product
GFD	gross fiscal deficit
GST	goods and services tax
HRD	Human Resources and Development
IDA	Industrial Disputes Act
IDA	International Development Association
IIM	Indian Institute of Management
IIT	Indian Institute of Technology
IMF	International Monetary Fund
IMR	Information Management Resources
IR/PS	International Relations and Pacific Studies
ISC	Inter-State Council
ISO	independent system operator
IT	information technology
ITES	IT-enabled services
KPO	knowledge process outsourcing
LMP	locational marginal prices
MFA	Multi-Fiber Arrangement
MMC	Monopolies and Mergers Commission
MOA	Memorandum of Agreement
MOF	Ministry Of Finance
MOU	Memorandum of Understanding
NAS	National Accounts Statistics
NBER	National Bureau of Economic Research
NCLT	National Company Law Tribunals
NCMP	National Common Minimum Programme
NDA	National Democratic Alliance
NDC	National Development Council
NDTL	net demand and time liabilities

NEP	National Electricity Policy
NERGA	National Employment Rural Guarantee Act
NETA	New Electricity Trading Arrangements
NIC	National Informatics Centre
NIPFP	National Institute for Public Finance and Policy
NJBPU	New Jersey Public Bureau of Public Utilities
NOPR	notice of proposed rulemaking
NRI	nonresident Indian
NSDL	National Securities Depository Limited
NSS	National Sample Survey
PSBR	public-sector borrowing requirements
RBI	Reserve Bank of India
RGGVY	Rajiv Gandhi Grameen Vidhyutikaran Yojana
SCID	Stanford Center for International Development
SEB	state electricity board
SERC	State Electricity Regulatory Commission
SEZ	Special Economic Zone
SITC	Standard International Trade Classification
SLR	statutory liquidity ratio
SSI	small-scale-industry
STP	Software Technology Park
T&D	transmission and distribution
TFC	Twelfth Finance Commission
TFP	total factor productivity
TIN	Tax Information Network
TRC	Tax Reforms Committee
UGC	University Grants Commission
UPA	United Progressive Alliance
USPTO	U.S. Patent and Trade Office
VAT	value-added tax
WTO	World Trade Organization

EDITORS' ACKNOWLEDGMENTS

Upon completion of the October 2006 *India: An Emerging Giant* conference, we knew that the content presented at the conference by the talented group of India experts assembled at the event should be shared with a wider audience. Through the efforts of the School of International and Public Affairs at Columbia University and Columbia Business School's Jerome A. Chazen Institute of International Business, the conference was an enormous success, attracting prominent businesspersons, government officials, policy makers, and academics. We wish to extend special thanks to Saroj and Sreedhar Menon for their support of the conference. Professor Arvind Panagariya, the Jagdish Bhagwati Professor of Indian Political Economy, International and Public Affairs and Economics, and a contributor to the volume, played a key leadership role in coordinating both the conference and the volume.

The dedication and assistance of Myles Thompson and Marina Petrova of the Columbia University Press was very valuable and helped us to achieve the important task of publishing the work in a timely fashion.

Our job as editors was made much easier than it otherwise would have been through the help of Jennifer Tromba at the Chazen Institute, who was charged with the task of keeping all the authors and commentators (and the editors) on track in meeting their respective deadlines, and coordinating the schedules and paperwork related to the conferences. Her assistance was invaluable, and she managed the get the book to the press remarkably quickly and cheerfully.

Sustaining India's Growth Miracle

INTRODUCTION

Jagdish N. Bhagwati and Charles W. Calomiris

Beginning in the second half of the 1980s and especially during the 1990s and beyond, India's development strategy underwent a fundamental transformation. Government controls over a variety of economic decisions were relaxed, markets were given greater play, and the door to imports was opened considerably wider. These reforms placed the economy on a higher growth path, shifting the growth rate first to 6 percent per year and more recently, during the last four years, to the 8–9 percent range. The central question on the minds of many observers of India today is whether India can sustain this upward shift in the growth rate and whether the country can push it up further to the double-digits level.

On October 13–15, 2006, the Jagdish Bhagwati Chair in Indian Political Economy at the School of International and Public Affairs and Columbia Business School's Jerome A. Chazen Institute for International Business jointly convened a conference to consider this central question. The conference brought together leading economic scholars and political figures from India and the United States who have been participating for many years in the ongoing dialogue and discussion of India's future. The organizers deliberately chose to focus on a selected set of issues and sectors and to analyze them in-depth rather than superficially cover the whole range of big and small issues confronting the economy.

A highlight of the conference was the opening panel that focused on two broad sets of issues: India's development strategy since its independence, including recent economic reforms; and India's relations with the United States, especially in the context of the India-U.S. nuclear cooperation agreement. The panel brought together four luminaries: former Privatization Minister Arun Shourie, India's Ambassador to the United States Ronen Sen, former U.S. Ambassador to India Frank Wisner, and

Columbia University Professor Jagdish Bhagwati. Another notable event of the conference was a celebratory dinner featuring India's Commerce Minister Kamal Nath, who addressed the participants on the important subject of the rising economic weight of the Indian economy in the world.

This volume brings together nearly all of the papers presented by scholars at the conference, several of the comments on them by the discussants, proceedings of the opening panel, and the address given by Minister Nath. The papers and discussants' comments offer in-depth analysis of the key bottlenecks India must overcome to sustain and accelerate its growth, thereby pulling more and more of its citizens out of poverty. The panel offers a richly informed perspective on the economic reforms and U.S.-India relations by some of the most influential participants in these events. The address by Minister Nath offers a vision of where India is headed in the years to come.

In Chapter 1, Arvind Panagariya poses what he considers the central economic problem facing India today: transforming its traditional, rural economy into a modern one. He notes that almost three-fifths of the workforce in India is employed in agriculture, which contributes less than one fifth of the national income. Even in industry and services, much of the workforce is employed in the informal sector, with the organized sector employing less than one-tenth of the workforce. Panagariya points to an entirely stagnant share of manufacturing in income as the key factor explaining the continuing large share of agriculture and the informal sector in the workforce. In turn, this stagnant share is accompanied by very poor performance of the unskilled/labor-intensive sectors such as apparel, footwear, toys, and other light-industry products. These are the very products that China exported in large volumes in the 1980s and the first half of the 1990s.

Panagariya argues that if India is to move a significant proportion of its workforce out of agriculture, it must undertake a number of policy reforms to allow unskilled labor-intensive industry to grow rapidly while maintaining its lead in the information technology sector. He points to labor-market rigidities, absence of a proper bankruptcy law permitting smooth exit of firms, and infrastructure bottlenecks, especially in the power sector, as the key obstacles to the rapid expansion of an organized sector of labor-intensive industry. He suggests the reforms necessary in these areas, especially focusing on the liberalization of the labor market. Panagariya also discusses a set of reforms necessary to maintain India's lead in the software industry, a topic considered in much greater detail in Chapter 2. Barry Bosworth and Mihir Desai offer commentaries on Panagariya's arguments at the end of the chapter. While both commentators agree with much of the broad overview provided by Panagariya, they raise additional concerns, particularly relating to fiscal policy challenges, and to the scarcity of skilled labor.

In Chapter 2, T. N. Srinivasan offers a detailed description and analysis of the institutional structure of Indian fiscal policy, its evolution over time, its shortcomings, and a consideration of the costs arising from a failure to address those shortcomings. This wide-ranging overview draws particular attention to political and institutional problems associated with Indian federalism, and to the stubborn political barriers to reforming fiscal policy (e.g., the subsidization of rural electricity users, which has both a huge fiscal cost and creates a barrier to the rationalization of the electricity industry). Srinivasan also makes concrete suggestions for ways to break through some of the political logjams that have prevented coordinated progress in fiscal reform (e.g., the proposed creation of a Fiscal Policy Review Council). At the end of the chapter, Govinda Rao, a prominent policy maker in the area of Indian fiscal affairs, reinforces the themes articulated by Srinivasan, emphasizes the need to improve intergovernmental coordination and to harden the budget constraints of subnational governments, and offers his own views on the prospects for reform.

In Chapter 3, Frank Wolak presents a detailed discussion of the Indian electricity sector to which Panagariya points as a major bottleneck in the rapid growth of organized-sector manufacturing. Electricity supply to Indian industry is expensive and unreliable. On the other hand, farmers receive electricity at highly subsidized prices, sometimes even entirely free. This leads to wasteful use not only of electricity but also of valuable water resources. Most water pumps in the rural areas operate on electricity, and since there is no charge for water pumped from the ground, the provision of electricity free of charge drives the marginal cost of pumping water to zero. This naturally leads to wasteful pumping of water.

After reviewing the extent of key problems relating to subsidies, theft, and production incentives, and, on the other side, the efficiency advantages relating to scale, Wolak offers a detailed blueprint for reform. In particular, he considers the appropriate sequencing of reforms and argues that opening the industry to greater competition should not be the immediate objective of policy. Indeed, until basic incentives are improved and appropriate servicing and rate standards are put into place, he argues, competition could be destructive to industry performance and consumer welfare. In her comments, Jessica Wallack agrees that India must address its distribution problems before moving to a competitive market. She argues, however, that this is not just an economic problem but reflects political constraints related to the federal division of jurisdiction among India's government agencies. She suggests some possible ways to resolve this problem, namely, either an act of parliament to override states' authority or a change in the rules that would shift states' incentives by connecting service quality with higher prices.

In Chapter 4, Ashish Arora shines a spotlight on the software industry, which has been hailed as the major success story of India's recent growth experience. He notes that a measure of success of this industry is the growth of software exports from less than $1 billion in fiscal year 1996–97 (April 1, 1996, to March 31, 1997) to $23.4 billion in 2005–6. He offers a detailed discussion of its evolution of and reasons for the industry's success. Arora points to a reserve army of underemployed engineers in the early phase of the expansion of the industry; liberalization of electronics imports starting in the mid-1980s and accelerating in the 1990s; the relatively modest scale of firms that helped the industry escape the travails of the licensing regime; telecommunications reform and the creation of technology parks; and the existence of entrepreneurs, many of whom had useful overseas (mainly United States) connection or experience. He places special emphasis on the superior ability of local firms to exploit the pool of relatively inexpensive local engineering talent that India had to offer. Looking to the future, Arora voices some skepticism regarding India's ability to increase its importance as a global software innovator, but sees alternative strategies for moving up the value chain as more promising, particularly in the area of organization-intensive services. Arora recognizes that a crucial prerequisite for sustained growth in the information technology sector will be the continuing expansion of skilled labor, which will require further relaxations of regulatory limits on education. Frank Levy offers comments at the end of the chapter, focusing on barriers that confront information technology firms from countries like India when they seek to break into the global market. Levy highlights reasons not to project too far into the future from previous experience when judging the long-term comparative advantage of any country in the information technology supply chain.

Chapter 5 presents the panel discussion, chaired by Arvind Panagariya. The discussion is divided into two parts. First, the panel assesses progress in Indian economic policy and performance and identifies salient contributors to India's growth. Second, it considers the progress in India-U.S.

relations. Jagdish Bhagwati and Arun Shourie offer the principal perspectives on the first topic, and Ronen Sen and Frank Wisner lead the discussion of the second topic. Additionally, Sen and Wisner offer comments on the presentations by Bhagwati and Shourie, and Bhagwati and Shourie reciprocate by reacting to the presentations of Sen and Wisner.

Bhagwati argues that India failed to grow rapidly and reduce poverty in the early decades because it adopted an inward-looking and anti-market model of development. Slow growth meant that the direct benefit to the poor through employment growth was limited. It also meant that revenue growth was slow, making it harder to finance antipoverty programs. It was not until India introduced major reforms that effectively abandoned this policy framework, opened the economy to world markets, and gave entrepreneurs freer play that growth acceleration and significant poverty reduction began. Looking to the future, Bhagwati believes that the central question today is whether the Congress Party can deliver on the reforms that are stalled. Can it revive the privatization program and introduce labor market reforms that "introduce some obligations and not just rights for workers and which would be more compatible with an element of flexibility"? Bhagwati goes on to develop the broader perspective that openness, economic freedom, and political freedom constitute the ultimate keys to achieving sustained rapid growth.

Shourie concurs with Bhagwati, noting that liberalization under prime ministers Rao and Vajpayee had given a freer hand to entrepreneurs and resulted in massive restructuring in manufacturing while allowing many services sectors to takeoff. Indian entrepreneurs are now acquiring firms abroad in a major way. He also noted that privatization done during approximately three years of his tenure as Privatization Minister had been a major success. Production in the privatized enterprises has gone up by between 30 percent and 250 percent.

Shourie points to the crucial importance of the will of the prime minister in bringing about the policy change and implementing economic reforms. The critical question is whether he will take a firm stand. He cites the example of Prime Minister Vajpayee who faced serious opposition to some of the reforms from within his own party. But he stood firm and challenged the members to vote against him, and thus called their bluff. Shourie goes on to discuss other obstacles to reforms such as resistance within the relevant ministries, the nature of discourse that does not go beyond slogans, political culture that rewards opposition for the sake of opposition, and an entirely splintered electorate.

In his comments, Ambassador Sen emphasizes the importance of innovation, debate, and dissent, which have been important characteristics of Indian civilization. Echoing Bhagwati, he believes that democracy and market reforms are inseparable. He concludes by emphasizing the importance of investment in infrastructure, primary education, and health and nutrition. Ambassador Frank Wisner then offers some thoughts on economic developments in India from the viewpoint of U.S. business owners. He reminds us that the United States is currently the largest foreign investor in India and is likely to remain so for some years to come. Ambassador Wisner believes that while there is growing awareness among business professionals in the United States that India is growing rapidly, it is unlikely to grow as rapidly as China. He points out that "we have heard a very convincing argument tonight that the structure of Indian politics is going to lead to slow delivery of policy, which effects macroeconomic change." He also sees infrastructure bottlenecks, fiscal deficit, and skill shortages as key obstacles to pushing the growth rate to the Chinese level.

In the second half of Chapter 5, panelists turn to India-U.S. relations. Ambassador Sen begins by debunking the myth that during the Cold War era, India-U.S. relations were all bad and since the Cold War ended, everything has been hunky dory. He offers several examples of cooperation between the two countries during the 1980s, including the first non-NATO sale of supercomputers to India (before any other country), General Electric supplying engines for light combat aircraft, and the first science and technology agreement permitting the imports of dual-use technologies by India. Symmetrically, there was a period of benign neglect after the end of the Cold War until President Clinton's visit to India in 2000. Pointing to the Clinton visit as a "real watershed," Sen goes on to carefully describe increased cooperation between India and the United States in such areas as nanotechnology, biotechnology, information and communication technology, and defense technology. He concludes by describing India-U.S. cooperation in the economic field, especially through the instrumentality of the CEO Forum.

Ambassador Wisner describes the India-U.S. relationship as "extraordinary," adding that "a dramatically important page has been turned in the relationship and it will not be turned back." Tracing the origins of the change in the relationship, Wisner states, "The real change came, in an ironic manner, out of an act over which we both disagreed sharply. The great black cloud over the relationship since the 1970s, the nuclear test in India, caused hostility for a brief period but then actually changed the relationship for the better. For India was newly strengthened in her own sense of her position in the world, her self-regard; and the United States realized it had run its course in trying to hold back India's nuclear capability."

Referring to U.S.-India nuclear cooperation, Wisner expresses optimism for the conclusion of an agreement, "opening a major new chapter in American's life with India and, in my opinion, removing a major impediment to the nature of the relationship that has existed for many years." He also points out, however, that it will require considerable more work on each side to figure precisely where they take the relationship and how. While the two sides have declared their relationship to be strategic, ordinary people, government officials, and intellectuals on both sides have yet to figure out what it means.

In his comments, Bhagwati notes that the relationship between India and the United States has certainly matured in one important way: each side appreciates the constraints facing the other and is willing to be patient. This was best illustrated by the manner in which they both handled the nuclear test by India. On the U.S. side, when writing about the sanctions, President Clinton essentially said that his wife Hillary loved India, his daughter Chelsea loved India, but unfortunately he had to impose the sanctions. In turn, India took the sanctions in stride and did not become confrontational. India is now keen on moving forward and the United States sees a little better the value of democracy in a partner.

In the final comment, Shourie emphasizes the importance of multidimensional contacts: from cargo planes to open-skies to academic institutions. This will ensure that no single issue turns into a be-all-and-end-all of the relationship. In the early 1990s, the Dabhol power project became so central to the relationship that, after it closed down, the resumption of dialogue between the two sides became difficult. Shourie expresses the fear that a failure to conclude a nuclear cooperation agreement might lead to a similar outcome. He advises that each side should understand that in the end the other side will act in its own self-interest.

Chapter 6 presents the keynote speech by Minister Kamal Nath. He highlights several aspects of India's recent development that he argues will persist, including the end of state domination over the economy, the emergence of major new cities, the change in mind-set toward entrepreneurship, and the growing intolerance for corruption, laziness, and shoddy products. He emphasizes (as many of the contributions to this volume do) the interplay of economic and political factors affecting reform, and the special challenges that India faces as the world's largest democracy—notably the need for politicians to explain and defend reform and to deliver concrete accomplishments commensurate with the rising expectations of the electorate. Nath touches on virtually all of the themes raised elsewhere in the volume. He acknowledges the importance of infrastructure improvement, and shares Panagariya's view that manufacturing growth will be crucial for absorbing unskilled labor and that changes in labor laws will help to realize that objective. He advocates the use of special economic zones to spur foreign direct investment in India. He also argues that relaxation of trade barriers through a successful WTO round is important for the growth of India and other developing countries, and that Europe and the United States need to play a crucial leadership role in coordinating a successful negotiating round. Minister Nath ends his overview on an optimistic note, suggesting that India's engagement in the global economy has produced irreversible positive changes in expectations that will translate into sustainable growth: "In India today, the biggest changes are a change in perception and a change in government. Today, in government, there is a consciousness of never before; a consciousness of the expectations of the people of India and the expectations of the world from India, to which India must respond."

CHAPTER 1

Transforming India

Arvind Panagariya[1]

1. INTRODUCTION

India's economy has been growing at a rate of more than 6 percent since the late 1980s. In the last three years, the growth rate has been even higher—8 percent—bringing it close to East Asian levels. While skeptics argue that this shift merely represents a strong upswing in the business cycle, optimists see it as representing an upward movement in the trend growth rate. If optimists are right and the 8 percent growth rate is sustained, possibly even accelerated, we can truly begin to see the emergence of a giant economy in India. Even at the 8 percent rate, the economy will double in a matter of nine years.

In this chapter, I begin by presenting a cautiously optimistic view of the current growth. Some fundamental changes in the economy do seem to be occurring that suggest the growth rate may have crossed yet another milestone. As one example, the economy has moved toward integration into the world economy as never before: within the last three years, the ratio of exports of goods and services to the GDP has risen from 14.6 percent to 20.5 percent. Even more remarkable, this increase has taken place with the simultaneous growth in GDP in current dollars at the rate of 16 percent per annum.

Yet, even as the economy picks up pace and poverty continues to come down, doubts remain about the transformation of India from a primarily agricultural and rural economy to a modern one in the next two decades. Despite substantial growth and reduced poverty, this transformation has not progressed as far as one would expect based on the experience of other countries. For example, census data show that the proportion of rural population declined from 79 percent in 1991 to 77 percent in 2001. The share of the farm workers in the total workforce fell more—from 67 percent to 58 percent. However, much of this shift is accounted for by the expansion of the informal, unorganized sector. Unskilled jobs in the organized sector have simply not grown.

The main culprit behind this phenomenon is the slow growth of manufacturing in general and of unskilled labor-intensive manufacturing in particular. Whereas virtually all rapidly growing developing economies, such as those of Korea, Taiwan, and China, have seen declining shares of agriculture in their GDPs replaced by rising shares of manufacturing in the initial stages of development, India has witnessed an entirely stagnant share of manufacturing in its GDP since 1991. The decline in the output share of agriculture has been entirely absorbed by the growing share of services since 1991.

Therefore, the challenge of transformation facing India is that of creating an environment that allows unskilled labor-intensive manufacturing to grow rapidly and rise as a proportion of GDP. Such growth would pull workers from agriculture into gainful employment more rapidly than is the case currently, and it would reduce the burden of labor on the land. Agricultural wages would also rise faster than would be the case if there were not a rapid expansion of unskilled labor-intensive manufacturing.

Some have argued that the transformation to the modern economy need not require a switch to manufacturing. After all, according to the traditional growth pattern, once manufacturing reaches a certain stage, its share declines and that of services rises. India could simply skip the transitional stage and jump directly to the final stage of specialization in the services sector. The flaw in this argument, however, is that if workers are to be employed in the formal-service sector, they must be given college education. But the vast majority of the farm workers that need to be moved into the formal sector of the economy lack even high-school level education. Moreover, given the countrywide gross college enrollment ratio (the number of individuals in college as a proportion of the population in the 18-to-24 years age group) of 12 percent and the relatively poor prospects for further expansion of higher education, the idea that a large proportion of the population could receive a college education in the next two decades is tentative at best.

Therefore, if the objective is to achieve significant transformation of the economy within two decades, India must undertake the reforms necessary to allow faster growth of unskilled labor-intensive manufacturing. The argument developed in this chapter is that this requires significant reforms in two areas: labor markets and infrastructure. The chapter then goes on to advocate a "walk on two legs" approach whereby India must sustain the current high growth in the information-technology sector while improving the prospects for manufacturing.

2. IS INDIA FLYING? BUSINESS CYCLE UPSWING OR HIGHER TREND GROWTH?

In Panagariya (2007, Chapter 1), I argue that the performance of the Indian economy between 1951–52 and 2003–4 can be best related to the operative economic policies if we divide these fifty-three years into the following four phases: 1951–65, 1965–81, 1981–88 and 1988–04.[2] While this is not the place to repeat that discussion, the average annual growth rates during these four phases, shown in Figure 1.1, provide a useful starting point for this chapter. The figure shows that during the first two phases spanning 1951–81, India grew at what has come to be called the "Hindu" rate of growth of 3 to 4 percent. The growth rate shifted to 4.8 percent in the third phase spanning 1981–88 and to 6.1 percent in the fourth phase.

There are now indications that the trend growth rate in India may be shifting upward yet again. During the last three years, 2003–4 to 2005–6, the GDP at factor cost has been growing at the impressive rate of 8.1 percent. While it is too early to tell conclusively whether this shift

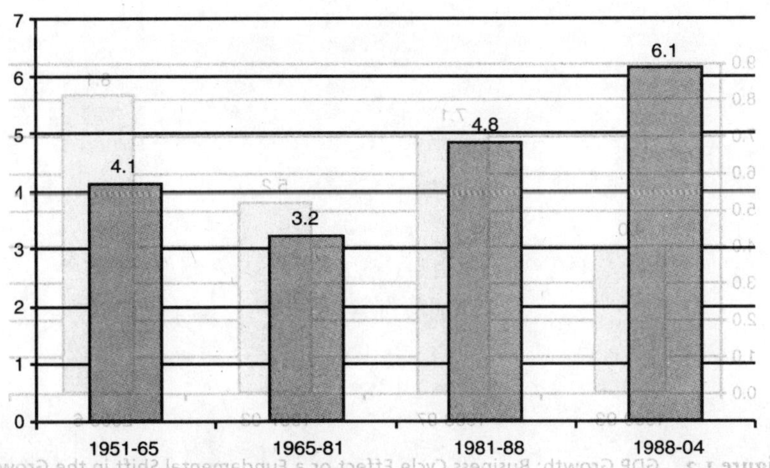

Figure 1.1 Growth Rates During Four Phases

represents an especially strong upswing in the business cycle or a jump in the long-term trend growth rate, on balance, evidence favors the latter hypothesis.

Before I explain the reasoning behind this assertion, it is useful to consider why the change may merely represent an upswing in the business cycle. Consider Figure 1.2, for example, which divides the period 1990–06 into four subperiods with high and low growth rates. The growth rate during 1990–93 was 4 percent. It rose to 7.1 percent during 1993–97 but fell again to 5.2 percent during 1997–03. Starting with 2003–4, the growth rate has risen once again, reaching the high average rate of 8.1 percent. It is not unreasonable to speculate that the rise is temporary and that the growth rate will drop yet again to the 5 to 6 percent range in a year or two.

Other evidence offers a more compelling case for the possibility that this growth rate would be sustained over a much longer period of time. In the last three years, the economy has produced some spectacular successes not witnessed in the empirically recorded history of India—successes that almost rival the performance of the Chinese economy. In turn, these successes are bringing fundamental changes in conditions that are likely to help the economy sustain the current growth rate. As an aside, these successes also raise doubts about the fears expressed by some observers that the high growth rate may largely reflect rising errors in the measurement of services, which account for a disproportionately large and rising part of the GDP. Evidence from some sectors that we are able to measure with reasonable accuracy points to very strong growth in the economy.

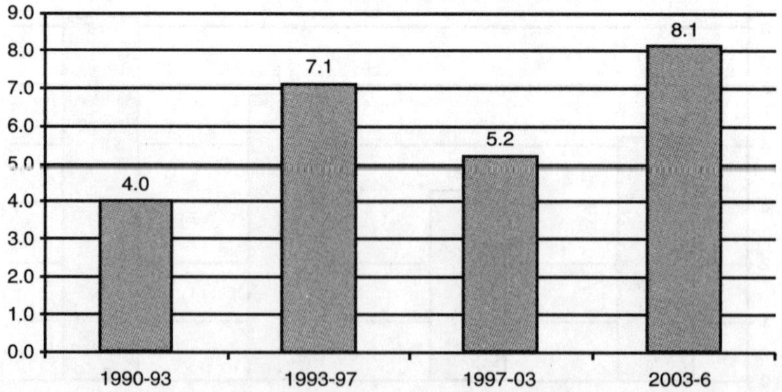

Figure 1.2 GDP Growth: Business Cycle Effect or a Fundamental Shift in the Growth Rate?

Let us consider first GDP in current dollars at the market exchange rate, which highlights a dramatic aspect of the current growth. GDP in current dollars is obtained by dividing GDP at current consumer-goods prices in rupees by the exchange rate. Because GDP in current rupees has risen at extremely high rates and the value of the rupee in dollars has also risen 9.3 percent during the last three years, GDP in current dollars has shown growth not seen before.[3] As Figure 1.3 shows, GDP rose from $506 billion in 2002–3 to $798 billion in 2005–6. This represents a 58 percent growth. The annual growth rate of GDP in current dollars during 2003–6 turns out to be a phenomenal 16.4 percent. Allowing for 3 percent inflation in the United States, this works out to a 13.4 percent annual growth in real U.S. dollars. If this growth rate could be sustained, GDP in India would surpass the U.S. GDP of $11.5 trillion in 2005 in just twenty-two years! While the likelihood of this outcome is close to nil, it remains true that given the stability of the rupee in terms of the dollar, the progress achieved in dollar terms will be largely retained rather than reversed by a massive depreciation.

An important distinguishing feature of the growth achieved during the last three years is that despite 9.3 percent appreciation of the rupee

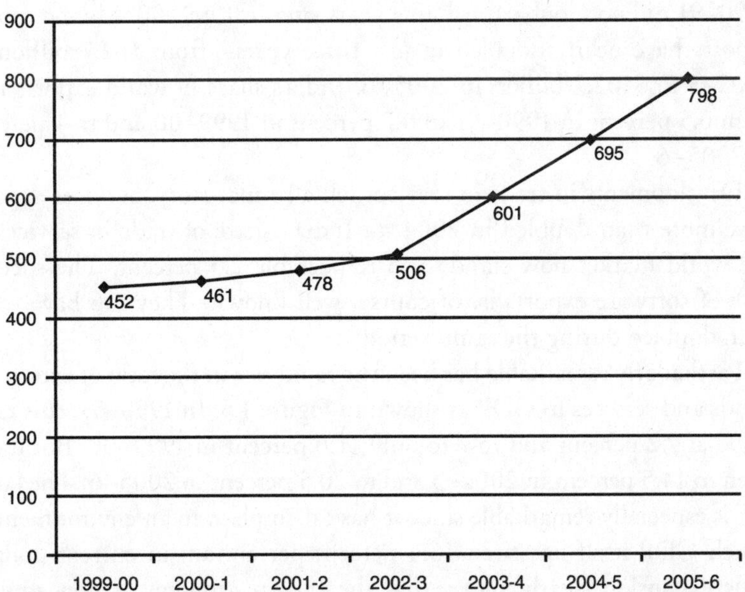

Figure 1.3 Dramatic 16.4% Annual Growth in the GDP in Current Dollars During 2003–6 ($billion)

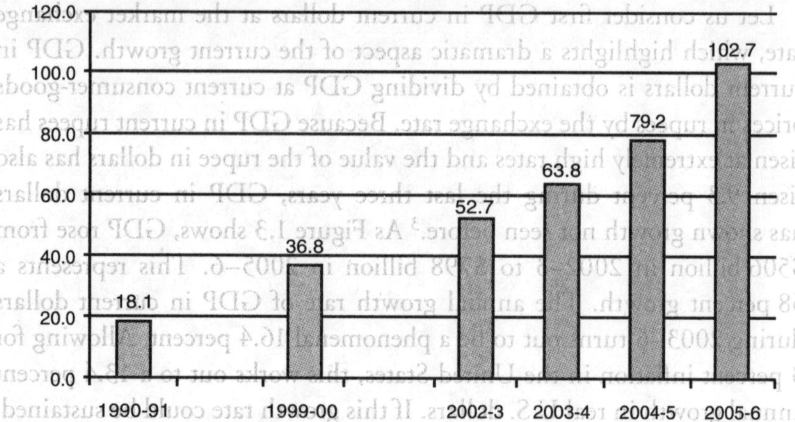

Figure 1.4 Merchandise Exports Have Doubled in Three Years ($billion—Current)

since 2002–3, trade has grown at an extraordinary pace. This is shown in Figure 1.4, with respect to merchandise exports. In 1990–91, India's merchandise exports in current dollars stood at $18.1 billion. During 2005–6, the increase in exports over the previous year alone topped that amount. To put the comparison slightly differently, in current dollars, exports in 1990–91 did not double until nine years later in 1999–00. More recently, exports have nearly doubled in just three years—from $52.7 billion in 2002–3 to $102.7 billion in 2005–6. India's share in world exports rose from 0.5 percent in 1990–91 to 0.7 percent in 1999–00 and to 1 percent in 2005–6.

Developments in trade in services tell a similar story. Services exports have more than doubled in 2004–6. India's share of trade in services in the world market now stands at a respectable 2.5 percent. The specific case of software exports is, of course, well known. They too have more than doubled during the same period.

Particularly remarkable has been the rapid rise in the ratio of exports of goods and services to GDP as shown in Figure 1.5. In 1990–91, this ratio stood at 7.2 percent and rose to only 11.6 percent in 1999–00. But it has risen to 14.5 percent in 2002–3 and to 20.5 percent in 2005–6. The latter rise is especially remarkable since it has taken place in an environment in which GDP itself has risen 16.4 percent per annum in current dollars. This expansion clearly shows that the Indian economy is now rapidly integrating into the world economy. To put this in perspective, the exports of goods and services as a proportion of GDP in China, at 26 percent as

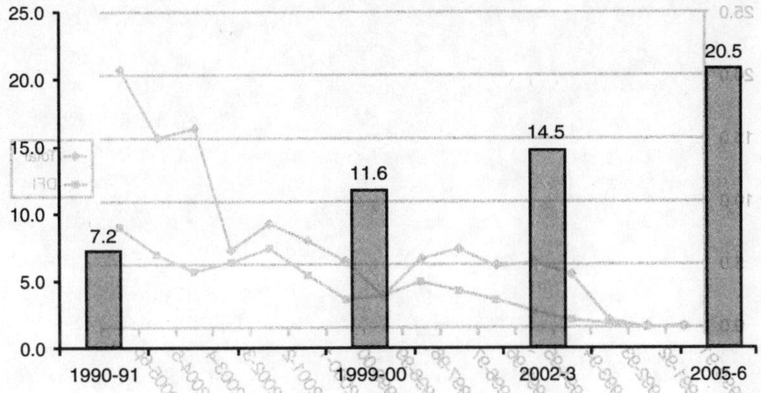

Figure 1.5 Exports (Goods + Services) to GDP Ratio

recently as 2000, were not wildly higher. At the current pace, India would catch up with that ratio in another three years.

Foreign investment inflow, which had remained sluggish for many years after initial liberalization in 1992, has also seen a major upward shift in the last three years. From just $6 billion in 2002–3, the total foreign investment into India has risen to $20 billion in 2005–6. Though direct foreign investment has also received a boost in the past three years, for reasons to be explained later, the bulk of the foreign investment into India has taken the form of portfolio investment. When we add even larger inflows of remittances that bring no foreign liabilities abroad with them, inflows of foreign resources in 2005–6 amount to $45 billion, a figure that exceeds that for direct foreign investment in China up until 2001. Figures 1.6 and 1.7 show the evolution of foreign investment and remittances, respectively, since 1990–91.

Similar dramatic changes have taken place in some sectors that are currently serving virtually exclusively the domestic market and do not have significant presence in the external sector. The story of the expansion of telecommunications is perhaps the best known of these successes. In 1990–91, India had just five million telephone lines in total. During April to July 2006, telephone lines expanded at the rate of more than five million *per month*.

Figure 1.8 shows the dramatic expansion of telephones between July 31, 2005, and July 31, 2006, and relates it to the total telephone lines in 1990–91. At the end of July 2006, the total number of telephone lines stood at 158 million. Of these, 117.2 million lines were cellular. The nationwide

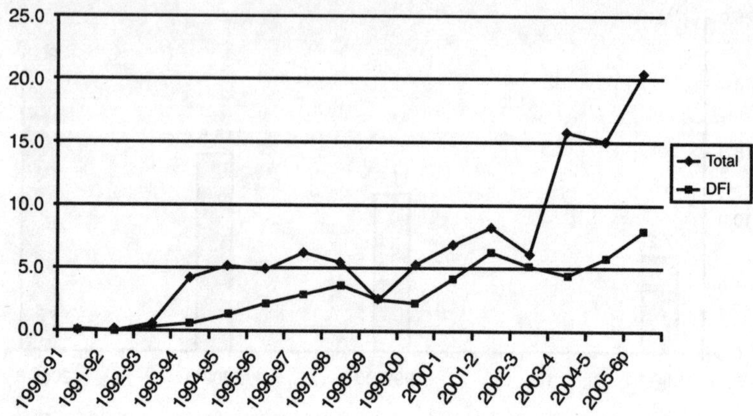

Figure 1.6 Total Foreign Investment Has Picked Up though not DFI ($billion)

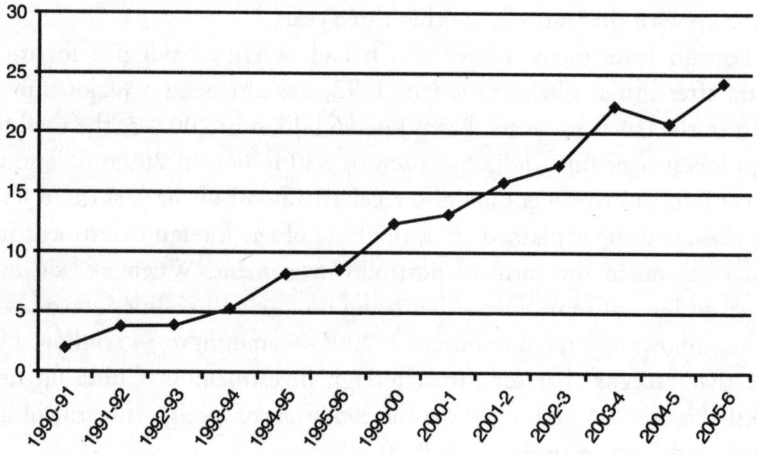

Figure 1.7 Remittances Have Continued to Rise Rapidly ($billion—Current)

teledensity—the number of phone lines per 100 of population—stood at 14.1 at the end of July 2006.[4] At the end of calendar year 2005, urban teledensity was already 31—a level unthinkable even five years ago—and rural teledensity was 2. The latter figure is low, but to put the matter in perspective, as recently as 1991 urban teledensity was below this figure. The communication sector as a whole has been growing 24 percent per year in real terms since 1999–00. Its share in GDP has more than doubled from 1.6 percent in 1999–00 to 3.5 percent in 2004–5.

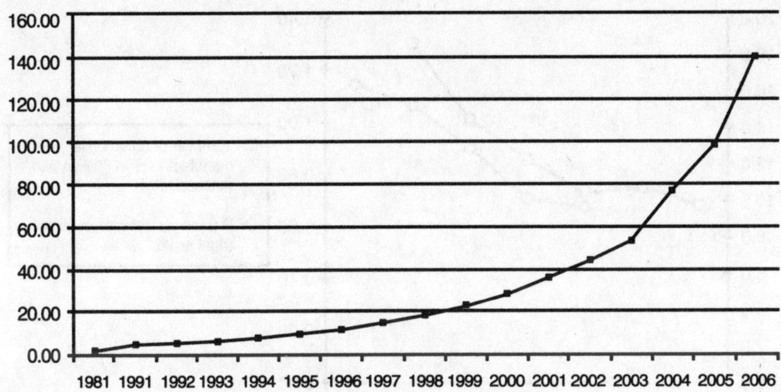

Figure 1.8 The Explosive Growth in Phone Lines (million lines)

The automobile sector offers another example of dramatic expansion. Figure 1.9 shows the total turnover of the sector from 1999–00 to 2004–5 and also the number of passenger vehicles sold between 2000–1 and 2005–6. The total turnover of the sector rose from $12.3 billion in 2002–3 to $19 billion in 2004–5. The sales of passenger vehicles have risen from 707,000 in 2002–3 to 1.14 million in 2005–6.

To conclude this section, let me note three distinguishing features of the current expansion as compared to the one observed during 1993–97. First, trade and foreign investment expansion, and therefore integration into the world economy, has been much more rapid and much deeper in the current phase. For the first time in the last fifty years, the economy has the appearance of an open economy in terms both of trade and investment policies and of outcomes. Second, the exchange rate in the current phase has been either stable or has appreciated. This has meant a very rapid growth in GDP in dollar terms when converted at the market exchange rate. Given a very large stock of foreign exchange reserves—$165 billion on August 11, 2006—prospects for a large depreciation are extremely low. This means that the expansion in the dollar value of GDP will sustain itself. Finally, after three consecutive years of more than 7 percent growth, the previous phase (1993–97) saw the growth rate plummet to 4.8 percent in 1997–98. The current phase, in contrast, has shown no signs of slowing down. According to all available projections, despite the occurrence of natural disasters and therefore of very low agricultural growth, GDP growth in 2006–7 is expected to hit the 8 percent mark. Indeed, the growth rate during April–June 2006, the first quarter

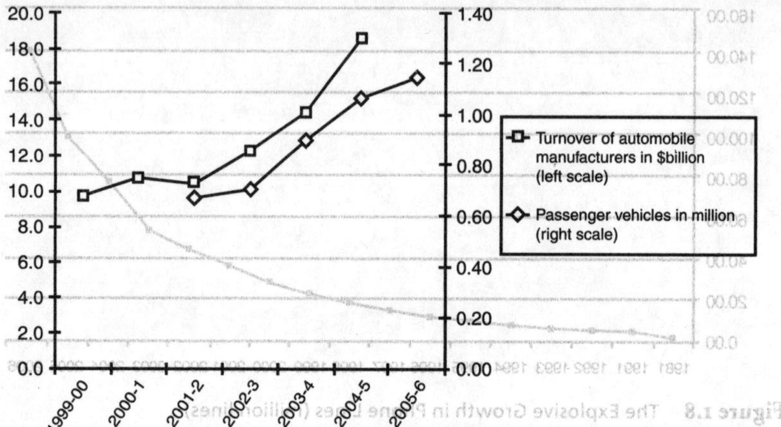

Figure 1.9 Automobile Sector: Total Turnover ($billion) and Passenger Vehicle Sales (million)

of 2006–7, has been 8.5 percent and has come on the heels of 9.3 percent growth during January–March 2006, the last quarter of 2005–6. All these factors persuade me to stand on the optimistic side of the debate regarding growth prospects in India, as advocated most strongly by Kelkar (2004) and as questioned most vigorously by Acharya (2004).[5]

3. THE PROBLEM OF TRANSFORMATION

While disagreements remain among specialists on the precise decrease in poverty achieved during the last two decades, there is agreement among scholars that considerable progress in poverty reduction has been achieved.[6] According to official government figures, the proportion of those living below the national poverty line in India fell from 39 percent in 1987–88 to 26 percent in 1999–00. But even if we go by the more conservative (and careful) estimates in Deaton and Drèze (2002), which correct for an important change in the design of the 1999–00 expenditure survey questionnaire, the ratio came down to 28.5 percent.[7] If we also accept Deaton and Drèze's correction to the poverty line through the utilization of more appropriate price indexes, the poverty ratio in 1999–00 turns out to be far lower at 22.2 percent. Unlike the impression created immediately following the victory of the United Progressive Alliance (UPA), poverty has fallen in both rural and urban areas, though more so in the latter. As Bhagwati and Panagariya (2004) have argued, the defeat of the National Democratic Alliance was brought by an anti-incumbency vote at the state level, voters having been motivated by rising expectations triggered by recent rapid GDP growth and a decline in poverty.

In terms of poverty reduction, the Indian experience is no exception to the Bhagwati (1988) "pull-up" hypothesis, which emphasizes that rapid growth does not simply trickle down but in fact "pulls up" the poor in large numbers into gainful employment. Nevertheless, as Bhagwati (2004, pp. 56–57) argues, the *type* of growth still matters for poverty reduction. How much poverty reduction is achieved from a given aggregate growth depends crucially on the precise pattern of growth: rapid growth in unskilled labor-intensive industry is likely to create many more opportunities for the poor than will growth in capital-intensive and skilled labor-intensive sectors.[8] It is with respect to the former that India has been unsuccessful in taking full advantage of its growth.

There is no doubt that if the trend growth rate in India does shift up to 8 percent, poverty reduction will accelerate further. Yet, there are several interrelated features of the current pattern of growth that undermine its ability to reduce poverty even faster and transform the economy from its current traditional character into a modern one within the next two decades. Let us consider five important features of the recent growth experience.

3.1 THE CURRENT GROWTH PATTERN

In looking at the current situation, one can say, first, that India's growth process has been unique in that in spite of a very substantial reduction in the share of agricultural output in GDP, the share of industry and, in particular, manufacturing, has not grown since 1990–91. This is shown in Table 1.1, which reports the evolution of the shares of agriculture, industry, and services in GDP at 1993–94 prices since 1970–71. The share of agriculture in Indian GDP fell from 46 percent in 1970–71 to 32 percent in 1990–91 and to 21 percent in 2004–5. Yet over this period, the share of industry has moved very little. It rose from 22 percent in 1970–71 to 27 percent in 1990–91 and has stayed there. Correspondingly, the share of manufacturing rose from 13 percent in 1970–71 to 17 percent in 1990–91 and has remained at that level to date. The entire decline in the share of agriculture since 1990–91 has been absorbed by services. The latter have expanded their share in GDP from 32 percent in 1970–71 to 41 percent in 1990–91 and to 52 percent in 2004–5.

Table 1.1 Sectoral Shares in the GDP

Year	Agriculture, Forestry and Fishing	Industry	Manufacturing	Services
1970–71	46	22	13	32
1980–81	40	24	14	37
1990–91	32	27	17	41
2000–1	24	27	17	49
2004–5RE	21	27	17	52

Source: Author's calculations from data in the RBI Handbook 2006.

Second, within the formal, organized sector, industry and services in India have been and remain either capital intensive or skilled-labor intensive.[9] Beginning in the 1960s, India gradually shifted to the autarkic path to development, which necessitated the creation of a large machinery sector. But, in addition, starting with the Second Five Year Plan, the promotion of heavy industry was adopted as an explicit goal by the government. Later, in the early 1970s, the government confined the successful, large business houses (the so-called "dominant" undertakings) to a group of nineteen heavy-investment sectors. This naturally created further bias in favor of capital-intensive industries and scuttled the growth of the labor-intensive industry. India also encouraged the engineering-goods and chemical industries, which made intensive use of skilled labor.[10]

Unfortunately, liberalization during the last two decades has not been able to correct the bias against unskilled labor-intensive industry. For reasons I will discuss later in the chapter, rapidly expanding sectors in India remain capital intensive or skilled-labor intensive. Two of the fastest growing sectors—telecommunications and automobiles—share this characteristic. Two other major successes—pharmaceuticals and the software industry—are highly skilled-labor intensive. Moreover, as I document systematically in Panagariya (2006), at the two-digit Standard International Trade Classification (SITC) level, two of India's fastest growing exports, petroleum and petroleum products, and iron and steel, are highly capital intensive. Among other leading exports of India—textiles, gems and jewelry and apparel—only apparel is unskilled-labor intensive. But its share in India's merchandise exports has been declining.

Table 1.2, which shows the shares of various industry sectors in GDP and in the total labor force in 1999–00, sheds some light on the relative patterns of output and employment. The first point to note is that the share of agriculture and allied activities in the labor force in 1999–00

Table 1.2 GDP and Employment Shares of Various Sectors, 1999–2000

Industrial Category	Output Share	Employment Share
1. Agriculture, forestry, and fishing	25.3	60.3
Nonagricultural	74.7	39.7
2. Mining and quarrying	2.3	0.6
3. Manufacturing	14.7	11.0
4. Electricity, gas, and water supply	2.5	0.3
5. Construction	5.9	4.4
6. Trade, hotels, and restaurant	14.2	10.3
7. Transport, storage, and communication	7.4	3.7
8. Finance, insurance, real estate, and business services	13.0	1.2
9. Community, social, and personal services	14.7	8.3
Gross Domestic Product at factor cost (1 to 9)	100.0	100.0

Source: Author's calculations using the GDP data (at 1999–2000 prices) from the CSO and employment data from the PowerPoint file "Informal Sector in India" at www.wageindicator.org/documents/wwwmeetingjune06/informalindia.

was 60 percent, but its GDP share was only 25 percent.[11] On the other hand, manufacturing accounted for 15 percent of output but only 11 percent of employment in 1999–00. It is also evident from this table that fast-growing sectors such as communications, construction, and software (included in business services) are not big employers. Remarkably, finance, insurance, real estate, and business services, which accounted for 13 percent of GDP in 1999–00, employed only 1.2 percent of the labor force.

Third, as a consequence of the highly capital-intensive and skilled labor-intensive character of the organized sector, the transition of the labor force from agriculture to nonagricultural activities has been extremely slow. For example, according to the census data, farm workers (cultivators plus agricultural workers) accounted for 67.1 percent of the total workforce in 1991. This proportion fell to only 58.5 percent in 2001. Because the total workforce itself rose during the period, the absolute number of farm workers still rose from 210 million to 233 million over this period.

Fourth, while nonfarm employment has increased more rapidly than farm employment, as reflected in the declining share of the latter, the bulk of this increase has been absorbed in the informal, unorganized sector.[12] Some indirect evidence supporting this assertion can be gleaned from the fact that the share of the rural labor force in the total labor force has grown by only a tiny amount. According to the census data, even though the share of the farm workforce fell by 9 percentage points during 1990–00, the share of the rural workforce in the total workforce fell by

2 percentage points: from 79.3 percent in 1990–91 to 77.2 percent in 1999–00. Therefore, the bulk of the shift away from the farm workforce was accounted for by rural industry or rural services, which are predominantly in the informal sector. More directly, according to the available data, employment in the private organized sector in India has been low and stagnant. It stood at 7.5 million (out of the total number of workers of 313 million) in 1991, peaked at 8.7 million in 1998, and fell back to 8.4 million in 2003.

Table 1.3, constructed from Saha, Kar, and Baskaran (2004, tables 1 and 2), shows the output and employment shares of the informal sector in various industry categories in the year 1999–00.[13] It is remarkable that outside of agriculture, as much as 88 percent of the labor force continued to be in the informal sector in 1999–00 though the output generated there was only 44 percent. Within manufacturing, 94 percent of the labor force was in the informal sector, though only 39 percent of the manufacturing

Table 1.3 Shares of Informal Sector Output and Employment by Industry Categories

Industry	Percentage Shares in GDP by Sectors		Percent Share of Informal Employment
	Formal	Informal	
Agriculture	3.2	—	99.2
Forestry and logging	5.6	—	98.3
Fishing	0.1	—	98.5
Agriculture, forestry, and logging and fishing	3.1	—	99.1
Mining and quarrying	91.6	8.4	90.7
Manufacturing	60.8	39.2	94.9
Electricity, gas, and water supply	93.8	6.2	90.1
Construction	41.8	58.2	85.8
Trade	18.1	81.9	84.7
Hotels and restaurants	41.2	58.8	90.7
Transport and storage	35.2	64.8	79.3
Communication	91.4	8.6	92.8
Banking and insurance	90.5	9.5	88.7
Real estate, ownership of dwelling and business services	18.6	81.4	89.9
Public administration and defense	100.0	0.0	0.4
Other services	69.5	30.5	87.4
Nonagricultural other than paid domestic workers	56.0	44.0	88.3
Hired domestic workers	—	—	100.0
Total	42.0	32.4	95.6

Source: Saha, Kar, and Baskaran (2004, tables 1 and 2). This table reproduces table 2 in Saha, Kar, and Baskaran (2004) with two modifications: it eliminates their third column and replaces the last column by the last column in their table 1.

output originated there. Indeed, except in public administration and defense, this pattern held across the board.

Yet one more piece of evidence that reinforces this picture comes from the Economic Census, which covers *all* entrepreneurial units located in India regardless of size or sector (excluding crop production and plantation). According to the latest of these censuses, conducted in 2005, of the 42 million enterprises countrywide, only 1.4 percent employed ten or more workers.[14] The total number of workers employed in all enterprises was 99 million. Even under the conservative assumption of two workers per enterprise, approximately 81 million workers would belong to the informal-sector enterprises (enterprises with fewer than ten workers). All evidence points to a highly fragmented production structure of nonfarm activity in India, whether in the industry or services.

Finally, the pattern of savings also reinforces this picture. Corporate savings in China have risen from the hefty 22 percent of GDP in 2000 to 30 percent in 2005. In contrast, corporate savings in India are tiny: strictly below 5 percent in the last five years. Even more dramatically, even the GDP share of the Indian corporate sector is far less than 30 percent in India. Instead, it is household savings that supply the bulk of the investment funds in India. Astonishingly, of the 24.3 percent of GDP in household savings, household investment accounted for as much as 13 percent of GDP. Household investment of this magnitude is yet another indicator of very substantial informal sector in the economy. Moreover, recognizing that the bulk of the financially intermediated household savings are absorbed by the fiscal deficit, corporate sector investment is relatively limited.

3.2 A COMPARATIVE CASE: KOREA

To put the matter in perspective, I conclude this section by briefly summarizing the experience of South Korea starting in the 1960s. Korea's annual per-capita GDP at current prices was barely $79 in 1960. But it rose to $248 in 1970, $1,632 in 1980, and $5,199 in 1989 (Harvie and Lee 2003, table 1). In 1960, Korea started with a real per-capita income below that of Haiti, which is currently classified as a Least Developed Country by the United Nations, and comfortably crossed the upper-middle-income level by the late 1980s.[15] The Korean economy took off in 1963 and went on to register average growth rates of real GNP of 9.5 percent during 1963–73, 7.2 percent during 1974–82 and 9.9 percent during 1983–90.[16]

Table 1.4 Korea: Sectoral Shares in the GDP and Employment

Year	Agriculture	Mining	Manufacturing	Other
A. Gross domestic product by sector (as percent of the GDP)				
1960	36.9	2.1	13.6	47.4
1965	38.7	1.8	17.7	41.8
1970	25.8	1.3	21	51.9
1975	24.9	1.4	26.6	47.1
1980	15.1	1.4	30.6	52.9
1985	13.9	1.5	29.2	55.3
1990	9.1	0.5	29.2	61.2
B. Employment by sector (as percent of total employment)				
1960	68.3	0.3	1.5	29.9
1965	58.6	0.9	9.4	31.1
1970	50.4	1.1	13.1	35.4
1975	45.7	0.5	18.6	35.2
1980	34	0.9	21.6	43.5
1985	24.9	1	23.4	50.7
1990	18.3	0.4	26.9	54.4

Source: Economic Planning Board, *Major Statistics of Korean Economy*, various issues, and Bank of Korea, *Economic Statistics Yearbook 1962* (as cited by Yoo [1997, table 2] from which this table is taken).

During these years of rapid growth, the Korean economy also underwent a dramatic structural transformation with shares of agriculture in GDP and employment declining and those of manufacturing rising sharply. Table 1.4, excerpted from Yoo (1997), captures this transformation. The share of agriculture, forestry, and fisheries in Korean GDP fell from 37 percent in 1960 to 26 percent in 1970, to 15 percent in 1980, and to 9 percent in 1990. While the share of industry in general rose, the most dramatic gains were made by manufacturing, which rose from 14 percent in 1960 to 21 percent in 1970 and to 31 percent in 1980.[17] In an economy that had been growing 8 percent per year overall, the sharp rise in the share of manufacturing during 1960–80 implies a very rapid expansion of manufacturing in absolute terms. According to Yoo (1997, p. 8), manufacturing growth averaged a hefty 16 percent during the 1960s and 1970s.

These changes in sectoral output shares were also reflected in employment shares. According to Table 1.4, the employment share of manufacturing rose from 9.4 percent in 1965 to 22 percent in 1980 and to 27 percent in 1990. The share of agriculture, forestry and fisheries declined from 58.6 percent to 18.3 percent of the total employment between 1965 and 1990. This shift in employment was accompanied by substantial increases in wages—approximately 7 to 8 percent annually during 1961–81. Thus,

Korea was entirely transformed from a primarily agricultural to a primarily industrial nation, and from a basket case to an upper-middle-income economy, in a matter of thirty years.

4. TRADE AND DIRECT FOREIGN INVESTMENT

In Panagariya (2006), I compare the evolution of external trade and investment liberalization by India and China. The discussion there leads me to conclude that whereas China had a much more open trade and foreign investment regime until the early 1990s, aside from agriculture, India has now caught up with it. Currently, the highest industrial tariff in India, with a handful of exceptions applying to the auto sector, is 12.5 percent. In 2005–6, custom duty as a proportion of the total merchandise imports was less than 5 percent. In agriculture, India remains more protected than China with its tariffs averaging 30 percent compared with 15 percent for the latter.

Services imports have been liberalized considerably as part of the liberalization of foreign investment policy. The foreign investment regime now operates on the "negative list" approach, meaning that unless there are specific restrictions spelled out in the foreign direct investment (FDI) policy, subject to sectoral rules and regulations, up to 100 percent foreign investment is permitted under the automatic route. Exceptions include retail trading, where no foreign investment is allowed (except single-brand product retailing, where foreign investment up to 51 percent is permitted), and insurance, defense and publishing of newspapers and periodicals dealing with current affairs, where foreign investment is limited to 26 percent.

A puzzle, however, is that despite very similar factor endowments, the response of merchandise exports and inward direct foreign investment to this opening up has been much more muted in India than in China. Even if one takes the view that India is somewhat less open than China, and takes account of the fact that India has had a late start, these differences would not be sufficient to explain the differences between their performances. At the aggregate level, China currently accounts for 5 percent of the world merchandise trade and India only 1 percent. Direct foreign investment in India currently stands at $8 billion, while FDI in China is $60 billion. Even adjusting for the time lag in the opening up by India relative to China, it is almost inconceivable that India would reach the current levels of China's trade and foreign investment in ten years' time.

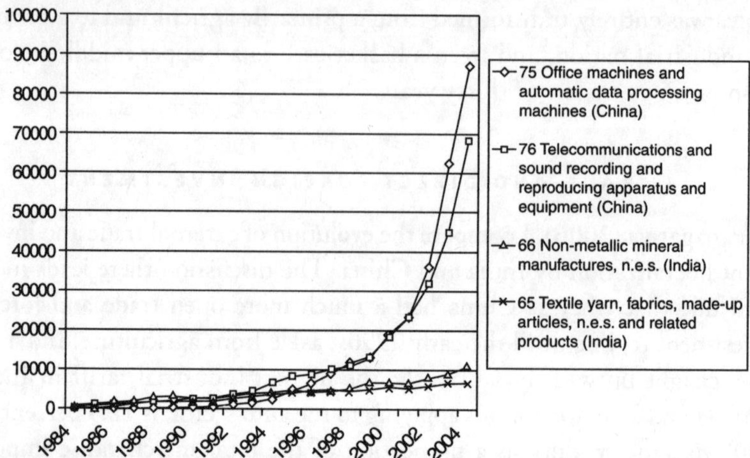

Figure 1.10 Top Two Exports of India and China

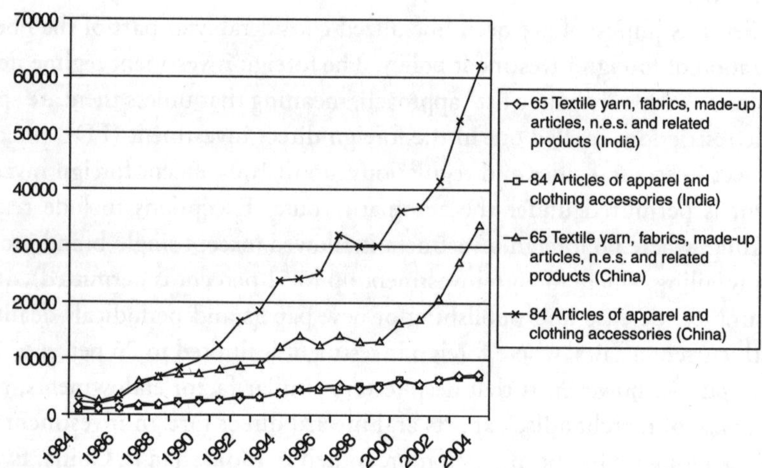

Figure 1.11 Textiles and Clothing Exports of India and China

Figures 1.10 and 1.11 offer dramatic illustrations of the difference between the relative performances of India and China in exports. Figure 1.10 shows the evolution of the value of exports of the top two items in each of India and China in current dollars between 1984 and 2004. Figure 1.11 traces the exports of textiles and apparel by the two countries. Surprisingly, the top two exports of China are no longer textiles and apparel, or toys and footwear. Instead, they are (a) office machines and automatic data processing machines, and (b) telecommunications and sound-recording and reproduction equipment. What is remarkable is that, until as late as 2000, exports of both of these items stood below $20 billion. By 2004, they had reached $87 billion and $68 billion, respectively. In comparison, India's top two exports, nonmetallic mineral manufactures (mainly gems and jewelry), and textile yarn and fabric, stood at only $11 billion and $7 billion, respectively. As Figure 1.11 shows, these are levels that textiles and apparel had surpassed in China more than ten years earlier.

5. IT IS THE DOMESTIC POLICIES, STUPID![18]

The features of the Indian economy that I have discussed in Sections 3 and 4 have a common explanation: a set of domestic policies that discourage the entry of large-scale manufacturing firms in unskilled labor-intensive sectors.[19] It is the unwillingness of the large-scale manufacturing firms to enter the unskilled labor-intensive sectors that explains the virtual lack of growth of employment in the organized sector. The same phenomenon also explains the muted response of merchandise exports and the relatively small inflows of foreign direct investment. Few foreign firms are willing to locate their manufacturing facilities of unskilled labor-intensive products in India. A quick look at the destination data shows that foreign direct investment has gone predominantly into services sectors whose capacity to absorb such investments is limited.

Recall that prior to the beginning of the reforms, virtually the entire policy regime had been designed to force bigger firms to concentrate on capital-intensive products and to set aside the production of labor-intensive products for small-scale firms. The tightening of the licensing policy in the early 1970s excluded the big business houses—entities with $27 million or more in investment in fixed assets (land, buildings, and machinery)—from all but nineteen heavy-industry sectors. The Foreign Exchange Regulation Act (FERA) of 1973 did the same to foreign firms. These restrictions were complemented by a very tight import-licensing regime.

But the policy that turned into the greatest obstacle to exports was the reservation of virtually all unskilled labor-intensive products, exported by China in massive volumes in the 1980s and 1990s, for exclusive production by small-scale units. The latter were defined in 1969 as entities with investment in plant and machinery not exceeding $100,000. Although this limit was raised in subsequent years, increases in limits were gradual and small: even today investment by the small-scale-industry (SSI) enterprises is limited to less than $225,000.

The SSI reservation policy alone was sufficient to ensure that India would exclude itself from the exports of labor-intensive products. Foreign firms interested in buying labor-intensive products from cheaper sources demanded a scale and quality standard that the SSI units were typically incapable of supplying. Their huge cost advantages did allow some SSI enterprises to succeed but not on a scale justified by the cost advantage India potentially enjoyed. Even the successful small-scale entrepreneurs would find that they quickly hit the ceiling on investment. And of course, at such a small scale, individual enterprises had no incentive to explore world markets. Exports had to be organized through intermediary export houses. But that requirement severed the critical buyer-seller link.

With access to high-quality foreign inputs virtually denied, foreign investment tightly controlled, and regulatory limits on the pursuit of comparative advantage, the prospects of major successes in exporting heavy-industry products were limited, as well. Unsurprisingly, India found itself excluded from the world markets across the board. Its organized sector came to be dominated by heavy industry that was incapable of competing in world markets. Its labor-intensive manufacturing came to consist of millions of tiny enterprises spread all across the country and serving principally local markets. Other than durable products such as automobiles, scooters, and refrigerators, which were, in any case, capital intensive, India produced few consumer goods that had national appeal.

The reforms undertaken since 1991 have brought about four important policy changes that open the door wider to the entry of large-scale firms in unskilled labor-intensive products:

- Imports have been liberalized so that the access to high-quality inputs is no longer a constraining factor.
- With the end to the investment-licensing regime, big business houses are no longer confined to heavy industry.
- FERA 1973 has been repealed and the door has been opened to foreign investors.
- The list of products reserved for exclusive production by small-scale industry has been progressively trimmed.

Unfortunately, however, these reforms have not produced a major breakthrough in manufacturing. Excluding the last three years, manufacturing output has grown at only 6 percent per annum, a rate already achieved in the 1950s and early 1960 and recovered in the 1980s after a major drop in the intervening years. More importantly, even including the last three years, neither large-scale manufacturing nor major success in the exports of unskilled labor-intensive products has been achieved.

It is tempting to attribute this outcome to the delay in launching the process of de-reservation, which got under way only in 1997, and to piecemeal progress in trimming the SSI list. Out of 821 items on the list in 1998–99, approximately 239 items still remained subject to the small-scale reservation in January 2007. But this explanation fails to withstand closer scrutiny.

Many of the textiles and apparel products have been off the reservation list for several years now. More importantly, even for products still on the SSI list, large-scale production has been permitted since at least March 2000 as long as the enterprise exports 50 percent or more of its output. This latter change means that firms predominantly interested in exporting their output have been effectively freed of the SSI reservation in all products since at least March 2000.

Given these facts and the anticipated end to the quotas under the Multi-Fiber Arrangement (MFA) on January 1, 2005, a logical outcome would have been the entry of at least some large-scale manufacturers in some of the unskilled labor-intensive products and a major upsurge in their exports. But this has not happened. Instead, it is the capital-intensive and skilled-labor-intensive products that have continued to grow rapidly. The removal of the SSI reservation constraint was a necessary condition for the rapid expansion of unskilled-labor-intensive manufacturing but it has not turned out to be sufficient.

In my view, two critical factors constrain the Chinese-style breakthrough in the production and export of unskilled labor-intensive manufacturing products in India: highly inflexible labor markets in the organized sector and infrastructure bottlenecks, especially power and ports.

5.1 LABOR-MARKET RIGIDITIES IN THE ORGANIZED SECTOR

In India, a firm has two options: it can choose to employ less than ten workers (twenty if it does not use power) and stay in the unorganized sector, or it can employ ten or more workers (twenty or more if not using power) and operate in the organized sector. If it chooses to operate in the unorganized sector, its workers are not covered by most of the national labor legislation. It does not have to offer formal employment contracts or the usual benefits such as paid annual leave, sick leave, or medical and pension benefits. It can also fire workers without notice and does not owe any severance pay. Minimum wage regulations may apply, depending on the state and the sector, but these are not vigorously enforced. As shown in Table 1.3, 88.3 percent of nonagricultural workers were employed in the unorganized sector under precisely this set of conditions in 1999–2000.

The firm's alternative option is to employ ten or more workers (twenty or more if not using power) and accept obligations toward workers that become increasingly onerous with size. At twenty workers or more, the firm must establish a pension fund for the workers. At fifty workers or more, it must offer mandatory health insurance under the Employee State Insurance Act of 1948 and also be subject to a worker-management dispute resolution process that is heavily tilted in favor of workers and the rules that make the reassignment of workers to a different task virtually impossible under the Industrial Disputes Act (IDA) of 1947 (see below). And, once the firm reaches one hundred workers or more, it effectively loses the right to fire workers, even if it goes bankrupt.

Historically, India always has had a very high level of protection of labor rights. Even in the 1950s, labor legislation in India was at par with that in most developed countries along most dimensions. Although the obstacles that this posed to growth prospects were recognized by at least some scholars very early on, little was done by way of damage control. In his comprehensive essay on economic reforms, Srinivasan (2003) offers the following striking observations by his teacher, P.C. Mahalanobis (1969, p. 422):[20]

> in certain respects, welfare measures tend to be implemented in India ahead of economic growth, for example, in labor laws which are probably the most highly protective of labor interests, in the narrowest sense, in the whole world. There is practically no link between output and remuneration; hiring and firing are highly restricted. It is extremely difficult to maintain an economic level of productivity, or improve productivity. At early stages of development in all countries there has been a real conflict between welfare measure and economic growth. Japan is an outstanding example; the concept of minimum wages was introduced only about ten or twelve years ago when per-capita income had reached the level of $250 or $300 per year; and minimum wages were fixed more or less at actual average levels. In India with a per-capita income of only about $70, the present form of

> protection of organized labor, which constitutes, including their families, about five or six per cent of the whole population, would operate as an obstacle to growth and would also increase inequalities. It is a serious problem not only in India but in other under-developed countries.

Although Zagha (1998) mentions the existence of forty-five different national- and state-level labor-law enactments, the most critical one relevant to the issue of the entry of large firms in the unskilled labor-intensive industries is the IDA, which applies to firms with fifty or more workers. The legislation governs relations between workers and management and the settlement of disputes between them; rules relating to the reassignment of a worker to a different task; and the conditions of layoff, retrenchment and closure. In each case, the legislation stacks the deck disproportionately against management.[21]

First, the legislation confers on the state the power to regulate labor-management relations. This is unlike the laws of most other countries, where the state can move to intervene only after bilateral negotiations between workers and management break down. Labor departments of the central and state governments have responsibilities to implement various provisions of the IDA. Once the Labor Department, with jurisdiction over a firm, decides that a certain dispute merits its intervention, it initiates a process aimed at reconciling the two sides. If this process fails, the matter is sent to the labor judiciary. The latter has predominantly ruled in favor of workers.[22] Labor unions prefer this system to alternatives because it greatly increases their bargaining power vis-à-vis management. Indeed, an effort in 1950 to replace the IDA with alternative legislation that would have largely freed labor-management relations from state intervention was defeated by the trade unions.

Second, under Section 9A of the IDA an employer must give three weeks' written notice to a worker of any change in his or her working conditions. These changes include (a) changes in shift work, (b) changes in grade classification, (c) changes in rules of discipline, (d) a technological change that may affect the demand for labor, and (e) changes in employment, occupation, process, or department. The worker has the right to object to these changes, which may culminate in an industrial dispute with the associated costs in terms of time and financial resources. This provision makes it very difficult for the firm to respond quickly to technological changes or changes in demand conditions.

Finally, and most importantly, an amendment to the IDA in 1976 added Chapter V.B., which made it mandatory for firms with three hundred or more workers to seek the permission of the Labor Department for layoffs, retrenchment or closure. The permission is seldom forthcoming, however. A further amendment in 1982 made this provision applicable to firms with one hundred or more workers. Therefore, under current provisions, a firm with one hundred or more workers has effectively no right to retrench or layoff workers. Even when it is bankrupt, it must pay its workers out of profits from other operations.

The IDA and other labor-market rigidities have had a detrimental effect on the entry of large-scale firms in the unskilled labor-intensive sectors in at least two mutually reinforcing ways. First, firms are afraid that should they go bust for some reason, they will be stuck having to pay full wages to a large workforce despite bankruptcy. Second, various labor laws have disproportionately strengthened the hand of the unions in wage negotiations. Consequently, the wages in the organized sector are now several times those in the unorganized sector. These high wages are less of an issue for the firms in the capital-intensive industries since labor costs are only a tiny proportion of their total costs. But for unskilled labor-intensive firms, such high wages result in a very large increase in their unit costs and render them uncompetitive.

Skeptics sometimes argue that low growth in the employment prospects of unskilled workers cannot be attributed to labor-market rigidities in the organized sector since the bulk of the workforce is in the unorganized sector where workers have virtually no rights. For example, Bardhan (2006) makes the following argument:

> There are serious differences on the empirical judgment on the adequacy of growth trickle-down. In particular employment growth at the low-skill levels has been quite disappointing so far, and to blame this on the restrictive labor laws (applicable to the large factory sector) is asking the tail to wag too large a dog (in a country where more than 80 per cent of workers even in the non-agricultural sector work in informal activities where the labor laws do not apply).

But this is a spurious argument. Those of us advocating labor-market reform do not blame labor-market rigidities for the slow growth of unskilled employment *in aggregate*. That would indeed be silly since even 20 percent growth in 10 percent of the total jobs located in the organized sector produces only 2 percent growth in aggregate jobs. Instead, we hold labor-market rigidities responsible for the slow growth or nongrowth of unskilled employment *in the organized sector,* which has much greater potential for generating such employment than it has done so far. We also blame these rigidities for the slow pace of the *transition* of India from a traditional to a modern economy. The more favorable the environment for the growth of unskilled employment in the organized sector, the larger will be the base of well-paid, unskilled jobs and the more India will be able to promote overall growth in unskilled jobs. Recall that in 1991, exports of goods and services were only 7 percent of GDP. Today, they are nearly 21 percent.

Besides, the fundamental question to ask is not whether the tail can wag the dog but rather why the proportion of the nonagricultural labor force employed in the organized sector is so tiny after fifty years of development effort. If labor-market rigidities were as benign as Bardhan suggests, we should see many more firms manufacturing unskilled labor-intensive products in the organized sector, and on a large scale, than we do currently. Whereas large firms employing thousands of workers under a single roof in the apparel sector abound in China, shops with fifty tailors represent the large-scale end of the spectrum in India. India remains entirely divorced from global production chains in unskilled labor-intensive manufacturing.

Skeptics further argue that labor-market rigidities consistently fail to appear as the major constraint facing firms in business-environment surveys. This, too, is a spurious argument. The firms for which labor-market rigidities are crucial are simply absent from the samples on which these surveys are based. The small-scale industries reservation, the high organized-sector wages, and costly exit barriers have systematically kept large-scale firms out of the unskilled labor-intensive sectors. Large-scale firms are present in the capital-intensive or skilled labor-intensive sectors where labor laws do not constitute the most pressing problem. The fact that they have chosen to enter those markets is evidence that they are able to overcome these barriers. For instance, the CEO of Infosys, a software firm, is unlikely to complain about labor laws as the most pressing problem. For him, a high-quality labor force, and shortcomings related to airports and urban infrastructure, are likely to be more important. A proper survey would ask the existing entrepreneurs why they chose not to go into manufacturing apparel, footwear, or toys on a massive scale. Anecdotal evidence suggests that when the question is put this way, CEOs are quick to point a finger at labor unions and high wages, which result in low profit margins.

Several econometric studies done at various times evaluate the effects of labor laws on employment in the organized sector.[23] In my view, all of these studies are subject to the same criticism offered above regarding the business-environment surveys: large-scale firms producing unskilled labor-intensive products are missing from the sample. Some of the studies relate to the period when investment licensing was in full force. During that period, labor laws mainly redistributed the rents on the licenses in favor of workers with minimal employment effects. These studies cannot capture the effect of labor laws on entry and employment in the license-free environment of today. Even the studies based on more recent data suffer from the absence of large-scale firms in the unskilled labor-intensive sectors on account of small-scale-industries reservation and the IDA of 1947. Some studies rely on differences in labor laws across states, but they use rather crude indexes of labor-market regimes. More importantly, they cannot capture the effect of the stringent national laws within which state laws must be enacted.

In reforming the labor laws, ideally, it would be desirable to return to the attempt made in 1950 to replace the IDA by an entirely new legislation that would redefine worker-management relations and rebalance the rights and obligations of workers in accordance with international best practices. Given the political realities, however, no government is likely to attempt such a reform in one go. Instead, the government could reform the law for newly hired workers, with the rights of the workers currently employed in the organized sector remaining unchanged. The reform could also offer more substantial unemployment and retraining benefits and severance pay than currently available in return for the restoration of the employer's right to retrench or layoff workers. The conditions under which workers can be reassigned to other tasks must be made more flexible. In the globalized world of today, with technology and demand conditions shifting rapidly, flexibility in the reassignment of workers to different tasks is an important condition for the survival of a firm.

To further balance the rights of workers, India also needs a proper bankruptcy law. Under the current system, the bankruptcy procedure involves first declaring the firm sick on the ground that its liabilities exceed its assets, then referring it to the Board of Industrial and Financial Rehabilitation (BIFR). BIFR then makes a determination whether the firm can be restructured, and if not, it initiates the liquidation proceedings. The BIFR process is extremely slow and often takes ten years or more.

The National Democratic Alliance (NDA) government had introduced a major reform in this area that would replace the BIFR process with a more expeditious channel for the winding up of firms through the Companies (Second Amendment) Act of 2002. The amendment proposes to create National Company Law Tribunals (NCLT) and a National Company Law Appellate Tribunal. All legal proceedings relating to the winding up and restructuring of companies would be placed under the NCTL and its decisions would be subject to appeal before the Appellate Tribunal only. The latter would be required to give its decision within sixty days. The verdicts of the Appellate Tribunal would be subject to appeal in the Supreme Court only. This process would take the civil courts, which are the primary source of the delay under the existing BIFR procedure, entirely out of the process. Unfortunately, the implementation of the Companies (Second Amendment) Act of 2002 has been challenged in the Supreme Court, where the matter still awaits a final ruling.

5.2 INFRASTRUCTURE

Bottlenecks in the area of infrastructure are well recognized. While some notable successes have been achieved in this area in India, much remains to be done. I have already described the success achieved in telecommunications. Similar success has also been achieved in domestic civil aviation. With virtually free entry, several new airlines have entered and helped push up air traffic. Annual growth in passenger travel during each of 2004 and 2005 touched 25 percent. A major hike in the share of private airlines accompanied this growth. From just 0.4 percent in 1991, this share rose to 52.8 percent in 2000 and to 68.5 percent in 2005. Success has also been achieved in road construction with the newly completed Golden Quadrilateral project involving the conversion of the national highway connecting the metropolitan cities of Delhi, Mumbai, Chennai, and Kolkata into a four-lane road. There has been some slowdown in construction since the United Progressive Alliance (UPA) came to power, but conversion of the North-South and the East-West national highways into four-lane roads is now under way, as well. Recently, railways have seen some improvements in performance under the dynamic leadership of Railway Minister Lalu Prasad Yadav. Progress has also been made in port management through public-private partnerships.

Electricity is the most important area of infrastructure in which progress remains slow. Industry in India not only pays punishing prices for electricity in order to subsidize the lower prices offered to households and to cover the enormous transmission and distribution (T&D) losses, but the available power supply to industry is often irregular and unreliable. This has led some large firms to opt for in-house generation of electricity but this is a highly inefficient and costly alternative. Moreover, small and medium-sized firms cannot afford this alternative. This places the firms in the unskilled labor-intensive sectors at a particular disadvantage, since they are predominantly small or medium-sized.

The NDA government had taken a major step toward reforming the electricity sector through the Electricity Act of 2003, which replaced the three existing legislative enactments in the sector dated 1910, 1948, and 1998. This legislation offers a comprehensive framework for restructuring the power sector. It builds on the experience in the telecommunications sector and introduces competition through private-sector entry side by side with public-sector entities.

Under the act, the Transmission Utility at the central as well as the state level is a government company with responsibility for planned and coordinated development of the transmission network. The private sector is allowed to enter distribution through independent distribution networks and has open access to transmission at the outset. Open access in distribution is to be introduced in phases, with a surcharge for the current level of cross subsidy to be gradually phased out along with the obligation to supply. State electricity regulatory commissions, made mandatory by the act, are to frame regulations within which transmission, distribution, and generation companies operate.

The act fully de-licenses generation and freely permits captive generation. Only hydro projects require clearance from the Central Electricity Authority. Distribution licensees are free to undertake generation, and generating companies are free to take up distribution businesses. Trading has been recognized as a distinct activity with the regulatory commissions authorized to place ceilings on trading margins, if necessary.

A second track of reforms has involved the states signing memorandums of understanding (MOU) with the center under which states are offered financial resources contingent on satisfying certain performance criteria. The MOU milestones include consumer metering, energy audit, control of theft, tariff setting by the state electricity regulatory commission, and timely payment of subsidies.

The change in the government at the center, which brought the UPA to power, led to a considerable slowdown in the implementation of the Electricity Act. Parties on the left were not warm to the idea of private-sector involvement and insisted on a review of the act. The implementation of the act has now resumed, but progress has been slow and success of the kind achieved in telecommunications remains a dream. A key problem is that the implementation in this area is in the hands of the state governments, which are generally far less capable than the central government. In particular, the bureaucracy of the old State Electricity Board remains powerful with the result that the state electricity regulatory authorities are often unable to act independently. Moreover, collection of dues in the electricity sector is inherently more difficult than in telecommunications. The temptation on the part of the politicians to offer free electricity to farmers also remains a barrier to improving the financial health of the state electricity boards or their successor distribution and transmission companies.

Finally, despite some progress in recent years, the congestion at ports and airports owing to capacity constraints, bureaucratic red tape, and poor administration hampers swift movement of goods into and out of the country. In the supercompetitive global marketplace, this bottleneck can seriously hamper the chance of success of industry. This is particularly true of the apparel industry that operates on a very tight time schedule dictated by the seasons, which determine the sales in the large, developed-country markets of the United States and the European Union.

Table 1.5, taken from Roy and Bagai (2005), documents the striking delays that characterize the Indian ports and airports when compared with international norms. India not only needs to undertake rapid expansion of its port capacity, it needs also to streamline the procedures. Exporters and importers currently must file the same information separately to a multiplicity of agencies relating to transport, agriculture, health, and custom departments or ministries. In the modern electronic age, this information gathering can be organized through a single window, as it is in Singapore.[24]

Table 1.5 Delays at Ports and Airports in India

Transaction	Location	Norm
Air freight	Delhi airport	
Export	2.5 days	Less than 12 hours
Import	15 days	Less than 12 hours
Containerized sea freight	Mumbai	
Ship waiting time	3–5 days	Less than 6 hours
Export dwell time	3–5 days	Less than 18 hours
Import dwell time	7–14 days	Less than 24 hours

Source: Roy and Bagai (2005, Box 2).

6. WALKING ON TWO LEGS

The previous section has emphasized the role of unskilled labor-intensive manufacturing in the transformation of India to a modern economy. But unlike countries such as Korea, China, Taiwan, and Brazil, India does not have to walk on just one leg to achieve this transformation. India is also uniquely placed to rely on a second leg: the modern services sector composed of information technology (IT) and IT-enabled services (ITES).

One of the best things that happened in India during the 1990s was the growth of the IT sector. Gradual liberalization in the electronics industry, which started in the mid-1980s and accelerated in the 1990s, gave the sector access to world-class hardware. Moreover, it was largely free from other regulations, including the draconian labor laws, since it principally employs white-collar workers. Therefore, when the world markets offered growth opportunities, the IT sector was able to take advantage of them. The key question confronting the sector now is whether it can continue to grow at its current pace.

There is some reason to fear that despite its current leadership status, even in this sector, India may be crowded out by China. For example, India's advantage in English over China has been eroding rapidly in recent years. The Chinese students coming to the United States today are much more fluent in English than those coming fifteen years ago, so the gap in language skills between the two countries has been declining. China has also been bridging the gap in technical education. The impact of these developments is reflected in the growth of the IT sector in China and exports of software and IT-enabled services.

But potential competition from China is perhaps not the major source of worry for India for two reasons. The total demand for outsourcing activities from developed countries will continue to grow sufficiently rapidly that India is unlikely to experience a major slowdown in the expansion of its demand. Moreover, India will continue to enjoy the advantage emanating from its relatively greater cultural and institutional affinity with Western nations, compared with China.

Bottlenecks in the growth of the Indian IT sector are likely to arise from the supply side. Most jobs in this sector require some college education. Unfortunately, India's higher-education system is starved for resources and currently incapable of producing the large number of high-quality students that will be demanded at the current wages by the outsourcing industry. According to the 2001 census, there were only 12.6 million workers with nontechnical undergraduate or higher degrees and 2.3 million workers with technical undergraduate or higher degrees in urban areas. These workers represent less than 4 percent of the total workforce of 398.8 million counted by the census. Moreover, at present, even with only 12 percent of the population in the college-going age group (eighteen to twenty-four years) in colleges, India's colleges and universities are overcrowded and underfunded.

While there are no quick fixes to solve the problem of higher education, India must begin the work on four fronts. First, entry of private universities, so common around the world, including in Bangladesh and China, must be introduced. The government has no resources to expand higher education at a pace consistent with demand. Nor is it in a position to create many more institutions like the Indian Institute of Technology (IIT) and Indian Institute of Management (IIM) using public resources. Only private universities that can charge hefty fees and attract private sponsors from home and abroad will be able to afford the salaries necessary to retain top-tier scholars and teachers and to create the facilities needed to promote excellence in research.

To be sure, there has been at least an intellectual recognition of this need at the official level, as evidenced by the Private Universities (Establishment and Regulation) Bill of 1995 and by the recommendations of the so-called Core Group of six members appointed by the Human Resources and Development (HRD) Ministry in 1999. Additionally, the issue has been widely discussed in various forums, with the Education Committee of the Federation of Indian Chamber of Commerce and Industry offering excellent ideas within the Indian context. The sad reality, however, is that there has been little real action by the government and the 1995 bill has been "pending" for many years in the Rajya Sabha (Upper House of the Parliament). The UPA government had appointed a Knowledge Commission, which could have taken the lead, but to-date it has done precious little in this direction. Moreover, following the recent expansion of caste-based quotas in educational institutions, two of its prominent members have resigned.

Second, even at the college level, where the private sector is currently permitted to operate, there is need for deregulation. The process of entry should be relatively simple and transparent. The state-imposed limits on the number of students that these colleges can admit should be abolished. Under the current rules, private engineering colleges usually lack the freedom to choose their own students or to charge fees to students beyond a tiny fraction of those admitted. As a result, fees from a very small percentage of admitted students pay for the entire college. While a strong case can be made for admissions on merit and scholarships cum loans to the admitted students unable to afford the fees fully, there is little justification for a blanket exemption or near exemption from fees for a large number of the students at the private colleges.

The third necessary step is to loosen the stranglehold of the University Grants Commission (UGC) and give greater autonomy to universities and colleges. In this respect, India's own experience has been consistent with that of the rest of the world: notably, the successful institutions, such as the IIT and IIM. These are the highest-quality institutions in India largely because they have been outside the purview of UGC. The Education Committee of FICCI has rightly suggested giving greater play to unitary (rather than affiliating) universities. Like the IIT and IIM, such institutions will be better able to maintain uniform and high-quality standards.

But India needs to go farther. After more than fifty years of independence, India should be willing to confer greater responsibility on the universities, in general, so that they can make informed decisions on courses, curricula, degrees, research centers, and types of academic appointments based on local needs and competitive pressures from peer institutions. It is possible that the initial impact of autonomy on a wide scale would be adverse in part, but it is time to begin laying down the groundwork for a modern education system, which requires increasing decentralization and local responsibility. In the 1950s and 1960s, when India was dealing with a small number of universities and colleges, it was possible for the UGC to centrally control and regulate the process. But with more than 250 universities and 10,000 colleges, this is no longer an efficient form of organization.

It is also essential to state the obvious: India needs to gradually raise tuition fees from their existing negligible levels. Unlike primary and secondary education, the benefits of higher education accrue largely to those who receive it. While provisions for loans and scholarships for the talented among the poor must be made, there is little justification for burdening the taxpayer with expenses that lead to private gains for those lucky enough to find spots in colleges or universities. According to the Justice Punnayya Committee, appointed by UGC in 1992 to advise on how to fund higher education, tuition fees accounted for 15 to 20 percent of university expenditures in the early 1950s. Today, they account for less than 3 percent. This is ironic since rising incomes should have increased rather than decreased the contribution from tuition.

Finally, it bears noting briefly that the IT industry will also benefit greatly from infrastructure development. The rudimentary roads and airport in Bangalore—a city that is so much feared by professional workers in developed countries—invariably shock a first-time visitor to this city. The city stands in sharp contrast to the premises of its major suppliers of IT services such as Infosys and Wipro, which rival their developed-country counterparts. Building the urban infrastructure in the major hubs of the IT industry should be a national priority.

7. CONCLUDING REMARKS

We can be cautiously optimistic that the trend growth rate in India has moved further up, reaching the 8 percent annual mark. A key feature of the rapid growth at this higher rate in the last three years has been very rapid expansion of exports of both goods and services. Unlike in the past, this time India has taken advantage of the rapid growth in the world economy and its open markets. With the export base somewhat bigger, future prospects for a rising share for India in world trade are even better.

Nevertheless, rapid growth in both output and exports has happened without the expansion of the share of the unskilled labor-intensive industrial sector in GDP. This has meant that the movement of the workforce out of agriculture has been slow. Moreover, whatever movement has taken place has been into the informal, unorganized sector of the economy. Modernization of the economy requires the expansion of employment opportunities in the organized sector.

During the last two decades, India has removed many of the barriers to the entry of medium-and large-scale firms into unskilled labor-intensive sectors. Most importantly, the vast majority of the unskilled labor-intensive products have been removed from the small-scale-industries reservation list. Even in the case of the products still on the list, medium- and large-scale firms have been allowed to enter production at least since March 2000 as long as they export more than 50 percent of their output.

The removal of these restrictions has not proved sufficient to speed up the transition of workers into the modern, organized sector. This inevitably points to the presence of remaining barriers to the entry of large firms into the unskilled labor-intensive sectors. I have argued that various labor-market rigidities and infrastructure bottlenecks account for the continued muted response of unskilled labor-intensive industries to the reforms undertaken to date. Unless the government brings relief to the firms in these two areas, the transformation will be slow and poverty reduction will be less than what is practically feasible.

I have also argued in this chapter that unlike countries such as Korea, Taiwan, and China, which have relied principally on manufacturing to transform their economies, India has the prospect of walking on two legs: manufacturing and services in the information-technology industry. Indeed, stimulated by the liberalization of hardware imports in the 1980s and free of labor-market rigidities (since white collar workers are not subject to the draconian Industrial Disputes Act of 1947), the IT industry provided the initial impetus to growth.

But the IT industry also faces major constraints in the medium to long run on the supply side. This is reflected in the very rapid expansion of skilled wages in India in the last three years. Therefore, India also needs to undertake major reforms in its higher-education system to ensure a steady stream of qualified IT workers. These reforms include giving genuine entry opportunities to private universities, the introduction of proper tuition fees to give the existing universities the necessary resources to provide quality education, and a drastic downsizing of the University Grants Commission, which has outlived its usefulness.

NOTES

1. The author is the Jagdish Bhagwati Professor of Indian Political Economy at Columbia University. This chapter was originally written for presentation at the conference "India: An Emerging Giant," October 13–15, 2006, at Columbia University.

2. India's fiscal year begins on April 1 and ends on March 31. Accordingly, a year such as 1951–52 refers to the period from April 1, 1951, to March 31, 1952. Unless otherwise specified, throughout the chapter, an expression such as 1951–65 refers to the period beginning with 1951–52 and ending with 1964–65.

3. The average exchange rate in the year 2002–3 was 48.4 rupees per dollar. It changed to 46, 44.9, and 44.3 rupees per dollar in the subsequent three years.

4. Comparative figures at the same time are: 23 for China, 60 for the United States, and 73 for France. As of February 28, 2007, the number of telephones has touched the 200 million mark, with the nationwide teledensity reaching 18.

5. In an article entitled "My Millennium Wish: Double Digit Growth," published in January 2000 (Panagariya 2000), I had concluded that although the reforms were getting into rough territory, double-digit growth was "within the grasp of the country."

6. See Deaton and Kozel's (2005) provocatively titled "Data and Dogma: The Great Indian Poverty Debate" for a careful review of the debate on poverty.

7. Deaton and Drèze calculate that poverty in the rural areas fell from 39.4 percent in 1987–88 to 30 percent in the rural areas and from 39.1 percent to 24.1 percent in the urban areas over the same period. I have calculated the national poverty figures using these figures assigning the weights of 0.714 and 0.286 to rural and urban poverty, respectively. In turn, these weights are calculated from the official poverty figures available at the national level as well as for the rural and urban areas separately.

8. The pattern of growth will in general interact with the rate of growth. Here I would argue, however, that a shift in favor of unskilled labor–intensive products in a labor abundant country would reinforce rather than impede growth.

9. Officially, the organized sector includes the firms with ten or more workers using power and firms with twenty or more workers otherwise.

10. Kochhar et al. (2006) provide systematic empirical evidence demonstrating the high capital and skilled-labor intensity of the Indian production structure.

11. Employment data in Table 1.2 are from the Employment-Unemployment Survey of National Sample Survey (NSS) from the 55th Round. These data do not match identically to those from the census quoted immediately below. Likewise, the shares in the GDP are based on the GDP data at the revised 1999–00 prices and need not match those in Table 1.1, which is based on the GDP data at 1993–94 prices.

12. In the Indian context, "informal sector" refers to unincorporated household units engaged in the production of goods and services with the primary objective of generating employment and income for the household concerned. These units do not have legal status independently of the households and lack a complete set of accounts that will distinguish their incomes and expenditures from those of the households owning them. The closest analogue to the informal sector officially reported in India, including in the National Accounts Statistics (NAS), is the unorganized sector as contrasted with the organized sector. The unorganized sector includes unincorporated household enterprises or partnership enterprises as well as enterprises run by cooperative societies, trusts, and private and limited companies. Therefore, the informal sector is a subset of the unorganized sector.

13. This table is identical to Table 1.1 in Bosworth, Collins, and Virmani (2007), who additionally cite CSO (2006, February) as the source.

14. This census has been conducted five times so far on an intermittent basis: in 1977, 1980, 1990, 1998, and 2005.

15. This comparison is based on the real per-capita incomes of Korea and Haiti reported in the data set posted on the World Bank website under the title "Global Development Network Growth Database." In turn, the database cites Penn World Table 5.6 as the source.

16. All data on Korea in this chapter relate to the calendar year. Periods such as 1963–73 are inclusive of the beginning and ending years. This means that 1963–73 refers to the eleven-year period inclusive of both 1963 and 1973.

17. During the 1980s, manufacturing share saw a slight downturn, declining to 29 percent in 1990.

18. I draw heavily on Panagariya (2006) in Sections 4 and 5 except subsection 5.1.

19. I had offered this hypothesis earlier in Panagariya (2002).

20. For even earlier views along these lines, see Lewis (1962, p. 226–27).

21. I rely heavily though not exclusively on Datta Chaudhari (1996) for the discussion of the IDA.

22. In this context, Datta Chaudhari (1996, p. 16) offers the following insightful quotation from the High Court judge I. B. Mehta (1994): "Some judges are overwhelmed by the view that the only object and purpose of the Industrial Disputes Act is to take a view favorable only to labor, ignoring other facts and circumstances as also the necessity of preserving industrial peace. It is sometimes forgotten that the problem confronting industrial adjudication is to promote two-fold objectives: (1) security of employment of the workers; and (2) preservation of industrial peace and harmony so that industry can prosper and employment can increase. Any lopsided view, that to favor labor is the only goal of the statute, is counterproductive in as much as it ultimately harms the cause of labor itself."

23. For example, see Fallon and Lucas (1991, 1993), Dutta Roy (2004), Besley and Burgess (2004), and Ahsan and Pages (2005).

24. See Roy and Bagai (2005, box 5).

REFERENCES

Acharya, Shankar. 2004. "India's growth prospects revisited," *Economic and Political Weekly* (October 9).

Ahsan, Ahmad and Carmen Pages. 2005. "Helping or Hurting Workers? Assessing the Effects of *de jure* and *de facto* Labor Regulations in India," Washington, D.C.: World Bank.

Bardhan, Pranab. 2006. "Globalization Hits Road Bumps in India," *Yale Global Online* (October 3), http://yaleglobal.yale.edu/display.article?id = 8246

Besley, T. and R. Burgess. 2004. "Can Regulation Hinder Economic Performance? Evidence from India," *Quarterly Journal of Economics* 119:91–134.

Bhagwati, Jagdish. 1988. "Poverty and Public Policy," *World Development* 16:539–55.

———. 2004. *In Defense of Globalization* (New York: Oxford University Press).

Bhagwati, Jagdish and Arvind Panagariya. 2004. "Great Expectations," *Wall Street Journal* (May 24), op-ed page.

Bosworth, Barry, Susan Collins, and Arvind Virmani. 2007. "Sources of Growth in the Indian Economy." *India Policy Forum.* Forthcoming.

Datta Chaudhari, Mrinal. 1996. "Labor Markets as Social Institutions in India," IRIS-India Working Paper no. 10. Center for Institutional Reform and the Informal Sector. University of Maryland at College Park.

Deaton, Angus and Jean Drèze. 2002. "Poverty and Inequality in India: A Reexamination." *Economic and Political Weekly* (September 7), 3729–48.

Deaton Angus and Valerie Kozel. 2005. "Data and Dogma: The Great Indian Poverty Debate," *World Bank Research Observer* 20(2):177–99.

Dutta Roy, S. 2004. "Employment Dynamics in Indian Industry: Adjustment Lags and the Impact of Job Security Regulations," *Journal of Development Economics* 73:233–56.

Fallon, P. and R.E.B. Lucas. 1991. "The Impact of Changes in Job Security Regulations in India and Zimbabwe," *World Bank Economic Review* 5:295–413.

———. (1993). "Job Security Regulations and the Dynamic Demand for Labor in India and Zimbabwe," *Journal of Development Economics* 40:241–75.

Harvie, Charles and Hyun-Hoon Lee. 2003. "Export-Led Industrialization and Growth—Korea's Economic Miracle 1962–1989," *Australian Economic History Review* 43(3):256–86.

Kelkar, Vijay. 2004. "India: On the Growth Turnpike." 2004 Narayanan Oration, Australian National University.

Kochhar, Kalpana, Raghuram Rajan, Arvind Subramanian, and Ioannis Tokatlidis. 2006. "India's Pattern of Development: What Happened, What Follows?" NBER Working Paper no. 12023.

Lewis, John P. 1962. *Quiet Crisis in India* (Washington, D.C.: Brookings Institution).

Mahanalobis, P. C. 1969. "The Asian Drama: An Indian View," *Sankhy&amacr, The Indian Journal of Statistics*, series B, 31(3&4):435–58.

Mehta, T. U. 1994. "Contribution of Judiciary to Industrial Equity," in D. S. Saini, ed., *Labor Judiciary, Adjudication and Industrial Justice* (New Delhi: International Book House Publishing).

Roy, Jayanta and Shweta Bagai. 2005. "Key Issues in Trade Facilitation," World Bank Policy Research Working Paper no. 3703. Washington, D.C.: World Bank.

Panagariya, Arvind. 2000. "My Millennium Wish: Double-Digit Growth," *Economic Times*, January 12.

Panagariya, Arvind. 2002. "Why India Lags behind China," *Economic Times* (May 22).

———. 2006. "India and China: Trade and Foreign Investment." Paper presented at the Pan Asia 2006 Conference, Stanford Center for International Development, June 1–3.

———. 2007. "Why India Lags Behind China and How It Can Bridge the Gap," *World Economy* 30(2):229–48.

Saha, V., A. Kar and T. Baskaran. 2004. "Contribution of Informal Sector and Informal Employment in Indian Economy." Paper presented at 7th Meeting of the Expert Group on Informal Sector Statistics, New Delhi (February).

Srinivasan, T. N. 2003. "Indian Economy: Current Problems and Future Prospects." Lecture delivered under the auspices of the ICFAI Business School, Chennai, India, January 3.

Yoo, Jungho. 1997. "Neoclassical versus Revisionist View of Korean Economic Growth." Development Discussion Paper no. 588, Harvard Institute for International Development, Harvard University.

Zagha, Roberto. 1998. "Labor and India's Economic Reform," *Journal of Policy Reform* 2(4):403–26.

COMMENT I

Barry Bosworth

Arvind Panagariya has provided a very useful assessment of the current condition of the Indian economy. It highlights the contradictions that arise in any discussion of India's economic prospects. There is much to be positive about; but there is also an intimidatingly long list of severe problems. The primary conclusion of the chapter is that the fundamental challenge is to achieve an accelerated growth of employment for the unskilled portions of India's labor force. That is, growth must be broadened beyond the current emphasis on skilled labor and capital-intensive industries. To Panagariya, that means expanding the role of the manufacturing sector, particularly in the area of low-tech assembly where China has done so well. He argues that India's restrictive labor laws and weak infrastructure are significant barriers to such growth, but that the small-firm reservation system is no longer important.

The first portion of the paper documents the positive developments. Clearly there has been a sustained acceleration of GDP growth that began sometime in the 1980s and which seems to have gained momentum in recent years. Most recently, growth has been supported by a phenomenal expansion of trade in both merchandize and services. In fifteen years, exports have grown from only 7 percent of GDP to over 20 percent. India has also begun to attract significant amounts of foreign capital, though much of it is portfolio capital rather than foreign direct investment. India is clearly integrating with the global economy at a rapid pace. Panagariya also points to telecommunications and automobiles as areas of major domestic success.

However, the paper also identifies a long list of problems that threaten the sustainability of growth. Poverty has been reduced, but there is concern about the lack of obvious gains in rural areas. The economic acceleration

Table 1.6 Growth of GDP and Employment by Sector, 1960–2004

	Annual Percentage Rate				
Period	Total	Agriculture	Industry	Services	Mfg
		GDP Growth			
1960–80	3.4	1.9	4.7	4.9	4.6
1980–2004	5.8	2.8	6.4	7.6	6.6
1993–2004	6.5	2.2	6.7	9.1	6.8
		Employment Growth			
1960–80	2.2	1.8	3.1	2.8	2.7
1980–2004	1.9	1.0	3.5	3.6	2.6
1993–2004	1.7	0.6	3.8	3.3	2.9

Source: Central Statistical Office, various publications.

has been remarkably concentrated among the high-skilled capital-intensive industries with a corresponding concentration of the gains among an emerging middle and upper class. And while GDP growth has clearly accelerated since 1980, it is harder to see that anything has changed in terms of the overall growth of jobs. This last contrast is highlighted in Table 1.6. GDP growth, shown in the top panel, has clearly accelerated in all three major sectors, with the largest increase in services. However, a focus on employment change in the lower panel leaves an impression of far more modest gains. Employment growth in industry and services has accelerated by less than a percentage point in each, with no improvement in the critical area of manufacturing.

I believe that it is also easy to exaggerate the role of services in driving the economic expansion. Business services are a very small industry that employs a limited number of highly educated workers who comprise a small proportion of the Indian workforce. Communications and finance have also been areas of strong growth, but, again, they do not employ low-skilled workers. Traditional services—transportation and trade—have responded to growth in the rest of the economy, but they are not drivers of growth.

Furthermore, the statistics on trade in business services, which have attracted so much attention in both the United States and India, have large problems. In recent years, India has consistently reported a level of exports to the United States in the category of business, professional, and technical (BPT) services that is more than twenty times that recorded by the United States as an import—$8,700 million versus $402 million, for example, in 2003. The General Accountability Office sent a team to India and issued a report in 2005 that identified most of the discrepancies.[1] To begin with, the U.S. estimates are too low: the Bureau of Economic Analysis reports country-specific data only for unaffiliated trade because it believes that multinational companies cannot accurately account for their intra-firm trade by country. Given the importance of affiliated trade, it would be reasonable to increase the U.S. estimate by a factor of 3 to 4. Also, the importation of computer software embedded in imported computers is classified as part of goods trade rather than as services.

Issues with the Indian data account for most of the discrepancy. The India balance of payments deviates from international standards in two major respects. First, India's service exports include the earnings of Indian workers resident in the United States, whereas they are excluded by the United States if they intend to stay more than one year. That activity is believed to represent about 40 percent of total BPT exports. Second, India reports the internal sale of services to local affiliates of U.S. firms as part of its exports. That is estimated to be about 30 percent of the total. Thus, the GAO concluded that the reported level of service exports to the United States was overstated, relative to international standards, by a factor of 2 to 3.

I agree with Panagariya that the greatest challenge is the striking lack of interest on the part of both domestic and multinational firms in India's unskilled workforce. Unless this situation can be changed, India's growth is likely to flounder for both economic and political reasons. There are already signs of shortages in the markets for more skilled workers, and without more widespread participation, it will be difficult to sustain political support for the process of liberalization and integration with the global economy. Thus, the central question is why is the demand for India's unskilled, low-wage workers so low?

The major candidate in earlier decades would have been the small-firm reservation strategy, but Panagariya argues that it was largely eliminated during the 1990s and cannot explain the continued weakness of the low-skill end of the manufacturing sector in recent years. Instead, he points to the labor protection policies and infrastructure bottlenecks. Regulations governing employment conditions differ dramatically between firms in the unorganized (fewer than ten employees) and the organized (ten or more employees) sectors. The obligations of employers in the organized sector increase with the size of the firm and are comparable to those in most high-income economies—employer provision of pensions and health care, minimum-wage standards, and restrictions on job terminations and reassignments. In the international market for low-skilled labor, businesses are likely to go elsewhere.

Some business groups have argued that the labor laws are not all that constraining because the regulations can be easily avoided by relying on contractual workers. It makes sense to me that the labor regulations would be a severe disincentive to locating industry in India, but there is a surprising shortage of empirical research on the issue. I would have liked to see some data, for example, comparing the size distribution of Indian manufacturing firms with that of other countries at a comparable stage of development. Also, since some large enterprises are doing well, what is the differentiating feature?

Panagariya also criticizes the bankruptcy laws that force some firms to pay the workers of failed enterprises out of the income of other activities. He advocates a reform of the bankruptcy laws that would expedite the process but also give workers priority over creditors in the disposal of assets. This is a more complex matter than he suggests, and individual clauses could have unintended consequences. For example, his proposal would seemingly vitiate loan terms that incorporate collateral requirements.

We have heard a lot about the severity of India's infrastructure problems, particularly in the areas of transportation and electric power. It is unclear, however, whether the problem is one of capacity or poor management. In electric power, it certainly seems as though the difficulty is management; and without reform, the expenditure of more funds may simply lead to even more waste. Panagariya correctly emphasizes the reform aspects. On the other hand, I was surprised by his advocacy of moving freight traffic away from the railroads to highways. In many other countries, I thought that there was agreement that the promoting of highways over rail for the long-distance movement of freight had been a mistake. Would not India be better served by promoting an integrated railroad system of freight transportation?

Overall, I agree with Panagariya's emphasis on the need to promote low-skill manufacturing; however, the barriers to the development of competitive firms in these areas appear daunting. In the meantime, the global production system has evolved into a sophisticated network of intra-industry specialization. It may be difficult for India to become an effective new entrant into that network.

The chapter ends with a brief discussion of the problems in India's system of higher education. The sad state of the educational system in India will come as a surprise to many outsiders who have heard much about the success in ITC services. Developing a consensus on the need for reform and providing the requisite magnitude of resources strikes me as another major challenge to sustained future growth.

I am greatly impressed by the breadth of this chapter. At the same time, I found the underlying message to be a sobering one, leaving me with a concern over the difficulties and challenges of sustaining future growth rather than the optimism one might expect to result from an extrapolation from the recent past.

NOTE

1. United States General Accountability Office. 2005. "International Trade: U.S. and India Data on Offshoring Show Significant Differences," Report to Congressional Committees (October). Available at: http://www.gao.gov/new.items/d06116.pdf

COMMENT II

Mihir A. Desai

Arvind Panagariya has written an exhaustive and very helpful review of the state of the Indian economy and its future prospects. As a good two-handed economist, Panagariya assures us that there is reason for optimism but much to fret about. The rising importance of trade and foreign investment during a period of rupee stability underlie his optimism for continued strong economic growth. Panagariya views the absence of a more important manufacturing sector with associated employment in the organized sector as the fundamental roadblock to a more fundamental transformation of the Indian economy. That absence, in turn, is traced primarily to labor regulations and inadequate infrastructure. In short, Panagariya tells us to "be happy and do worry."

There are many reasons to be happy and yet worry in India today, but has Panagariya isolated the most important ones? The growth narrative that runs through Panagariya's paper is one in which manufacturing in the organized sector is required for "transformation" and long-term growth. A comparison to the growth experience of Korea in the 1960s and China in the early 1990s is employed to make this point. This comparison may be misleading owing to the changing nature of manufacturing around the world. Using data from the World Bank, it is hard to find a grouping of countries by income where manufacturing has grown over the last decade. Indeed, in various emerging markets (including China), rising services shares of value-added are the norm over the last decade. Comparisons with South Korea's experiences from the 1960s may no longer be relevant in this regard. It is not clear what has happened to manufacturing and its measurement but it seems that it has not been critical to many growth success stories in the last decade.

Fetishizing manufacturing and the role of employment in the organized sector may be a particularly worrisome idea in India, as such arguments can be used to motivate interventionist policies to spur manufacturing employment—not unlike the recent employment guarantee scheme. In fact, manufacturing is already enjoying a renaissance, as evidenced by sharply rising merchandise exports and strong investment levels. While it is not keeping pace with the continued meteoric growth of services, it is not clear that this is an important source of concern.

An emphasis on the organized sector, manufacturing, and the policies that appear to hinder such employment also obscures other concerns. The social infrastructure of public health and educational services, and the fiscal demands of creating such an infrastructure, is the critical challenge of the next several decades. Managing macroeconomic stability and inflationary pressures when the current account deficit, adjusted for private transfers, is at a level that approximates what it was in 1991, is perhaps the most daunting short-term concern.[1] Understanding that remarkable levels of global liquidity and a benign global environment have contributed mightily to India's recent experience also suggests that bracing for a change in those conditions should be a primary concern.

There is much to be happy about and yet to worry about in India today. Labor regulations and the shortage of required infrastructure are surely hurting India and merit attention. The transformation narrative, however, may obscure other, more worrying concerns and inspire the kinds of interventionist policies that India has, most happily, recently abandoned.

NOTE

1. Speech by Y.V. Reddy titled "Dynamics of Balance of Payments in India," available at http://www.rbi.org.in/scripts/BS_SpeechesView.aspx?Id = 319

CHAPTER 2

Unfinished Reform Agendum: Fiscal Consolidation and Reforms

T. N. Srinivasan[1]

1. INTRODUCTION

1.1 ACCELERATION OF REAL GDP GROWTH PER CAPITA SINCE 1980

The growth rate of real GDP (at factor cost) of India increased significantly in the 1980s (the precise initial date of the increase is unimportant) compared to the previous decades. With the rate of growth of population steadily going down, the rate of growth of real per-capita GDP more than tripled from 1.5 percent per year during 1950–80 to 4.7 percent since then. In the three years ending in March 31, 2006, the rate of growth of real GDP per capita was a little under 6 percent, with it rising even higher to 7.7 percent in 2006–7. Table 2.1 provides the relevant data.

The step-up in growth that began in the decade of the eighties was no accident. As is well known, India's development strategy since 1950, until the systemic reforms after 1991 and some hesitant piecemeal reform in the mid-eighties, was articulated through five-year and annual plans put together by the Planning Commission. The state played a dominant role in three ways: first, by emphasizing import substitution across the board and general industrialization as core strategies; second, by appropriating a large share of the savings of the economy for its own use, largely for public investment until the eighties and also for public consumption thereafter; and third, by attempting to steer the private sector to conform to the priorities and targets set in the plans through various instruments of control, many of which were in the form of quantitative restrictions rather than taxes and subsidies. Moreover, most of the instruments of control were exercised on a discretionary, case-by-case basis, rather than through a set

Table 2.1 Average Real GDP Growth (Percent per Year)

	GDP	Population	Per Capita GDP
1951–61[1]	3.9	2.1	1.8
1960–70[1]	3.4	2.3[2]	1.1
1970–80[2]	3.6	2.1[2]	1.5
1980–90[1]	5.7	2.1[6]	3.6
1990–2000[1]	6.0	1.8[6]	4.2
2001–3[5]	4.6	1.7[1]	2.9
2003–4[5]	8.5	1.7[1]	5.8
2004–5[7]	7.5	1.7[1]	5.8
2005–6[7]	9.0	1.7[1]	7.3
2006–7	9.4[7]	1.7[1]	7.7

[1] MOF (2006a), Appendix Tables 1.2 and 1.6
[2] World Bank (1982), Table 2, Table 17
[3] World Bank (2005a), Table 4.1
[4] World Bank (2006), Table 4.1
[5] RBI (2006a), Table 1
[6] World Bank (1993), Table 26
[7] RBI (2008), Table 1

of rules, and in effect insulated producers from domestic and international competition. The 1980s saw some liberalization of the regime of controls. The liberalization in combination with an expansionary fiscal policy accelerated growth.

1.2 FISCAL PROFLIGACY, DEBT ACCUMULATION, AND THE BUILDUP TO THE CRISIS OF 1991

Until the 1980s, macroeconomic policy was stable and indeed conservative. In the three decades 1950–80, only in three years did current expenditures of the central and state governments exceed current revenues and that too by very small proportions of less than 0.10 percent of GDP. With the Index of Consumer Prices rising fivefold between 1950 and 1980, the average rate of inflation in the three decades was a modest 5 percent per year. From then on, current expenditures exceeded current revenues in every year, with the excess, which is called the revenue deficit in Indian data, reaching 6.89 percent of GDP in 2001–2 (MOF 2006b, table 4.2). The revised estimates for 2006–7 show a revenue deficit of 2.1 percent of GDP, which is budgeted to fall to 1.3 percent of GDP in 2007–8 (RBI 2008, table 15). The gross fiscal deficit (GFD) data are available on a comparable basis only from 1980–81 on. These show that GFD rose steadily from 5.9 percent of GDP in 1982–83 to as high as 9.9 percent in

1986–87. In the year of macroeconomic crisis, namely 1990–91, it was 9.4 percent of GDP (RBI 2008, table 248). It is still high at 6.4 percent of GDP in the revised estimates for 2006–7 and is budgeted at 5.5 percent of GDP in 2007–8 (RBI 2008, table 15). The combined total outstanding liabilities of the central and state governments together rose from 48.4 percent of GDP in 1980–81 to 64.2 percent in 1990–91 (RBI 2007, table 249). In contrast, it was 80.6 percent at the end of 2006–7 and is budgeted to come down slightly to 74.6 percent by the end of 2007–8.

The external liabilities (at historical exchange rates) of the central government came down steadily from 7.9 percent of GDP in 1980–81 to around 2 percent of GDP in 2006–7. Total external debt at the end of 1991–92, immediately after the crisis, was 38.7 percent of GDP, with short-term debt having come down slightly from 10.2 percent of total debt to 8.3 percent (RBI 2007, table 163). At the end of March 2007, total debt was only 16.4 percent of GDP, with short-term debt at 7.7 percent of total debt (RBI 2008, table 150). The debt service ratio has fallen steadily from 35.3 percent of GDP in 1990–91 to 4.8 percent of GDP in 2006–7 (RBI 2008, table 163). Although the external debt situation has improved substantially since the crisis year of 1990–91, total debt of the government, at nearly 75 percent of GDP in 2007–8 is alarming.

The buildup toward the crisis of 1991 came from domestic and external sources. Most of India's external debt until the early 1980s was long-term and was owed to other governments and the multilateral banks. In 1980, three quarters of external debt was concessional. By 1990, this proportion had fallen to 47 percent. In 1980–81, out of $18.3 billion of public and publicly guaranteed external debt, $2.0 billion was owed to private creditors (World Bank 1990, table 4.1). On the eve of the macroeconomic crisis in 1990–91, external debt had nearly quadrupled to $71.1 billion, of which $23 billion was owed to private creditors (World Bank 2000, table 3.1a). Debt to external private creditors thus grew eleven-fold in ten years. What was left to finance of the gross fiscal deficit, after domestic and external borrowings, small savings, and provident funds, was monetized through the ad hoc sale of treasury bills to the Reserve Bank of India (RBI). For example, in 1988–89 and 1989–90, before the crisis year of 1991, the gross fiscal deficits of the center and states together were rupees (Rs.) 356.7 and Rs. 452.0 billion, respectively. Nearly Rs. 62.4 billion and Rs. 109.1 billion, respectively, of the deficits were financed by treasury bills (World Bank 2000, table A4.4). Domestic debt held outside of the banking system grew sixfold, from Rs. 290 billion to Rs. 1,752 billion in the decade 1980–81 to 1990–91. Debt held by the banking system grew roughly at the same rate from Rs. 257 billion to Rs. 1,419 billion during the same period (World Bank 2000, table A4.14).

In the eighties, besides the macroeconomic mismanagement, serious political instability emerged. Rajiv Gandhi, who succeeded his mother after her assassination in 1984 and won a massive electoral victory for his Congress Party in that same year, was soon caught up in a corruption scandal over military procurement (the Bofors episode). He was unable to overcome opposition to the few economic reforms he had initiated. The Congress lost the elections of 1989 and was succeeded by V. P. Singh as the head of a non-Congress coalition. Singh resigned in 1990 and was replaced by a minority government headed by Chandrasekhar with support from the outside by the Congress Party. He too soon lost support and resigned. New elections were called for June 1991, and during the campaign, Rajiv Gandhi was assassinated.

The rising fiscal deficits, together with the steep rise in oil prices during the Gulf crisis of 1990, put pressure on prices and the exchange rate, fueling expectations of an imminent devaluation of the currency. Political instability in 1990, as reflected in two changes of prime minister within a year, led to a lack of confidence among nonresident Indians (NRIs) in the government's ability to manage the economy. The expectation of a devaluation of the rupee and the decline in confidence led to the withdrawal by NRIs of their deposits in Indian banks and of other capital by external investors. Foreign exchange reserves dwindled to a level that was less than the cost of two weeks' worth of imports. The specter of default on short-term external loans loomed and led to a downgrading of India's credit rating.

Although the fiscal profligacy of the eighties and its financing through domestic and external borrowing inexorably led to the macroeconomic crisis of 1991, the eighties were also a period of hesitant reforms. Since the sixties, there have always been attempts at moderating the rigors and the unintended side effects, as well as distributional consequences, of the control system. The earliest of these liberalizations occurred after a severe macroeconomic crisis in 1966 that forced the government to approach the International Monetary Fund (IMF) and the World Bank for assistance. As part of the agreement with the two institutions, the rupee was devalued in June 1966 and, for a brief period of two years, controls on foreign trade were relaxed. Prime Minister Indira Gandhi, who had come to power less than six months earlier, was politically vulnerable. Many senior leaders in her own party as well as opposition parties were adamantly against devaluation and liberalization. Their opposition, and the failure of the World Bank to deliver the substantial non-project assistance it had promised in support of liberalization, led Mrs. Gandhi to abort ongoing liberalization. She did not attempt any liberalization thereafter until shortly before her assassination in 1984. The second liberalization, in the mid-eighties, was initiated by Rajiv Gandhi and the young economists appointed by him at senior levels in his office and economic ministries. They had served on the staff of the World Bank and were keen on releasing rigid controls. It so happened that reserves of food grains and foreign exchange were comfortable at the time. This enabled Rajiv Gandhi's government to experiment with relaxing a few of the restrictive trade and investment policies without fear of triggering a balance-of-payments crisis. This liberalization, though by no means comprehensive and systemic, did increase the potential output from existing capacity. But for the increased potential to be realized, demand had to be expanded. However, with no improvement in the international competitiveness of domestic producers, the demand increase would have to be domestic rather than from exports. Domestic demand was stimulated by fiscal expansion, financed by borrowing at home and abroad and by some monetization of fiscal deficits.

Clearly, the reckless fiscal expansionism of the 1980s was unsustainable. However, accompanied by the few liberalizing changes, it did generate growth. For some industries, these changes simply involved delicensing; others were allowed more flexibility in the use of their own capacities, thanks to the relaxing of some import restrictions and the permitting of changes in their product mixes within the licensed capacity (under so-called broad banding). Indeed, an industrial mini-boom took place from 1985 to 1990, with value added by manufacturing growing at an average rate of 8.3 percent per year, peaking at 11.7 percent in 1989–90. The average annual growth rates of real GDP under the sixth and seventh plans (which covered the 1980s) were 5.5 and 5.8 percent, respectively—much higher than the infamous Hindu growth rate of 3.75 percent during 1950–80. The 1980s also covered the period of a steep reduction in the proportion of poor in India's population—from 48.36 percent in 1977–78 to 34.07 percent in 1989–90 (World Bank 2000, Annex Table 1.1). Needless to say, a reduction in poverty achieved during a period of unsustainable debt-led growth could not have lasted.

1.3 REFORMS OF 1991

It is no surprise that India went to the World Bank and IMF again in 1991 as it had done earlier in 1966 after a severe balance-of-payments and macroeconomic crisis. The conditionalities of the two institutions for their assistance were also the same as in 1966: devaluation and liberalization. What was different this time was the government initiated a set of systemic reforms that went beyond the conditionalities. The reform agenda was broad and systemic. It included: fiscal consolidation, abolition of investment and import licensing, unification and largely market determination of exchange rates, relaxation of restrictions inhibiting foreign direct investment, and reforms of debt management, telecommunications, and the financial sector. The economy responded well to the reforms—the rate of growth of GDP rebounded from 1.5 percent in the crisis year of 1991–92 to reach a peak of 7.8 percent in 1996–97. Subsequently, the growth rate fluctuated, though in the three years ending in 2006–7 it has averaged 8.6 percent a year (Table 2.1).

In my view, the reasons that systemic reforms were undertaken after the 1991 crisis, rather than a return to the status quo as happened after 1966, were basically two: the collapse of the Soviet Union and its planned economy on which Indian planning was modeled, and the rapid growth of China since its opening in 1978. Having fought and lost a boundary war with China in 1962, India could not afford to be left behind by China. It is also the case that many in India—in government, in politics, in business, in media, and in the street—view China as India's only relevant economic rival and comparator. With the rapid growth of both economies since 1980, the outside world has also come to recognize the likely global impact of rapid growth in the two giants.

1.4 DOES FISCAL CONSOLIDATION MATTER?

The progress in fiscal consolidation and reform was checkered, with some initial success and subsequent reversal: the consolidated fiscal deficit[2] of the central and state governments came down from 9.3 percent of GDP in 1990–91 (6.61 percent at the center and 3.19 percent at the states) to 6.26 percent of GDP in 1996–97 (4.11 percent at the center and 2.66 percent at the states) (MOF 2006b, table 4.3). From then on the consolidated deficit reached a peak of 9.63 percent of GDP in 2001–2, as high as it was in the crisis year.[3] The pattern of the rise between 1996–97 to a peak, and then some fall thereafter, was different for the center and states: the post 1996–97 peak for the center at 6.18 percent (ignoring the 6.43 percent reached in 1993–94) was reached in 2001–2. For the states, the post 1996–97 peak was 4.61 percent in 1999–00. Clearly fiscal consolidation efforts had not been particularly successful. Indeed, to induce fiscal consolidation, Fiscal Responsibility and Budget Management (FRBM) Acts have been legislated by the national Parliament and many state legislatures after 2001. These laws set target dates for a phased elimination of revenue deficits and substantial reductions in fiscal deficits.

The lack of success in fiscal consolidation has not been associated with any perceptible signs of macroeconomic stresses such as inflationary pressures or a rise in interest rates or incipient threats to the (managed) floating exchange rate regime. This has led to a debate as to whether high fiscal deficits pose a threat to India's economic growth and, more narrowly, whether the deficits have crowded out private investment. Some have argued that not all policy measures (either for raising revenue and/or for reducing expenditure) that consolidate fiscal deficits are the same, and the deleterious effects of some measures could outweigh the beneficial effects of any consolidation so brought about. These arguments have also led to an examination not only of the levels of revenues and expenditures but also of their composition, and also to a discussion of efficiency of expenditures. In turn, attention has been drawn to tax and expenditure reform of public enterprises, including partial disinvestment of part of public equity, as well as complete privatization (i.e., sale of all the equity) and the disposition of revenues from disinvestment and privatization.

1.5 EXCHANGE RATE REGIME AND FISCAL SOUNDNESS

An important element of the 1991 reform agenda related to exchange rate policy. As mentioned earlier, the preexisting multiple exchange rate system was replaced by a unified exchange rate (the rupee was made convertible for current account transactions with India's acceding to the IMF's Article VIII) that was to be determined largely by market forces. Yet, as in many other countries (Calvo and Reinhart 2002), the Indian authorities were not comfortable with relatively free floating of the exchange rate and in fact managed the exchange rate through interventions. As the external and financial sector reforms took root, with exports expanding faster than ever and foreign capital inflows (particularly portfolio flows) increasing, the concern about the exchange rate appreciating too fast and hurting exports led the authorities to intervene in exchange markets to acquire foreign exchange and accumulate reserves.[4] To some extent, the reserve accumulation was also driven by self-insurance motives reflecting the fear that the IMF-centered system for managing financial crises and contagion would be inadequate. As reserves continued to accumulate and the external payments situation seemed comfortable, the possibility of making the rupee fully convertible by making it convertible on capital as well as current transactions was explored by a committee (Tarapore Committee I) appointed by the Reserve Bank of India (RBI) in 1996. In its report of May 1997, the committee "set out detailed preconditions/signposts for moving toward capital account convertibility (CAC) and also set out the timing and sequencing of measures over a three-year period ending in March, 2000" (RBI 2006b, Chapter 3, p. 17). The government did not act on the committee's recommendations, and controls on capital flows remained.

Almost a decade later, in March 2006, the Prime Minister, in a speech at the RBI on March 18, 2006, referred to the need to revisit the subject of capital account convertibility (CAC) and requested the finance minister and the RBI to "revisit the subject and come out with a road map based on current realities" (RBI 2006b, p. 1). The RBI again appointed a committee (Tarapore Committee II), on March 20, 2006, with the same chairman and almost the same membership as the 1997 committee. Its report, submitted on July 31, 2006, was published in September 2006. It recommended moving toward "fuller capital account convertibility" (FCAC) over a period of five years ending in March 2011. It set out once again a phased program, or road map, for achieving FCAC, with preconditions/signposts to be met along the path.

Since CAC is not the main concern of this chapter, I will not delve deeply into it. I draw on the committee's report only to the extent that it bears on fiscal consolidation. The report emphasized fiscal consolidation as a key concomitant for FCAC. Noting that the fiscal deficit as measured does not fully allow for several other implicit and explicit liabilities of the government, it argued that

> generation of revenue surplus to meet repayment of the marketable debt should be viewed but as a first step towards fiscal prudence and consolidation. A large fiscal deficit makes a country vulnerable. In an FCAC regime, the adverse effects of an increasing fiscal deficit and a ballooning internal debt would be transmitted much faster and, therefore, it is necessary to moderate the public sector borrowing

requirement and also contain the total stock of liabilities. . . . [T]he combined domestic liabilities of the Center and States rose from about 56 per cent of GDP in 1996–97 to an estimated 79 per cent of GDP in 2005–06. The large gross borrowing of the government has consequential effects of crowding out private sector requirements, particularly, long-term requirements for infrastructure and other investments. More importantly, it has the adverse effect of raising interest rates; this would, in turn, hurt investment, output and employment. At the present time, the comfortable liquidity in the system, following large capital inflows, has resulted in interest rates being moderate. Once these capital flows slow down or reverse, the large gross borrowing programme of the government would force interest rates up to undesirably high levels. To obviate such high interest rates, it would be imperative to make arrangements for repayment of loans progressively out of the revenue surplus, while ensuring that the overall fiscal deficit is contained within the parameters laid down by the FRBM/TFC. By 2010–11 the Center should endeavor to build a revenue surplus of 1.0 per cent of GDP. (RBI 2006b, Chapter 4, p. 30)

The Committee's concerns about high fiscal deficits from the perspective of FCAC seem to be basically two:[5] the deleterious effects of high fiscal deficits and ballooning domestic debt would be transmitted much faster under a regime of CAC; and domestic interest rates would rise much more with a fall in the volume of external capital flows from current levels if the public sector's borrowing requirement remained high. The Committee does not spell out the mechanism of transmission nor does it make clear its thinking about the possible response of the domestic private sector (in particular, of private investment) to a fall in external capital inflows. Nonetheless, its presumption that fiscal consolidation not only ensures a well-functioning domestic financial sector but is a prerequisite for moving to fuller CAC, seems reasonable. The relation between fiscal deficits and current account deficits, the so-called "twin deficits" issue, has been discussed in the open economy macroeconomics literature and also in the Indian context (Basu and Datta 2005). The Committee's report makes no mention of this literature, although it would seem very relevant.

The macroeconomic literature on the consequences of fiscal deficits, in general, and India's deficits, in particular, is vast. The IMF in collaboration with the National Institute of Public Finance and Policy, New Delhi, held a conference on India's fiscal situation in New Delhi in January 2004, and the volume of conference papers has been published (Heller and Rao 2006).[6] Since this volume and the relevant literature are widely accessible, I will not discuss the wide-ranging contributions in them. I will, instead, focus on what I consider to be the most pertinent issues and draw on the literature relevant to them. The issues range from the relatively narrow one of fiscal sustainability and solvency in the conventional sense, to a very broad one of redrawing the architecture of India's economic management system, including fiscal federalism. This architecture was designed in 1950 and reflected the then prevailing circumstances, economic and political. It has remained largely unchanged, although circumstances have changed enormously.

This chapter departs from and adds to the literature by its emphasis on the need to redesign the outmoded fiscal architecture and makes a few proposals for such a redesign. Since this is its main contribution, I start with a discussion of the case for redesign in Section 2. In Section 3, I cover the following topics: fiscal policy and debt sustainability (Section 3.1); the role of fiscal policy in cyclical stabilization and in sustaining the target of an average annual rate of growth of real GDP of 8 percent or higher in the medium term (Section 3.2); the potential contribution of the FRBM legislation by parliament and state legislatures for achieving fiscal consolidation (Section 3.3); tax and expenditure reform (Section 3.4); and external sector implications, in particular whether the values for India for some of the indicators of vulnerability to financial crisis should be a cause for concern (Section 3.5). Except in the context of redrawing the architecture of economic management, I will not be offering any new proposals. I will conclude by highlighting the lessons that seem to be emerging from the literature (Section 4). I will not be presenting any formal theoretical model or econometric analysis.

2. RETHINKING OF INDIA'S ECONOMIC MANAGEMENT AND FISCAL SYSTEMS[7]

The basic political structure of the Indian Republic and of its fiscal federalism was set in the Constitution of India, adopted by India's Parliament in 1950. This structure has largely been left unchanged over five and a half decades, though its functioning has changed enormously. The system of economic management through central planning, with most economic policies (e.g., fiscal and monetary, foreign trade and payments) oriented toward the implementation of five-year plans, also dates back to 1950. However, the policy instruments used for the management of the economy have changed much more since 1950 than the structure of fiscal federalism.

2.1 FEATURES OF INDIA'S CONSTITUTION

India's Constitution, though federal, has strong unitary features that in fact date back to the colonial era Government of India Act of 1935. These features, in large part, reflected the political consensus among members of the Constituent Assembly that a strong central government was essential to address the trauma of partition of colonial India into the successor states of India and Pakistan, the problem of integrating former princely states with diverse socioeconomic and administrative features into the union, and the ever-present threat of "fissiparous" tendencies in the body politic. The constitution also created the architecture of fiscal federalism. It spelled out in some detail the assignment of taxation powers and expenditure responsibilities among states, mandated the appointment by the President of India of a Finance Commission every five years, and described its core duties—which require it to recommend the sharing of central taxes between the center and the states and of grants from the center to the states. On the advice of the central government, the President appoints the Commission and specifies its terms of reference. In all, twelve finance commissions have been appointed since 1950. The Twelfth Finance Commission (TFC) was appointed on November 1, 2002, and submitted its report on November 30, 2004. After the passage in 1993 of the 73rd and 74th amendments to the constitution on local governments, some state governments have appointed their own Finance Commissions to recommend devolution of finance to local governments.

Besides the constitutionally mandated Finance Commission, an extra-constitutional body, the Planning Commission, was established by a resolution of the central cabinet in March 1950, within three months of the adoption of the constitution. State governments appointed their own planning commissions or boards later on.

2.2 INCREASING DOMINANCE OF THE CENTRAL GOVERNMENT

Although the constitutional structure of economic relations between the center and state did not anticipate or require it, during the long era of central planning for national development the center has acquired through various channels substantial authority over the allocation of financial resources among the various levels of government and the private sector. First, the development plans of the states had to be formally approved by the Planning Commission. Second, in addition to the grants from the center to the states, as recommended by the Finance Commission under Article 275 of the constitution, the Planning Commission began making grants to states in support of their five-year plans. Third, central ministries made their own grants in support of centrally sponsored schemes to be implemented by the states. Presumably these were meant to subsidize states for undertaking schemes that had positive spillovers to other states and to the economy as a whole. The TFC (2004, p. 1) reports that transfers to states through all channels increased from 31.4 percent of gross revenue receipts of the center during the First Finance Commission to a high of 40.3 percent during the sixth commission, before they fell to 37.3 percent during the first two years of the eleventh.

Control of money and finance has also been an important centralizing feature of the Indian system. First, money creation was the exclusive privilege of the central government so that the revenues from seignorage accrued only to it. Second, with the nationalization of insurance companies and commercial banks in 1969, the central government acquired a large part of the investable resources of the financial sector for its use, either directly through lending or indirectly through cash reserve ratios (CRRs) and statutory liquidity ratios (SLRs). Selective credit controls and requirements of lending to priority sectors left little effective room for discretionary lending by financial intermediaries. Third, interest rates were also controlled by the central government. Of course, reforms since 1991 have brought about substantial changes: interest rates are no longer controlled (although the mandated rate on small savings sets a floor), CRRs and SLRs are well below their infamously high previous levels, and public equity in insurance companies and commercial banks has been partly divested. Still, the public sector (mostly the central government) owns 75 percent of the assets of commercial banks, and priority sector lending requirements have not disappeared. Besides the center owning a dominant share of assets of the banks, the central and state governments have vastly expanded their role in the economy, particularly by producing goods and services for which more cost-effective alternatives in the private sector have always existed or could have come into existence. Moreover, the center owned a dominant share of public enterprises in vital industries such as railways, telecommunications, air transport, steel, and heavy machinery.

Concentration of powers in the hands of the central government did not create serious conflicts in the early years of the functioning of the constitution, since the same political party, the Indian National Congress, ruled the center and states. Any potential interstate or center-state conflict was resolved within the party. During the seventeen years (1947–64) of Jawaharlal Nehru's prime ministership, the chief ministers of the states had strong local power bases within the party, and, as such, the Prime Minister could not impose central will on the states. After a brief period of political weakness during her prime ministership, Indira Gandhi managed to split the party and took the majority with her. She then systematically eliminated anyone with local political strength from chief ministership and installed in their place individuals personally loyal to her. This made local government beholden to her and the central government led by her. In fact, the rise of dynastic politics in the Congress Party dates back to her being made the Prime Minister. Similar tendencies are also seen in regional parties started and subsequently controlled by charismatic individuals and their family members. Resolving interstate conflicts through intraparty bargaining became irrelevant after Nehru's death in 1964.

Periodic attempts at reexamining center-state relations (e.g. the Sarkaria Commission in 1988) have not led to any fundamental changes in the constitution. The Inter-State Council (ISC) and also the National Development Council (NDC), which discusses and approves national five-year plans, however, have been constructive institutional additions.

2.3 CHANGES IN POLITICAL AND ECONOMIC LANDSCAPE SINCE 1950

The framers of India's constitution opted for a relatively centralized, "quasi-federal" system because of concerns about unity and stability as well as inequality and the potential for local elites to capture resources.[8] Implicit in this choice was the assumption that the central leadership (politicians and bureaucrats) would be more skilled and more honest than state and local politicians. Initially, therefore, state governments functioned basically as "corporate divisions" of the central ruling party, with local governments having little or no role to play in political or economic decision making. The size and distinct cultural homogeneity within most of India's major states and significant heterogeneity across states, combined with the constitutional decentralization of key government expenditure responsibilities, have been sources of tension. With a single party no longer controlling the governments at the center and the states, the rise of regional parties in the states and their participation in coalitions at the center, and above all, the changing political landscape (an increase in the political muscle of certain groups, particularly former untouchables called Dalits), many of the unitary features of India's constitution have become increasingly irrelevant.

The political story, revolving around the organizational decay and reduced political influence of the once-dominant Indian National Congress, coupled with the rise of the Bharatirya Janata Party (BJP) as a national "right-wing" party, and the emergence of regional and caste-based parties, has been extensively analyzed (Singh and Srinivasan 2006b).[9] Corruption and rent seeking spawned by the license-permit raj have also been analyzed. I will not summarize this literature except to note that the framers of India's constitution did not anticipate the emergence of a culture of corruption and the nature of political competition based on populism and caste. The circumstances then prevailing that led them to create a strong central government and a federal constitution with these strong unitary features no longer prevail.

The economic environment has changed enormously since 1950 when the Planning Commission was established to implement a consensus across the political spectrum on the need for planning that had been established prior to India's independence in 1947. Groups including the Indian Federation of Labour on the left end of the spectrum, as well as private business leaders on the right, and then the dominant Indian National Congress in the middle, accepted the need for planning as a means for articulating and implementing a national development strategy. They agreed on the desirability of a dominant role for the state in the economy, as well as for insulation of the economy from world markets (see Srinivasan and Tendulkar 2003, pp. 5–7 for details of the development plans published in the 1940s by these groups). This consensus also reflected the disastrous experience of the world economy between the two world wars. Prime Minister Nehru in particular, and also other leaders, believed in central planning (modeled after the Gosplan of the Soviet Union) and in a strong role for the state in the economy.

The circumstances that motivated the adoption of planning and the state's taking a dominant role in the economy no longer exist. Within three years after independence, the immediate problems arising from partition (in particular the absorption of millions of refugees from Pakistan) and problems from the Second World War had been addressed. The

Soviet Union collapsed in 1991, and central planning as a mode of articulating and implementing a development strategy had gone out of fashion even earlier. The need for economy-wide planning with the private sector playing only a limited role no longer exists. Markets have come to play a far greater role in the economy since the reforms of 1991. Besides emphasizing state control over the economy, the Indian development strategy from the 1950s until the mid-1980s was extremely inward-oriented, with across-the-board import substitution, implemented though a plethora of controls driving the investment pattern of the public and private sector. Foreign investment was actively discouraged and foreign borrowing was primarily from concessional loans of multilateral development banks and bilateral foreign aid. The economy has moved away from this dysfunctional strategy toward a new strategy with much greater openness to external competition and active pursuit of foreign investment (direct and portfolio). This shift was also accompanied by reforms in the financial sector along with making the rupee convertible for current transactions.

With the economy becoming integrated more and more with the world economy, both in trade in goods and services and in finance, the roles of domestic fiscal and monetary policies (and also of public investment in social and economic infrastructure, to the extent that the public sector continues to be the supplier of infrastructure services) have changed. They no longer serve to ensure that the public and private sectors conform to the targets of five-year plans. They now have to be consistent with foreign-sector policies, particularly with respect to the exchange rate and capital flows. Evidence from other federations (e.g., Argentina) suggests that the political economy conflicts of federalism in the fiscal arena can trigger an external payments/exchange rate crisis. As Indian policy makers are considering a road map for making the rupee fully convertible, they have to ensure that fiscal aspects of India's current federal system do not pose such a threat, and undertake appropriate actions to reform the system, if necessary, for this purpose.

Raja Chelliah, the doyen of Indian public finance economists and founder of the National Institute of Public Finance and Policy, pointed out that

> the root causes of the endemic fiscal crisis, especially in the states, are to be found in the simultaneous pursuit of fiscal objectives and policies which are in themselves incompatible. Carry-overs from the central planning era, these policies proceed on the basis that finances

> can be managed without reference to incentives, financial capacity of sub-national governments or fiscal discipline. Fiscal responsibility cannot be planned from above; rather rules and conditions must be created so that it will have to be practiced by states. Subject to this condition, state autonomy should not be affected by the system of central transfers rewriting the constitutional provisions regarding center-state fiscal relations. (Chelliah 2005, Abstract)

However, this will require considerable thought and debate and, in any case, will take a long time to accomplish. As a contribution to this debate, and based on the experience with the twelve Finance Commissions, let me discuss some problematic aspects of the commissions before turning to my proposals for institutional reforms, consisting of the creation of a Fiscal Review Council and reconstitution of the Planning Commission into a Fund for Public Investment.

2.4 FUNCTIONING OF FINANCE COMMISSIONS

The recommendations of each Finance Commission apply to the five-year period until the next commission is appointed. However, the sustainability of existing domestic and external debt of the central government, and the debt of state governments, cannot be judged without a perspective on revenues and expenditures and interest rates in the indefinite future beyond the five-year horizon of each commission. More importantly, even if the current commission does make its recommendations based on its perspective about the future, there is no way it can commit to preventing future commissions from having their own and possibly different perspectives about the future, even if there are no changes in the economy in five years to warrant it. Furthermore, the governments in power who are to act on the commission's recommendations, which have implications for future revenues and expenditures, cannot commit future governments, even if the party in power wins the election. In sum, myopia and short-term considerations would tend to bias the thinking of the commission and governments.

There is also a continuing problem with coordinating transfers recommended by the Finance Commission and the Planning Commission. In the past, an attempt was made to coordinate the approaches of the Finance and Planning Commissions by having a member of the Planning Commission serve as a member of the Finance Commission as well, but this had limited impact. The Twelfth Finance Commission (TFC 2004, Chapter 14) has recommended the creation of a permanent secretariat for itself and also of a research committee to undertake relevant studies for the commission. It has also recommended that each state set up a high-level monitoring committee to ensure proper utilization of the commission's grants. While these are unexceptionable, more could be done to ensure some depth and continuity in the analytical approach across commissions as long as the present constitutional arrangements remain.

The TFC, like its predecessors, and like conventional public finance economists, viewed its mandate as

> to recommend a scheme of transfers that could serve the objectives both of equity and efficiency, and result in fiscal transfers that are predictable and stable. These transfers, in the form of tax devolution and grants, are meant to correct both the vertical and horizontal imbalances. Correcting vertical imbalance relates to transfers from the central government to the state governments taken together, whereas the correction of horizontal imbalances is concerned with the allocation of transfers among the state governments. The vertical imbalance arises since resources have been assigned more to the central government and states have been entrusted with the larger responsibilities. The horizontal imbalance has its roots in the differential capacities and needs of the states as also the differences in the costs of providing services. (TFC 2004, p. 9)

Clearly, the vertical imbalance reflects in large part the constitutional provisions relating to taxes and expenditure responsibilities. Horizontal imbalances depend not only on differential capacities, needs, and costs but also on the efficiency with which capacities are used to deliver services at the least possible cost. Various commissions themselves have recognized that the "gap filling approach" of some past commissions seriously eroded the incentives to improve efficiency.

Successive Finance Commissions have studiously avoided getting into the question of the rationale for the existence of many public enterprises, partly as a result of their being given narrow terms of reference.[10] Their existence and operation have significant impacts on the revenues, expenditure and borrowing of governments at all levels. Indeed, the use of such enterprises for borrowing under state guarantees has created contingent liabilities for the states, besides being a nontransparent device outside of the formal budget to raise resources. Nonetheless, the Finance Commissions have not raised the question of whether public sector enterprises for which there is no social rationale for their being in the public sector (based on a consideration of their producing public goods or generating positive externalities) should be privatized. Instead of delving into the question of social rationale, the Indian debate on privatization has degenerated into whether public enterprises that are profit-making (at market prices) should be privatized. Given the impact on the economy of the existence and operation of public enterprises, and on fiscal deficits in particular, a serious analysis of their social rationale is needed. Protecting the jobs of those currently employed in these enterprises is not a convincing social rationale.

The narrow traditional approach of correcting vertical (between center and states) and horizontal (among the states) imbalances, without examining the broader question of the social rationale for the involvement of governments at various levels in the economy, can no longer be justified. The economics of fiscal federalism provides answers to the question of whether there is a legitimate rationale for public firms using public goods theory, applied to the case of different loci of benefits (Olson 1986). Based on this approach, many public enterprises in India are engaged in activities that would not even fall under the category of quasi-public or merit goods.[11] One area where the eleventh and twelfth Finance Commissions have played a constructive role is in making recommendations with respect to overall fiscal management: their broader terms of reference reflected a situation in which the central government executive, in an era of coalitions, may have lacked the direct power to rein in state fiscal deficits.

In its approach to horizontal imbalances, the TFC (2004, p. 10) refers to the concept of "equalization," considered in many federal countries to be "a guiding principle for fiscal transfers as it promotes equity as well as efficiency in resource use. Equalization transfers aim at providing citizens of every state a comparable standard of services, provided their revenue effort is also comparable." It goes on to add that, in Australia, the equalization principle has been defined to say that "states should receive funding . . . such that if each made the same effort to raise revenue from its own sources and operated at the same level of efficiency, each would have the capacity to provide services at the same standard . . . " and that, in Canada, equalization payments are meant to "ensure that provincial governments have sufficient revenues to provide reasonably comparable level of services at reasonably comparable levels of taxation."

The equalization concept seems eminently sensible if there is a social consensus on what should be included in the set of services to be provided by the government and at what level. The conventional argument for decentralizing their provision is that state (and local) governments are likely to be more informed about and more responsive to the heterogeneous preferences of their residents, and that competition among states could improve the quality and cost-effectiveness of services provided. But such competition, if it takes the form of subsidies or tax concessions to attract industrial investment, could turn into a ruinous "race-to-the-bottom."[12] Furthermore, the informational advantage of state governments with respect to the preferences of their residents may no longer be that important in the contemporary, informationally connected world. Incentives, however, still may favor decentralization, since a national government will tend to aggregate or balance across different constituencies. Hence, a state government's incentives may be better aligned with the preferences of constituents if they are heterogeneous, even if there is no difference in the informational asymmetry between the two levels.

It is evident that the architecture of fiscal federalism has to be reformed and the role of the planning commission has to be redefined to reflect the changes in domestic political structure and in the economic environment, domestic and global. I suggest the creation of a Fiscal Review Council and the reconstitution of the Planning Commission into a Fund for Public Investment.

2.5 FISCAL REVIEW COUNCIL

First, it would be very healthy if states and the center have means for discussing each other's fiscal policies in a common forum. No such forum exists now. The overall resource position of states, rather than their fiscal policies, figures in the discussions of state plans and their financing at the Planning Commission, and these discussions take place between the commission and each state separately. The National Development Council (NDC), in which state Chief Ministers are represented, on the other hand, discusses central plans, but the central government's fiscal policies are not part of these discussions. Even if the discussions at the Planning Commission and the NDC were expanded to cover fiscal policies, such discussions would become irrelevant once the system of five-year and annual plans is given up. There are ad hoc fora for discussion, such as the Empowered Committee of State Finance Ministers (ECSFM) and the meetings of state finance secretaries organized by the Reserve Bank of India, that do provide an opportunity for each state's representatives (finance ministers or finance secretaries) to be informed of, and to comment on, other states' policies. As is well known, the ECSFM under the leadership of Asim Dasgupta, Finance Minster of West Bengal, was instrumental in ushering in the value-added tax (VAT). But to the best of my knowledge, those fora do not discuss the central government's fiscal policies. It would be desirable to supplement, if not completely replace, these ad hoc fora by a formal Fiscal Review Council (FRC). The Prime Minster and Finance Ministers of India, the chief ministers and finance ministers of the states, and experts appointed by the Prime Minister in consultation with the chief ministers would constitute its membership. It could be patterned after the Trade Policy Review Mechanism of the World Trade Organization (WTO), which enables the members of the WTO to discuss, review and comment on each member's trade policies periodically.

The FRC could also learn from the experience of the European Union (EU). The EU introduced a new mechanism under which each member country submits to the European Commission each year a national reform action plan setting out how it intends to create jobs and growth, and in particular, how it will meet two or more specific economic targets: an employment rate of 70 percent of working-age population and an expenditure of 3 percent of GDP on R&D. Although the proposal of the former Dutch Prime Minister, Wim Kok, to use the EC review of action plans to "name and shame" countries that talked a good game but failed to deliver and "fame" those whose performance was exemplary, did not go far, there is something useful in this mechanism.

The FRC would meet at an appropriate frequency (certainly no more than once a year) to review the medium and long term fiscal policies of the states and center as well as make recommendations. Each state and the central government would submit to the FRC its plan (including specific tax and expenditure proposals) for achieving revenue and fiscal deficit targets (based on FRBM legislations) as included in its annual budget, and review its performance relative to the target in the previous fiscal year. Even if the FRC does not adopt a "name and shame or fame" approach, its report ranking the plans of states and the center based on their effectiveness and efficiency in achieving targets, if made public, would be very useful. To avoid political grandstanding and to encourage serious discussion, the meetings could be closed to the media. Whether the recommendations should be binding on all parties, or only advisory, is an issue that the FRC could decide. Each chief minister would have an opportunity to comment on and learn from the policies of other states and the center. Rankings and recommendations emerging from the review would have great political weight, and also would provide a commitment mechanism for each chief minister to undertake reforms in his or her state, which he or she may not be able to do unilaterally.

2.6 FUND FOR PUBLIC INVESTMENT

The center-state transfers through the Finance Commission, Planning Commission and the central ministries have to be looked at in a unified framework. Ignoring many details and simplifying a great deal, there are essentially three types of transfers: current revenue transfers as determined by the Finance Commission, capital transfers for financing investment (largely the domain of the Planning Commission), and transfers for internalizing positive externalities that one state's fiscal actions may have on other states and the economy as a whole (currently, the domain of centrally sponsored schemes).

In Section 2.3, I have discussed the transfers through the Finance Commission. Let me turn to the other two. In a unified framework, it would make sense for the center to assume full responsibility for financing investment and bear the operational costs of projects that have significant spillovers across states, regardless of the authority that implements them (center or state). The current system of centrally sponsored schemes, under which the center provides partial funding for a project's investment cost and for its operational cost for a limited period, has had the unfortunate effect that projects get started and completed but, once completed, are not fully utilized because states do not provide the funding to operate them once it becomes their exclusive responsibility to provide them. Assumption of full financial responsibility by the center would avoid this waste. Second, the current system of capital transfer for financing investment by states through the Planning Commission should be replaced by reconstituting the Planning Commission as a Fund for Public Investment (FPI) for both the center and states.[13] Its share holders will be the state and central governments. The FPI will operate much like a development bank for providing long-term development finance. It will borrow its loanable funds from domestic and foreign capital markets with guarantees from its shareholders, namely, central and state governments. It will appraise the projects for which the central or state governments wish to borrow from it for their feasibility, economic and social returns, and also for the soundness of the means by which the borrowing government (center or state) proposes to raise the rest of project investment, if the project is not to be fully funded by the FPI. In such an appraisal, the FPI will have to examine critically the issue of whether the central and state governments have taken advantage of the means of captive financing available to them. For example, the central government can park its deficits in the public sector banks, which must hold large quantities of government bonds. The states also have this luxury to some extent. Furthermore, they have been relying increasingly on access to small savings and pension funds to finance their deficits.

The TFC has argued that the center should not be the financial intermediary between state governments and capital markets at home and abroad, or between states and external aid agencies. Thus, states will have the freedom to borrow directly from capital markets and to negotiate with foreign aid agencies. Such freedom could lead to interstate imbalances in the flows and costs of financing. On the other hand, the potential for failure in being able to borrow at attractive terms or to solicit aid donors to fund them could also provide an incentive for states to undertake policies to make them more attractive to lenders and donors. The FPI will have an important role in this context for assessing whether a state's failure has occurred because of policy inadequacies or for reasons beyond the control of the failing state. To the extent that it finds the projects proposed by such states to be worthwhile from an economic and social perspective, the FPI could recommend capital transfers from the center to such states to make up for a failure due to reasons beyond their control to attract adequate funding from other sources. However, such FPI-recommended capital transfers should not carry any subsidy (relative to the cost of borrowing to the center) on interest rates. In other words, the FPI should not open a soft lending window similar to the International Development Association (IDA) window of the World Bank. There is no economic rationale for such a window. If a state is deemed "poor" for reasons of horizontal imbalance, such poverty should be addressed through the Finance Commission transfers and not through FPI.

The logic of the proposal for the FPI implies that each state replace its planning commission or board with its own fund for financing investment projects of local authorities along the same lines as for the central FPI. State level FPIs would, however, be restricted to borrowing only from domestic sources. The TFC's recommendation for limiting the role of the center as a financial intermediary and for letting the states borrow from the capital markets is being followed by the Reserve Bank. It is exploring the development of institutions to support this shift to market borrowing, including offering mechanisms, secondary markets for government debt, credit ratings, and methods of regulation and monitoring. Therefore, reforming financing states' capital expenditure through new borrowing mechanisms involves building on reforms already taking place in the financial sector. It is clear that there are imbalances across states in generating viable project proposals, identifying sources of finance and implementing them once approved. These "capacity" imbalances have to be addressed independently of proposals for project financing and transfers.

The creation of the FPI to replace the Planning Commission will not address some transitional issues such as restructuring the public debt of states. The TFC has also developed an elaborate scheme for restructuring the states' existing debts. Writing off any debt and/or rescheduling it, whether it is external debt of developing countries or the debt of states in India, can create a serious moral hazard—debt relief blunts the incentives to change behavior that led to the accumulation of debt in the first place. Although moral hazard cannot be eliminated altogether, conditionalities on debt relief, provided that they are credible, can alleviate moral hazard. The recommendations of TFC in this area do have conditionalities, making passage of FRBM legislation with specific debt-reduction targets a precondition for rescheduling and write-off. While the TFC has sensibly avoided confining the write-off only to the worst-off states, it should have been selective in other ways that do not create moral hazard.

3. PERSISTENT FISCAL DEFICITS: POSSIBLE CONSEQUENCES AND PROPOSALS FOR REFORM

3.1 FISCAL SUSTAINABILITY AND SOLVENCY

The trend in fiscal deficits of the center, the states, and the two consolidated together is visible in Table 2.2.

Six years prior to the beginning of the post-reform deterioration in fiscal deficits in 1997–98, Buiter and Patel (1992) presented an analysis of the sustainability of India's fiscal deficits, investigating whether their continuation would threaten fiscal solvency. Their analysis covered the period including the growth of fiscal deficits prior to the crisis of 1991. Not surprisingly, they found that unless corrective actions were taken, India faced fiscal insolvency. They returned to the issue several times, including most recently in 2006 (Buiter and Patel 1996, 1997, 2006). Buiter and Patel

Table 2.2 Fiscal Deficits (Percent of GDP)

	State			Center			Consolidated (Center and States)		
Year	Revenue	Primary	Fiscal (Gross)	Revenue	Primary	Fiscal (Gross)	Revenue	Primary	Fiscal (Gross)
1970–71	0.04	1.10	1.97	−0.36	1.76	3.08	–	–	–
1980–81	−1.03	1.73	2.58	1.42	3.96	5.77	0.4	4.1	6.3
1990–91	0.93	1.78	3.30	3.26	4.07	7.85	4.2	5.0	9.4
1996–97	1.18	0.85	2.72	4.88	0.53	4.88	3.6	1.3	6.4
1997–98	1.07	0.93	2.90	5.84	1.53	5.84	4.1	2.1	7.3
1998–99	2.51	2.20	4.27	6.51	2.04	6.51	6.4	3.7	9.0
1999–2000	2.78	2.39	4.72	5.41	0.75	5.41	6.3	3.8	9.5
2000–1	2.54	1.80	4.25	5.65	0.93	5.65	6.6	3.7	9.5
2001–2	2.60	1.50	4.20	4.40	1.50	6.20	7.0	4.0	9.9
2002–3	2.30	1.20	4.10	4.40	1.10	5.90	6.7	3.1	9.6
2003–4	2.30	1.50	4.40	3.60	−0.03	4.50	5.8	2.0	8.5
2004–5	1.30	0.70	3.40	2.50	−0.04	4.00	3.8	1.4	7.5
2005–6	0.20	0.20	2.50	2.60	0.40	4.10	3.1	1.6	6.7
2006–7 (Revised)	0.10	0.40	2.80	2.00	0.20	3.70	2.1	0.9	6.4
2007–8 (Budget)	−0.30	0.10	2.30	1.50	−0.20	3.30	1.3	0.2	5.5

Sources: RBI (2007), Tables 246, 247 and 248, RBI (2008), Table 15.

(2006) take on broad macroeconomic developments since 1991–92, including, in particular, the deterioration in fiscal deficits from 1997–98. They apply the conventional solvency criterion that the present discounted national value of debt, discounted by time varying default-risk free nominal interest rates, should be non-positive. Standard statistical tests are used to test for stability of parameters with no structural breaks, and also, conditional on an invariant structure being present in the data, to test whether the discounted debt process is covariance stationary or not. They note that non-stationarity of the debt-deficit process does not necessarily mean insolvency, but only that insolvency is inevitable with no change in fiscal policies. Also, a covariance stationary debt process, but with a positive deterministic trend, can also lead to insolvency. Finally, even with no deterministic trend, insolvency could arise if the unconditional expectation of the process is positive.

They conclude that: "on balance, our review (both informal and formal) indicates that the overall net public debt burden does not give cause for immediate alarm. There is also the possibility that the Indian sovereign has been helped to some extent by high GDP growth raising the denominator of the public debt (in rupees)-to-(nominal) GDP ratio . . . rather than the numerator being lowered by fiscal consolidation and restraint"

(Buiter and Patel 2006, p. 13). In their view, "the reasons India has remained fundamentally solvent are fast nominal GDP growth and financial repression" (ibid, p. 14). The authors recognize some limitations of their study: "Since we have not put forward a formal structural political-economic model of the evolution of debt and deficits, we are restricted to a mechanical description of the time series properties of the debt stock in terms of reduced form data generating processes" (ibid, p. 9). Even their use of the phrase "reduced form" is questionable, since a reduced form is derived from a structure that specifies exogenous and endogenous variables of a model. Given the admittedly mechanical description of the debt process, its sustainability may not even be necessary, let alone sufficient, for its optimality, from the perspective of an appropriate inter-temporal welfare indicator.

Debt and fiscal sustainability is also the theme of Rangarajan and Srivastava (2005). Their analytical framework is the simple and classic Domar (1944) model of the dynamics of debt accumulation. The model shows that given a constant rate of growth g of nominal GDP, nominal interest rate i, and primary deficit p (>0) as a ratio of GDP, the debt-to-GDP ratio b_t grows linearly over time if $g = i$, grows indefinitely if $g > i$ and converges to

$$b^{\cdot} = p\,\frac{(1+g)}{(g-i)} \text{ if } g > i.$$

In the last case, the fiscal deficit-to-GDP ratio f_t converges to

$$f^{\cdot} = p\left(\frac{g}{g-i}\right).$$

The authors note, correctly, that the Domar model defines "combinations of a stable debt-GDP ratio and fiscal deficit-to-GDP ratio but does not determine their best or most desirable values" (Rangarajan and Srivastava 2005, p. 2924).

The equation of motion for the debt-GDP ratio in the Domar model is

$$b_t - b_{t-1} = (p_t - p_t^s), \text{ where } p_t^s = b_{t-1}\left(\frac{g_t - i_t}{1+g_t}\right).$$

Thus, even if $g_t > i_t$, b_t will increase if the primary deficit/GDP ratio p_t exceeds its debt-stabilizing value p_t^s. For this reason, Rangarajan and Srivastava point out that once we depart from the assumption of constancy over time of g_t, i_t, and p_t, one has to consider the impact of debt and deficit levels on growth, which in turn requires consideration of their impact on savings and the investment of the private and public sectors.

The authors apply the Hodrik-Prescott filter to the time series of actual fiscal deficits to estimate its trend or structural component. The difference between the actual deficit and its structural component is its cyclical component. A similar break up of the actual primary deficits and interest payments is also computed. In all three, the structural component was by far dominant during 1990–91 to 2001–2. Concluding that large structural primary deficits and interest payment relative to GDP have had an adverse effect on growth in recent years, they urge that the debt-GDP ratio be brought down from its current high level in two phases, with an initial adjustment phase and a subsequent stabilization phase. In the first, the fiscal deficit would be reduced in each successive year until the revenue deficit is eliminated. In the second phase, the fiscal deficit would be stabilized at 6 percent of GDP so that the debt/GDP ratio stabilizes eventually at 56 percent, given that nominal GDP grows at 12 percent per year. Implicit in these numbers (and others in the paper on the ratio of interest payments-to-revenue receipts at 17 percent and the revenue receipts-to-GDP at 21 percent) are a nominal interest rate of 6 percent and a primary deficit of 3 percent of GDP. As far as I can judge, the authors do not provide any framework for deciding why these numbers are desirable except saying that "they would permit a large primary revenue expenditure to social sectors" (Rangarajan and Srivastava 2005).

It would seem from the analysis of Buiter and Patel (2006), as well as that of Rangarajan and Srivastava (2005), that the seeming sustainability of India's fiscal deficits should not lead to complacency. Some of the policies, such as aspects of financial repression that make deficits currently sustainable, are not desirable. If it is accepted, steps for containing fiscal deficits should be undertaken—the sooner the better.

3.2 FISCAL DEFICITS AND SUSTAINABILITY OF THE GDP GROWTH TARGET OF 8 PERCENT PER ANNUM

3.2.1 Relation Between Fiscal Deficits and Growth

The channels through which fiscal deficits could affect growth adversely can be seen from the perspective that there are three sources of growth: capital (human and physical) accumulation; improvement in the efficiency of resource use, and technical progress contributing to growth in total factor productivity (TFP). Public policies in general and fiscal policies (and deficits) in particular could influence all three sources.[14] First is the standard "crowding-out" channel that operates on physical capital accumulation. Financing fiscal deficits through borrowing could reduce private investment (at any interest rate) from its level in the absence of fiscal deficits. The source of financing both public sector borrowing and private investment is total savings, which consists of the sum of domestic private and foreign savings (i.e., foreign capital inflows). Ignoring some details, we can identify fiscal deficits with the public sector borrowing requirement or PSBR. Thus, any positive PSBR or an increase in it would mean that less of total savings would be available for private investment. Obviously, a reduction in private investment, *ceteris paribus* (in particular, with no change in public investment), would reduce the growth rate. However, if the public sector borrows for investment or for other growth promoting activities with higher returns compared to the private investment crowded out, the growth rate could go up, offsetting the negative effect of crowding out.[15]

Suppose, for simplicity, we ignore the existence of autonomous public sector enterprises. We can then equate PSBR with public investment expenditures net of the excess of current revenues over current expenditures. Thus, if current expenditures exceed current revenues, so that the public sector is running a revenue deficit, the government would be borrowing both for financing its investment and to finance the revenue deficit. This would violate the so-called "golden rule" of public finance that states that the public sector should borrow only for meeting its capital expenditures to the extent they exceed revenue surpluses. The Indian government has been violating the golden rule for a long time.

Public capital expenditure, such as spending on economic infrastructure, could be growth-enhancing in and of itself; and if the growth induced by such expenditures exceeds the growth that the private investment crowded out by it would have generated, the net effect on growth would be positive. More public investment in infrastructure could also increase private savings and investment, if such investment reduces private costs and increases the profitability of private investment. Private savings in the form of retained earnings of corporations could also rise to match investment in profitable opportunities. In other words, public infrastructural investment could "crowd in" rather than "crowd out" private investment. By the same token, fiscal consolidation achieved by compressing capital expenditures could have adverse growth effects (Rajaraman 2006). The point to take from all this is that a simplistic notion that fiscal deficits have "crowded out" investment and hence reduced growth needs to be qualified.

The fiscal deficit could influence growth through effects on human capital accumulation. In conventional budgeting, public expenditures on education and health (E&H) are classified as current expenditures along with those on wages and salaries of civil servants and others needed to operate the government. For example, an increase in E&H expenditures with no change in current revenues would raise fiscal deficits but could enhance growth, if such expenditures raise the growth of human capital (an assumption that will not hold if the system of the delivery of E&H services by the public sector continues to be wasteful and inefficient, as it currently is). By the same token, fiscal consolidation through a reduction in E&H expenditures, while keeping other current expenditures unchanged, could affect growth adversely.[16]

Fiscal deficits could, though not necessarily would, have an impact of the efficiency of resource allocation, including the allocation of factors. This effect is not from the fiscal deficits per se, but from the distortionary effect of the fiscal instruments (taxes and subsidies) in use. For example, attempts at fiscal consolidation by raising revenue through the use of a distortionary tax (or an increase of the rate of pre-existing one) would adversely affect the efficiency of resource allocation and total factor productivity growth.

Public policies towards R&D could obviously influence technical progress to the extent that these include direct expenditure on R&D by public agencies as well as subsidies for research development. Once again, if high fiscal deficits (or attempts at fiscal consolidation) constrain the options of the government in the pursuit of R&D by itself or its promotion of private R&D, technical progress and its contribution to growth would be attenuated.

3.2.2 Did Fiscal Deficits Crowd Out Private Investment in India?

Turning to the Indian situation, as noted earlier, fiscal deficits began rising from 1997–98 and the average annual growth rate of GDP during 1997–98 to 2001–3 was 5.3 percent (with significant year-to-year fluctuations), compared to an average of 6.8 percent (with an upward trend peaking at 7.8 percent in 1996–97) during the first five years (1992–97) after reforms. In the three years 2004–5—2006–7, according to the RBI (2008, Tables 1 and 15), not only did the GDP growth rate average 9 percent per year, but consolidated fiscal deficits began declining from a peak of 9.6 percent of GDP reached in 2002–3.[17] Moreover, private corporate sector investment, after rising from 6.28 percent of GDP at current prices in 1991–92 to 10.60 percent of GDP in 1995–96, began a steady decline thereafter, reaching a low of 5.80 percent of GDP in 2002–3. In the subsequent two years it rose to 6.8 percent and 8.2 percent, respectively. All this seems to confirm the widely held view that fiscal deficits have crowded out private investment.[18] Such a view needs to be heavily qualified, however, since the period of rising fiscal deficits from 1997–98 was also a period of falling interest rates in the economy. Prime lending rates of term lending institutions had been steadily falling from a range of 18 percent to 20 percent in 1991–92 to 11.5 percent to 12 percent in 2001–2 (RBI 2003, table 63). Clearly, if "crowding-out" occurred, its impact is not seen in the trend in prime lending rates. Further, commercial banks chose to invest in government securities to a greater extent than they were required to do under prudential regulations until recently. The RBI (2006c, pp. 37–38) points out that although "commercial banks holdings of government and other approved securities declined to around 31 percent of their net demand and time liabilities (NDTL) as on March 31, 2006, from around 38 percent a year ago," it was still "higher than the statutory requirement of 25 percent."

It is more plausible to argue that rising fiscal deficits since 1997–98, rather than crowding out private corporate investment, in fact shifted the investment schedule of the corporate sector to the left, by making an already poor investment climate poorer. According to the World Bank's project benchmarking the regulatory cost of doing business in 145 economies (World Bank 2004): it takes 425 days to enforce a contract in India as compared to 241 days in China and 27 days in Tunisia (the lowest); the cost of enforcing a contract is 43 percent of gross national income per capita in India as compared to 25 percent in China and 4 percent in Norway (the lowest); time to go through insolvency is ten years in India, 2.4 years in China, and 0.4 years in Ireland (the lowest); and recovery of assets is only 12.5 percent of value in India, as compared to 35.2 percent in China and 92.4 percent in Japan (the highest).

It is a poor investment climate, rather than increasing scarcity of investible resources due to rising fiscal deficits, that restricts India's private sector from investing more. One of the prime causes of the poor investment climate is the poor state of a crucial item of infrastructure, namely, electric power. The prospects in the near future of attracting significant private (domestic or foreign) investment is stymied by the continuing failure to clean up the mess in the state electricity boards (SEBs) and to allow truly independent regulatory agencies to function. It is a pity that the reforms promised in the Electricity Bill passed in 2003 appear to be still on hold. In the meantime, there seems to be no alternative to large public-sector investment in infrastructure, including in electricity generation. Such investment will not only raise growth by increasing the availability of infrastructural services but also crowd in private investment. Given the precarious fiscal situation of the country, deficit financing of even such a worthwhile investment is risky. However, increasing public investment by utilizing part of the resources held up in low yielding foreign reserves, without at the same time worsening the fiscal situation and affecting the exchange rate significantly, is a possibility.

3.3 FRBM ACTS AND FISCAL CONSOLIDATION

In the United States, attempts to force the executive and the legislature (Congress) to be fiscally responsible took various forms. These included proposals to amend the Constitution to mandate balanced budgets, to grant the President—like many governors of states—the power to veto specific expenditure proposals (the so-called line-item veto), and legislation requiring that proposals to increase any item of discretionary expenditure be accompanied by proposals for financing such expenditures either through cuts in other items of expenditure or revenue raising measures. Such proposals have been made at the federal and state levels and a few of the proposals (and more of them at the state level) have been adopted. To the best of my knowledge, the empirical evidence of the performance of enacted measures in achieving their goal of fiscal responsibility is not very encouraging.

In India, with the end of the dominance over the central government by a single political party, the Indian National Congress, in the 1990s, as regional parties became pivotal players in the coalitions that came to govern at the center, the central government could no longer exercise control over the fiscal deficits that its regional allies were running in the states under their control. Under these circumstances, as the fiscal situation at the center and states failed to improve, the need for new legislation, rather than political mechanisms, to impose fiscal discipline became apparent.

In response to this need the central government passed a Fiscal Responsibility and Budget Management (FRBM) Act in 2003. The Act laid down time-phased programs for deficit reduction. Many state governments have followed the center's lead since then to enact similar laws. The RBI provided model legislation, and the Twelfth Finance Commission has recommended tying debt relief and restructuring for the states to their passage and implementation of FRBM laws. There is understandable skepticism about the enforceability of such laws by sovereign governments, or by subnational governments that can count on being bailed out. A precondition for enforcement, namely, monitoring, is not trivial to implement.

Several aspects of FRBM laws have been analyzed in the literature: the quality of the fiscal adjustment in addition to its magnitude and the possible distortion of incentives (e.g., Rajaraman 2006); the need for an independent scorekeeper for monitoring (e.g., Hausmann and Purfield 2006), and possible monitors, such as the Finance Commission (e.g., Singh and Srinivasan 2006b); assessment of the initial impact of the state FRBM laws (Howes 2005); and the failure to tackle the fundamental underlying incentive problems (arising from the inability of the center to commit credibly not to bail out states) that can lead to poor fiscal decision making by subnational governments (Singh and Srinivasan 2006b).

Regardless of whether or not FRBM laws are the most appropriate means for achieving fiscal discipline, as long as they are on the statute books, any action by the government that undermines their credibility is not helpful. Unfortunately, there have been numerous unhelpful actions or proposed actions. For example, soon after the Central FRBM Act was passed in 2003 it was amended to move the target date for achieving revenue and fiscal deficit reduction goals set by FRBM to March 2009 and 2008 respectively from March 2008 and 2007. What is even more disturbing, the Finance Minister, while claiming the achievement of fiscal correction in 2004–5 as required by FRBM, said that he "was left with no option but to press the 'pause' button vis-à-vis FRBM Act" (GOI 2005, p. 23), largely because, in his view, accepting the recommendations of the Twelfth Finance Commission drastically changed the pattern of devolution and spending. Unfortunately, attributing the additional expenditures arising from the acceptance of the recommendations of the Twelfth Finance Commission as the reason for pressing the "pause" button is not convincing. After all, the Finance Commission is a constitutional body that is appointed every five years, and the record of recommendations of the previous eleven commissions was known when the FRBM Act was passed. It is hard to believe that the act formulated its targets without anticipating and taking into account the possible impact of recommendations of the Commission.

The Planning Commission (2006), in its approach paper for the Eleventh Five Year Plan, is suggesting a pause once again in meeting the amended FRBM target dates. After noting that, in principle, the resources needed for the plan could be mobilized in part by an increase in the fiscal deficit, it also recognizes that the scope for doing so is constrained by the target dates set by the amended FRBM for reaching the reduction of revenue and fiscal deficits. In its view, the constraints are two-fold: first, if the target date of March 2009 for achieving the fiscal deficit target is kept, "the increase in resource availability [for financing the plan] would be relatively modest in the first two years [2007–8 and 2008–9], followed by fairly sharp increases thereafter. This has the consequence that some of the plan expenditures needed for making growth more inclusive may have to be postponed. This time phasing may also present problems for infrastructure development, where there are long time lags, and delays could jeopardize growth with a corresponding effect on revenues. In addition, during these two years there would be very little, if any, scope to undertake countercyclical fiscal measures if circumstances so require. This raises the issue whether the FRBM targets should be shifted further out by say two years." (Planning Commission 2006, pp. 68–69).

> The second constraint relates to the achievement of the revenue deficit targets specified in the central FRBM, and also in various state legislations. These targets could prove difficult to achieve because the shift in Plan expenditure towards the social sectors has meant that a large proportion of the expenditure undertaken will be revenue expenditure as per the current budgetary definition. . . . it may not be easy for the Center to cut the revenue deficit from 2.1 percent in 2006–7 to 0 percent by 2008–9 while also achieving large increases in Plan expenditure with a high revenue component. . . . One approach would be to redefine the revenue deficit to exclude revenue expenditure which is clearly linked to asset creation. However, this may not be the appropriate solution especially since the concept of revenue expenditure is well defined in our accounting tradition and even recognized in the Constitution. A more basic approach is to question the rationale of including the revenue deficit as a fiscal control measure. Unlike the fiscal deficit, which at least has a clear economic implication, because it determines the increase in public debt, the revenue deficit is a pure accounting construct with no

> linkage to economically meaningful concepts such as savings and investment. A zero revenue deficit can be achieved merely by converting revenue expenditures to capital expenditures by showing grants to implementing agencies as a zero interest loan in perpetuity. (Ibid., pp. 69–70)

Neither of these arguments is persuasive. The first one implicitly assumes that the possibility of rearranging the time pattern of non-investment expenditure within the five-year plan period to accommodate the time pattern of investment expenditure on projects with long gestation lags is virtually nil and, moreover, there is no room for shortening the gestation lags. The commission offers no argument, let alone empirical evidence, in support of either of these implicit assumptions.

The second argument is more notable for its cleverness than for its persuasiveness. Creative accounting about grants notwithstanding, it ignores the basic economic rationale behind the "golden rule" of public finance that governments should borrow only for investment expenditures and not for current or revenue expenditures. The rationale is that current investments yield fruits in the future and it therefore makes sense for financing them through borrowing, with future benefits providing the resources for servicing the debt incurred. If the benefits, in part or entirely, accrue to the public at large, rather than to the government, then debt-service will call for future tax increases, thus making the generation benefiting from the investment pay for its cost. In the case of revenue expenditure, the benefits, if any, accrue to the current generation and it makes sense that the current generation pay the cost, rather than borrowing and shifting the burden to future generations.[19] Of course, the argument that benefits from some items of expenditure currently defined as current expenditures, such as on education and health, flow to future generations is well taken. By the same token, some items of expenditures, currently defined as capital expenditure (such as expenditures that in fact are maintenance and depreciation expenditures on capital, but were not fully included in revenue expenditures and hence do not add to productive capacity) do not generate future benefits. Unless an exercise carefully classifying expenditures based on the time pattern of the flow of their costs and benefits is done, it is hard to evaluate whether there is any merit to the suggestion that the dates targeted by FRBM for deficit reductions should be postponed once again. However, the damage to the credibility of FRBM done by such suggestions is substantial.

3.4 TAX AND EXPENDITURE REFORM

Tax reform in India faces its most difficult challenges at the subnational level largely from the constitutional assignment of tax powers between the center and the states based on the principle of separation, with tax categories being exclusively assigned either to the center or to the states. Most broad-based taxes, with greater revenue potential and lower collection costs, were exclusively assigned to the center. These included taxes on income and wealth from nonagricultural sources, corporation tax, taxes on production (excluding those on alcoholic liquors) and customs duty. Residual powers of taxation were also assigned to the center. With the central government emphasizing extreme progressivity (marginal tax rates on income and wealth were almost confiscatory) and narrow targeting,[20] a very inefficient tax structure was the outcome, with indirect taxes such as customs duties and excise generating the bulk of the revenue. Moreover, extensive tax evasion and corrupt tax administration were the inevitable consequences.

One of the triumphs of recent tax reform in India has been a substantial rationalization of the central government tax structure, which saw the lowering of marginal rates, simplification of the rate structure, and some degree of base broadening. This reform agenda was laid out by successive committees appointed by the Ministry of Finance. The first committee, headed by Raja Chelliah, filed its report in 1991. A decade later, two committees on direct and indirect taxes, headed by Vijay Kelkar, also filed reports. On tax administration, despite detailed analyses (e.g., Das-Gupta and Mookherjee 1998), less progress has been made.

Among taxes assigned to the states, only the tax on the sale of goods has turned out to be significant for state revenues, with taxes on agriculture having been allowed to erode (e.g., land revenue) or prevented from being imposed. In addition, the separation of the income tax powers of the center and the states based on source (agriculture vs. nonagriculture) created avenues for evasion, since the states chose not to tax agricultural income. The greatest inefficiencies arose in indirect taxes. Even though, in a legal sense, taxes on production (central manufacturing excises) and sale (state sales taxes) are separate, they tax the same base, causing overlapping and cascading, and leaving the states less room to effectively choose indirect tax rates. Also, the states were allowed to levy taxes on the sale and purchase of goods (entry 54 in the State list) but not on services. This provided avenues for tax evasion, and delayed the design and implementation of a comprehensive value-added tax (VAT). These issues have been the main subject of recent policy and institutional reform initiatives, and are discussed later in this section.

The initial assignment and subsequent evolution of tax powers effectively segmented India's markets. The framers of the constitution, aware of the need for a common market, enacted Article 286, which prohibited states from imposing taxes on trade with other states, and Article 302, which asserted the freedom of interstate commerce. But they effectively eroded this freedom by enacting an amendment to Article 302 empowering Parliament to impose restrictions on freedom of interstate trade in the "public interest" (a broad and ill-defined term). Further, Article 286 was effectively gutted by the Sixth Amendment to the Constitution in the late 1950s, which in effect authorized the central government to impose taxes on interstate trade.

The central government, in turn, authorized the states to levy a tax on interstate sales, subject to a specified ceiling rate (4 percent). Besides impeding the free movement of goods (through check-posts), this tax on the export of goods from one state to another converted the sales tax into an origin-based tax. This tax also has caused significant interstate exportation of the tax burden from the richer producing states to the residents of poorer consuming states.

Ideally, a coordinated consumption tax should be put in place instead of taxes on sales. Evolving such a system remains a major challenge (Rao 2000). Taxation of services, not explicitly mentioned in the Constitution, has remained implicitly in the exclusive domain of the central government (through the center's residual powers over such taxes). The central government has made this explicit through the 88th amendment to the Constitution, enacted in January 2004. The revenues from service taxes are to be shared with the states, in a manner yet to be determined by Parliament, and are therefore outside the "common pool" that is divided among the states by the Finance Commission. Indeed, it is possible that the sharing of service taxes will be completely outside the Commission's scope in the future. The Twelfth Finance Commission has properly raised this issue as a concern. One can conjecture that the move represents an attempt to establish more central control over the tax base in the face of broader sharing of centrally collected revenues as recommended by successive finance commissions.

In contrast to the noncooperative approach to service taxation, the center has been largely successful in persuading the states to replace taxation of interstate sales with a destination-based VAT, and this is well on the way to implementation (as of March 2006). This effort has taken a very long time, reflecting the difficulties of coordination of policy changes, as well as the practical difficulties of implementation.

A destination-based VAT will remove some of the internal barriers that have plagued the development of a true national market within India.[21] It will also mitigate the political problems associated with emerging interstate disparity in growth in the reform period by reducing tax exporting by richer states, although the growth impacts of tax exporting are hard to quantify. Studies commissioned by the Twelfth Finance Commission show that a properly designed state-level VAT would prove to be revenue augmenting over the medium to long term, with any transitory losses possibly compensated for by the center. The latest budgetary figures on the initial impacts of moving to VAT are consistent with this conclusion.

The Eleventh Finance Commission made a general recommendation to give the states more power to tax to reduce the vertical fiscal imbalance. This approach takes some pressure off the fiscal transfer system, encouraging states to seek internal political support for flexibly taxing their own constituents for delivering benefits to them. Another possible example of such a tax reassignment would be to allow states to piggyback on central income taxes.[22] With tax sharing no longer applied to specific tax "handles" but to tax revenues in total, this change would give states more flexibility at the margin, where they properly should have it. While states are already assigned the right to tax agricultural income, their use of this tax is minimal: the separation of agricultural income merely promotes tax evasion. Piggybacking, combined with a removal of the distinction between nonagricultural and agricultural income,[23] would represent a change in tax assignments that could increase efficiency as well as reduce the states' fiscal problems.

While services taxation and VAT represent the two most important aspects of sub-national tax reform, the potential reform agenda is much deeper. The World Bank study of state finances suggests attention to the professions tax, state excise duties, stamp duties and transport taxes, as well as to state-level tax administration. Ultimately, the real issue is how institutional reform can be achieved.

The tax reform process at the subnational level has proceeded through a combination of cooperative and competitive federalism. The central government has played an agenda setting and coordinating role in this process, and the states have managed to reach some level of agreement on tax rates and policies through bargaining by representatives of the executive branch. Strengthening and institutionalizing this process of bargaining could lead to a smoother reform process. Competitive benchmarking, sometimes spurred by individual states that initially go it alone (as in the case of Haryana with the VAT), is an aspect of competitive federalism that could be beneficial, in contrast to a "race-to-the-bottom" aspect. The center can broker interstate agreements by offering to compensate for lost revenue from a tax reform, with compensation capped to reduce moral hazard. All of the issues that have been raised in considering center-state tax reform apply to local governments. Their tax bases are inadequate, and property and land tax systems need to be developed and implemented more effectively for decentralization of expenditure authority to the local government level to make some headway. In doing this, the political process that governs reform needs to be given attention, including institutions that will allow local governments to share information, benchmark, and coordinate where possible and desirable.

With respect to expenditure reform, the three items that accounted for 52 percent of current expenditures (12.9 percent of GDP) of the center in 2004–5 were interest payments on debt (32 percent), subsidies (11 percent), and wages and salaries (9 percent) (IMF 2005, table 6). The share of salaries of central government employees in GDP has declined steadily from a peak of 1.8 percent of GDP in 1997–98 to 1.1 percent in 2005–6 (MOF 2006b, table 7.6). State government salaries reached a peak of 4.7 percent of GDP and declined to 4.2 percent of GDP in 2002–3 (Howes and Murgai 2006). The salaries of government servants are based on the recommendations of pay commissions periodically appointed by the central government. The Fifth Pay Commission reported in 1998, and the decision to appoint the Sixth was announced in 2006. Although the recommendations of the Central Pay Commissions, strictly speaking, refer to employees of the central government, it is no surprise that in due course the recommendations accepted and implemented by the central government for its employees are implemented by the state governments for their employees. Moreover, the salaries of the employees of quasi-governmental and government-aided agencies also are adjusted once salaries of government employees are adjusted. In the period between two consecutive payments, salaries are adjusted only for inflation. Thus adjustment of the level and structure of real salaries takes place only at the time of each pay commission but with retrospective effect. This means that the budgetary impact of the salary adjustment occurs at discrete intervals of time and is often large. A procedure for salary revision that smoothes its budgetary impact intertemporally is worth exploring.[24]

Given the political salience of public sector employees and their organization, it is no surprise that the government ignored the recommendation of the Fifth Pay Commission (FPC) to reduce the number of employees, while accepting its recommendation on upward revision of their salaries. In their very interesting analysis, Howes and Murgai (2006) conclude that notwithstanding the negative fiscal impact of the generous public sector pay rise after the implementation of FPC recommendations, "successful efforts to contain the wage hike can be observed . . . such salary bill reduction is not likely to come about by downsizing but a combination of hiring and wage restraint."

Unfortunately, the restraint on wage bill has not been replicated with respect to subsidies. Explicit subsidies from the central government's budget accounted for 1.3 percent of GDP in the revised estimates for 2005–6. The state governments probably spent as much or more on explicit subsidies. Indirect subsidies by way of recovering less than total cost of provision of goods and services are also substantial. When the present United Progressive Alliance (UPA) came to power in 2004, it announced a National Common Minimum Programme (NCMP 2004). It pledged that "all subsidies will be targeted sharply at the poor and the truly needy, like small and marginal farmers, farm labor and urban poor. A detailed road map for accomplishing this will be unveiled in Parliament within 90 days" (NCMP 2004). No such road map was unveiled within the stipulated 90 days after the assumption of office by the UPA in May 2004. Instead, the Finance Minister asked the National Institute for Public Finance and Policy (NIPFP) to prepare a report and promised to place it in Parliament in its winter session in 2004. NIPFP's report was published in December 2004 (MOF 2004). It suggested a three-tier (Merit I, Merit II, and Non-Merit) hierarchy of the government's social and economic services.[25] In its view, "while merit goods deserve subsidization in varying degrees, Merit I dominates Merit II in terms of desirability of subsidization. Furthermore, the case for subsidizing non-merit goods becomes a tenuous one" (MOF 2004, p. 2). Yet, non-merit subsidies accounted for 58 percent of the total subsidies in 2003–4! There has been very little change; in 1987–88 subsidies accounted for 4.53 percent of GDP, and in 2003–4 the percentage was 4.18 (MOF 2004, table 2.4). Explicit subsidies of 1.7 percent of GDP accounted for 40 percent of total subsidies.

The NIPFP report made several recommendations on addressing the subsidy problem. Unfortunately, given the strong opposition of the left parties in the UPA alliance to any subsidy reduction, not much concrete action followed. The Finance Minister admitted as much. After saying that the three main products that involve large explicit subsidies from the budget and otherwise were food, fertilizer and petroleum, he added, "However, we must now take up the task of restructuring the subsidy regime in a cautious manner and after a thorough discussion" (GOI 2005, p. 22), as if there has been no such discussion. In fact, there are various proposals, including those in the NIPFP report and others, for addressing the food and fertilizer subsidies without adversely affecting rural and urban poor, including small and marginal farmers. The NIPFP report covered only central government subsidies. The subsidies from the state government, particularly on electricity, are substantial. A comprehensive social cost-benefit analysis for explicit and implicit subsidies by governments at all levels most likely would show that the benefit/cost ratio is low. In any case, it is clear that not much progress is likely to be made to address the drain on the public exchequer from subsidies.

3.5 FISCAL DEFICITS, DEBT, AND EXTERNAL VULNERABILITY

In a provocative paper, Hemming and Roubini (2006) conclude that "while India's current debt path is unsustainable from a longer-term perspective, for the moment it appears to be financeable given that some of the vulnerabilities stressed by the balance sheet approach are, at first sight, not severe in India. However, a comparison with other emerging market economies that are either heavily indebted and have similar fiscal conditions and credit ratings or have episodes of financial crisis . . . suggests that balance sheet and other macroeconomic vulnerabilities are present and cannot be treated lightly" (p. 123). Their analysis was based on a data series ending in 2003. Three years have elapsed since. It is useful to examine whether some of the indicators of vulnerability used by them have improved or worsened.

Liquidity/external debt roll over risk, as measured by short-term external debt/reserves ratio has recorded a steady decline. It was at 5.8 percent as of the end of March 2006 (RBI 2006c, table 182). Solvency risk, as measured by the ratio of external debt-to-GDP, at 15.8 percent, was the lowest among top fifteen debtor countries, next only to China. The ratio of external debt service payments at $20 billion in 2005–6, accounted for about 12.5 percent of the estimated current receipts from exports of goods and services of $164 billion. Both indicators have improved significantly since 2003.

Balance sheet risk, reflecting a mismatch between the currency denomination of liabilities of government (or country) and that of its assets or revenues, is not significant. Although outstanding liabilities of the general government (including guarantees of 9.9 percent of GDP) as a share of GDP was 88.4 percent at the end of March 2006, this debt was overwhelmingly domestic—external liabilities of government are around 2 percent of GDP, far below the 8 percent level in the early eighties.

Capital structure risk, reflecting excessive reliance on debt-creating rather than debt-reducing capital inflows to finance current account deficits, is not significant. Paradoxically for a developing country, India ran a current account surplus for three years in a row from 2001–2 to 2003–4. FDI inflows averaged around $4 billion during 2001–2 and rose to around $8 billion in 2005. Portfolio flows have grown from around $2 billion in 2001 to over $10 billion in 2005 (RBI 2006c, Charts 1.47 and 1.48). As noted earlier, external debt as a share of GDP has been declining. It is evident that India has not been borrowing abroad to finance its current account. Still, Hemming and Roubini rightly caution against assuming simplistically that FDI, because it is not debt and is long-term, poses no risk of capital flight. They plausibly argue that FDI investors' attempts to hedge currency risk would create a problem if expectations of a fiscal crisis were to emerge.

Hemming and Roubini (2006) include among vulnerabilities the high fiscal deficit, which they estimate at 11.6 percent of GDP in 2003, a figure that is higher than shown in the official data. In any case, the deficit has come down to 7.5 percent in 2005–6 and is budgeted at 6.5 percent 2006–7. However welcome this improvement is, the deficit is still too high. The two authors noted the very high ratio of 430 percent of public debt to government revenue in India as compared to other countries similarly rated by credit agencies. This ratio continues to be high—at the end of March 2006 government debt inclusive of revenues accounted for around 88 percent of GDP, so that the ratio is 440 percent while current revenues were only roughly 20 percent of GDP. The high debt/revenue ratio also implies that interest payments as a share of revenue are also large—it was estimated at 33 percent in 2005–6, almost the same as the 34 percent that Hemming and Roubini cite for 2003.

The other vulnerabilities cited by Hemming and Roubini cannot be lightly dismissed. These include the possible reduction, if not disappearance altogether, of the positive differential between the rate of GDP growth and interest rates, the growing contingent liabilities of the government (as noted earlier, that government guarantees accounted for nearly 10 percent of GDP at the end of 2005–6) including pension liabilities, banking sector vulnerabilities arising from their excessive holdings of government paper, and lastly, the low levels of net foreign assets. In fact, India had net foreign liabilities of $41 billion, accounting for 6.3 percent of GDP, at the end of March 2005 (RBI 2006c, table 1.85).

While the analysis of Hemming and Roubini, and the vulnerabilities they enumerate, are enough to cause concern, there is another factor that they do not mention, but which potentially could be even more serious, namely, a possible adverse change in the global economic environment. In many ways the eighties and nineties (Rogoff 2006a,b) have been remarkable in terms of the fall in volatility in output growth and also the significant fall in inflation and interest rates. These trends were observed not only in advanced countries but, interestingly, in many developing countries as well. The exception to these trends was the high volatility in asset prices, which rose. Globalization, in the sense of integration of markets for goods, services and finance, and the ever-expanding depth and liquidity of global assets, is widely believed to be the major source of the benign trends in the global economy. In particular, according to Rogoff (2006a,b), the idea that "China is exporting deflation" has gained the most traction; although, as he rightly points out, it confuses trends in relative prices, or terms of trade, with trends in absolute prices. Unfortunately, there is no coherent overarching theoretical or econometric model that could be usefully deployed to analyze this belief on the effects of globalization.[26] This is not to say that there have been no theoretical and empirical analyses of the impact of globalization. Indeed, there are many studies cited by Rogoff (2006a,b). He has himself analyzed the possibly deeper and more durable impacts of globalization on inflation (Rogoff 2004). Yet, without detracting from any of these studies, it is fair to say that they have little to say on the likelihood of the benign trends continuing into the medium run. What if, in particular, the trends in inflation rates and interest rates reverse themselves? Already there are signs, including in India, of a rise in inflation and in interest rates (in part because of the policy response of monetary authorities to the actual or anticipated rise in inflation). If this were to happen, the vulnerabilities cited by Hemming and Roubini could seriously threaten India's macroeconomic stability.

A significant rise in interest rates would erode the value of government securities held by the banks and their capital adequacy. Also, private investment would most likely be adversely affected. The adverse consequences of the high fiscal deficits that had been masked in the benign environment would come into the open. The need to act on containing them is urgent and immediate, before any adverse turn in the benign environment may become pronounced and entrenched.

4. CONCLUSIONS[27]

The structure of India's fiscal federalism was defined in India's constitution of 1950. It has remained more or less intact since. The system of economic management through economic planning with a Planning Commission formulating five-year plans, extensive state control of the economy (license-permit-raj), including state ownership of enterprises, and insulation of India's economy from the world economy, all date back to the 1950s. State control intensified from 1966 to 1980. The controls and insulation remained virtually intact until the mid-1980s, when some of the more irksome controls were relaxed and the opening of the economy to imports began. Systemic reforms, including the abolition of import and investment licensing, had to wait until after the macroeconomic crisis of 1991.

In the five and a half decades since 1950, India's political and economic structure and the global economic environment have changed enormously. It is evident that the system of economic management based on economy-wide planning is incompatible with this changed environment. The political scene is also very different now; with the Congress Party governments at the center having been replaced by coalition governments. The coalitions include regional parties, with many, though not all, being in power in the states. A second wave of globalization (the first one, which dates back to the mid-nineteenth century, ended in 1913 at the outbreak of the first world war) gathered momentum in the early 1980s. Aided and abetted by the information and communication technology revolution, it is transforming international trade in goods and services and international capital flows. India has abandoned its insulation from the global economy and is actively participating in and benefiting from the second wave of globalization. The state control of the license-permit-raj is gone, with market forces and the private sector playing a much larger and more active role than during 1950–90.

Conservative fiscal and monetary policies of 1950–80 gave way in the 1980s to fiscal profligacy and rising fiscal deficits financed in part by domestic and foreign debt. This led to the macroeconomic crisis of 1991 and spawned systemic reforms. Although debt accumulation is no longer a serious problem, containing fiscal deficits, one of the most important items in the reform agenda, has not succeeded. This lack of success is in large part due to the fact that the structure set in the constitution for fiscal federalism has become inconsistent with the changed political reality of coalition governments and with the changed economic environment. This calls for a fundamental rethinking of the role of the Planning Commission and fiscal federalism.

I have made two specific proposals for institutional reform in this context. The first is the creation of a powerful Fiscal Review Council (FRC) as a forum for political and economic review of the fiscal policies of the center and states. The Council is patterned in part after the trade policy review mechanism of the WTO and also in part after the mechanism in the European Commission (EC) for reviewing the reform proposals of its members. Under the WTO mechanism, the members of the WTO have an opportunity to review and comment on the trade policies of individual members.

The Prime Minister and the Finance Minister of India, the chief ministers and finance ministers of states, as well as experts would constitute the membership of the FRC. The FRC would afford each state chief minister an opportunity to learn from and also comment on the fiscal policies of other states. Thus, any proposal for reform emerging from the deliberations of the Council would have greater political credibility and a greater probability of successful implementation. The FRC would also be a mechanism for monitoring the implementation of reforms. Moreover, with chief ministers having an opportunity to comment on the center's policies in the FRC, the current asymmetric situation in which the center has means for influencing state policies while the states have no direct means of influencing the center's policies, would be made symmetric.

The second proposal is to reconstitute the Planning Commission into a Fund for Public Investment (FPI). Although the Planning Commission still pretends at putting together an economy-wide national development plan, in fact the governments at the center and the states can control only those components of it that relate to public expenditures, both for implementing the public sector investment component of the plan and the so called "non-plan" current expenditures. Fortunately, with the license-permit-raj gone, the negative instruments that the government had through the denial of licenses or permits to force the private sector to conform to planned targets are no longer available. Thus, the private sector component of the plans has no operational significance, other than possibly as an indicative plan. It makes sense, therefore, to focus on public investment through FPI.

The FPI would concentrate on evaluating public investment proposals and their financing by the center and the state. It would also lend from the fund in support of the proposals it approves. The FPI would be set up in analogy to multilateral banks, with the center and states as shareholders and with authority to borrow from domestic and foreign capital markets with the guarantee of central and state governments.

Clearly, the proposals for the creation of FRC and FPI have to be discussed extensively by the polity and the public at large before they are given concrete shape. In the meantime, there needs to be some immediate short-run fiscal adjustment. Otherwise the probability of a crisis or collapse in the near term would increase dramatically. Furthermore, there are some obvious expenditures that could be reduced, such as, for example, reducing and reforming poorly designed subsidies, and improving the efficiency of public expenditures. Some steps can be taken to enhance revenues while simultaneously reducing the distortions in the tax system, including improvements in tax compliance and efficiency of tax collection. Since the efficient and smooth functioning of the financial sector is the foundation for sustaining rapid growth, further reforms of this sector must be pursued vigorously.

NOTES

1. Samuel C. Park, Jr. Professor of Economics, Yale University. This is a revised and updated version of a paper presented at the conference India: An Emerging Giant, held at Columbia University, October 13–15, 2006. I have drawn extensively from Singh and Srinivasan (2006a,b,c), Wallack and Srinivasan (2006, Introduction and Conclusion), and Srinivasan (2002) in writing this paper. I thank Dr. Govinda Rao, the discussant of my paper, and the participants of the conference for their comments.

2. Because of the netting out of the fiscal transactions between the central and state governments, the consolidated fiscal deficit is lower than the sum of the separate fiscal deficits of the center and states.

3. Data in RBI (2006a, Table 10) show a higher peak of 9.6 percent in 2002–3.

4. The cost to the economy of excessive accumulation of reserves has been analyzed by Lal, Bery, and Pant (2005) and Singh and Srinivasan (2005), among others.

5. David Burton, Director of IMF's Asia Pacific Department had the following to say about the evolution of the IMF's thinking on CAC, at a press briefing on the region's economic outlook on September 16, 2006: "In recent years, as an institution, I think we have done quite a lot of thinking about capital account convertibility. We have come to the conclusion that it is best to take it generally fairly cautiously, not something to be rushed into, and that there are important preconditions that need to be met. I would mention two, in particular. One is that the macroeconomic framework needs to be sound. Fiscal policy needs to be in good shape. You do not want to have strong external balance of payments pressures or potential pressures as one liberalizes the capital account. Secondly, and very importantly, you want the financial sector to be in good shape before you liberalize the capital account" (http://www.imf.org/external/np/tr/2006/tr060916b.htm). It is hard to think that aiming for FCAC by 2011, nearly fifteen years after the first report of Tarapore Committee (I), is "rushing into CAC"!

6. Let me mention a few other books: Acharya (2006), Joshi and Little (1996). Rao and Singh (2005), and Shome (2002). I should add that the annual economic surveys by the Ministry of Finance and the quarterly (and annual) reviews of macroeconomic and monetary developments by RBI always include a discussion of fiscal developments. There are also reports of committees appointed by the central and state governments. The reports of the Finance Commissions are relevant, as well. Of course, the World Bank and the IMF in their annual reports on India also discuss fiscal issues.

7. This section draws extensively from Singh and Srinivasan (2006a,b).

8. B.R. Ambedkar, in 1939, stated, "I confess I have a partiality for a unitary form of government. I think India needs it." Jawaharlal Nehru, initially less of a centralizer, changed his mind by 1946. The Union Powers Committee of the Constituent Assembly, over which he presided, wrote, "Momentous changes have since occurred. Now that partition is a settled fact we are unanimously of the view that it would be injurious to the interests of the country to provide for a weak central authority which could be incapable of ensuring peace, of co-ordinating vital matters of common concern and of speaking effectively for the whole country in the international sphere." Ambedkar made this statement about local government during the Constituent Assembly's drafting of the constitution: "What is a village but a sink of localism, a den of ignorance, narrow mindedness and communalism . . . ?" See Rao and Singh (2005) for more detail and references.

9. See, for example, Rudolph and Rudolph (1987); Brass (1990); and Kohli (1990).

10. In contrast to the past, recent commissions have played a greater role in articulating an agenda for fiscal federal reform, which then proceeds through a process of political bargaining.

11. The modern term is due to Musgrave (1959) and captures the idea that some goods may be rival goods but have positive externalities. While Musgrave introduced the term, it can be traced back to Adam Smith. There have been some controversies

over the precise meaning, but the externality perspective is analytically the clearest, tying in with public goods, which can also be formulated in externality terms.

12. The Prime Minister recently warned the state governments against what he called the unhealthy practice of providing "unsustainable tax breaks and fiscal incentives to industrial projects" in their bid for faster growth. He said that "The jury is still out whether these policies promote industrial growth. But in the process, in the excitement to have headline-grabbing MoUs [Memorandums of Understanding], we offer incentives, both fiscal and financial which our finances cannot sustain" (http://www.hindu.com/2006/09/29/stories/2006092915810100.htm, accessed September 29, 2006).

13. Interestingly, China seems to be ahead of India in recognizing the futility of old-fashioned central planning. It has abolished the Ministry of Planning, and the State Planning Commission has been renamed the National Development and Reform Commission. Moreover the development program for the five years 2007–12 is no longer called the 11th Five Year Plan! (Private communication from Nicholas Lardy, dated September 21, 2006).

14. I will ignore distinctions between the effects of an unchanging level of deficits as a proportion of GDP and of its change, both anticipated and unanticipated. The distinctions are indeed relevant, but their proper discussion would require spelling out a complete dynamic macroeconomic model. For such a model, admittedly simplistic, see Singh and Srinivasan (2005).

15. Rakshit (2005) takes a Keynesian perspective, arguing that fiscal consolidation through redirection in public expenditure would affect capacity utilization and growth by reducing aggregate demand. The argument that insufficiency of aggregate demand has constrained India's growth has a long history in India. Whatever its merit in the era of India's insulation from world markets, it does not make much sense now as India is far more integrated with world markets. On the so-called "demand constraint," see Srinivasan (1993).

16. It is time that public current expenditures, such as those on E&H, whose benefits flow over extended periods of time in the future, be treated as investment expenditures. If they were treated as such, the revenue deficit, fiscal deficit and PSBR would go up. This would make it easier to meet the FRBM target to eliminate revenue deficit by 2009. Indeed, the Planning Commission (2006) has suggested such recategorization of E&H expenditures.

17. RBI (2006c, Box 1.13, p. 59) reports a correlation coefficient of –0.42 between *change* in Gross Fiscal Deficit—GDP ratio and real GDP growth during 1990–00—2005–6, in contrast to a negligible –0.02 during the period 1971–72—1989–90.

18. In the Indian National Accounts Statistics, the private sector consists of households (including unincorporated enterprises) and the corporate sector. Investment by the household sector in physical assets is equal to its direct savings in such assets, and such savings are not available for use by corporate and public sectors. Only household savings in financial assets are available for such use through financial intermediation. In fact, household savings in physical assets constitute nearly half of total savings and investment. We exclude such investment from this crowding-out analysis because by being counted as part of both savings and investment, it cancels out and therefore is irrelevant for the discussion of crowding out.

19. I will ignore "Ricardian Equivalence" analysis of private-sector response of changes in intertemporal tax-expenditure patterns of the public sector. Hemming and Roubini (2006) suggest that Ricardian Equivalence phenomenon might be the source of the recent rise in private savings in India. I do not find this plausible.

20. The sharing formulas developed by the early finance commissions, which resulted in almost all central income tax revenue being devolved to the states, also likely distorted the pattern of central taxation, until it was replaced by general revenue sharing in 2000, after recommendations made by the Tenth Finance Commission.

21. There is the possibility that removing taxes on interstate sales could lead to evasion through false claims of interstate exportation: the evidence from the European Union suggests this as a possibility that would need to be guarded against (World Bank 2005b, Ch. 3).

22. This change would, of course, require a constitutional amendment.

23. This suggestion does not preclude provisions such as tax smoothing for farm income to mitigate the effects of greater risks associated with agriculture.

24. There is also a serious issue of rising pension obligations. Pensions are also revised as salaries are revised. Pension reforms that envisage moving away from defined benefit to a defined contribution program are under consideration. I will not touch on the issues of pension reforms in this paper.

25. The details of the three categories are:

- Merit I—Elementary education, primary health care, prevention and control of diseases, social welfare and nutrition, soil and water conservation, economy and environment.
- Merit II—Education (other than elementary), sports and youth services, family welfare, urban development, forestry, agricultural research and education, other agricultural programs, special programs for rural development, land reforms, other rural development programs, special programs for northeastern areas, flood control and drainage, nonconventional energy, village and small industries, ports and lighthouses, roads and bridges, inland water transport, atomic energy research, space research, oceanographic research, other scientific research, census surveys and statistics, and meteorology.
- Non-Merit—All others.

26. Let me repeat here a complaint that Nivikar Singh and I (2006b) voiced: "The classic Arrow-Debreu model of Walrasian general equilibrium in a world with a complete set of contingent (with respect to space, time, and state of the world) commodity markets, strictly speaking, does not require the existence of asset markets, let alone money and financial assets. There is no equally general, elegant and theoretical model of macroeconomics. Note that the integration of monetary theory and general equilibrium theory in available models is based on rather crude assumptions about the demand for money, such as cash-in-advance, or ad hoc approaches such as putting real balances in utility or production functions or a Cagan-style money demand function. Also, the fact that agents, domestic and foreign, have opportunities to invest in real and financial assets with varying risk-return characteristics is inadequately integrated in these models. Furthermore, models of sovereign

debt, public debt sustainability and growth (with or without public investment), and so on capture only some features of a far more complex reality. Finally, extrinsic and intrinsic uncertainties again are modeled in a more or less stylized fashion. On the other hand, the empirical literature has its own problems, including the lack of a sound theoretical foundation for the equations being estimated and often-unsatisfactory treatment of endogeneity and identification issues. We intend these remarks more as our understanding, albeit limited, of the state of the art and as a caution against taking the findings of some of the models (including those in our paper and others for this conference) too literally. Equally important to recognize is that sound policy analysis involves judgment by analysts that necessarily goes beyond the scope of the analytical models used."

27. I have drawn on Singh and Srinivasan (2006b) in this section.

REFERENCES

Acharya, Shankar. 2006. *Essays on Macroeconomic Policy and Growth in India* (New Delhi: Oxford University Press).

Basu, Suparna and Debabrata Datta. 2005. "Does Fiscal Deficit Influence Trade Deficit? An Econometric Enquiry," *Economic and Political Weekly* (July 23): 3311–18.

Brass, Paul. 1990. *The Politics of India Since Independence* (New York: Cambridge University Press).

Buiter, William and Urjit Patel. 1992. "Debt, Deficits and Inflation: An Application to the Public Finances of India," *Journal of Public Economics* 47:171–205.

———. 1996. "Solvency and Fiscal Correction in India: An Analytical Discussion," in S. Mundle, ed., *Fiscal Policy in India*, 30–75 (New Delhi: Oxford University Press).

———. 1997. "Budgetary Aspects of Stabilization and Structural Adjustment," in M. Blejer and T. Ter-Minassian, eds., *Macroeconomic Dimensions of Public Finance: Essays in Honour of Vito Tanzi*, 363–412 (London and New York: Routledge).

———. 2006. "Excessive Budget Deficits, a Government-Abused Financial System, and Fiscal Rules." *India Policy Forum 2005–06*. Washington, D.C.: Brookings Institution.

Calvo, Guillermo and Carmine Reinhardt. 2002. "Fear of Floating," *Quarterly Journal of Economics* 117(2):379–408.

Chelliah, Raja. 2005. "Malady of Continuing Fiscal Imbalance," *Economic and Political Weekly* (July 30):3399–3404.

Das-Gupta, Arindam and Dilip Mookherjee. 1998. *Incentives and Institutional Reforms in Tax Enforcement: An Analysis of Developing Country Experience* (New Delhi: Oxford University Press).

Domar, Evsey. 1944. "The 'Burden of the Debt' and the National Income," *American Economic Review* 34(4):798–827.

GOI 2005. *Budget 2005–2006: Speech of P. Chidambaram, Minister of Finance.* New Delhi: Government of India Press.

Hausmann, Ricardo and Catriona M. Purfield. 2006. "The Challenge of Fiscal Adjustment in a Democracy: The Case of India," in Peter Heller and Govinda Rao, eds., *Sustainable Fiscal Policy for India*, 283–321 (New Delhi: Oxford University Press).

Hemming, Richard and Nouriel Roubini. 2006. "A Balance Sheet Crisis in India?," in Peter Heller and Govinda Rao, eds., *Sustainable Fiscal Policy for India*, 114–42 (New Delhi: Oxford University Press).

Heller, Peter and Govinda Rao, eds. 2006. *Sustainable Fiscal Policy for India* (New Delhi: Oxford University Press).

Howes, Stephen. 2005. "Reforms to India's Federal Transfer and Borrowing Regime Proposed by the Twelfth Finance Commission: What Will They Mean for the States?" Presentation at Conference on Fiscal Responsibility and Intergovernmental Finance, Hyderabad, June 22–24: http://siteresources.worldbank.org/INTINDIA/Resources/Stephen.pdf

Howes, Stephen and Rinku Murgai. 2006. "Subsidies and Salaries," in Peter Heller and Govinda Rao, eds., *Sustainable Fiscal Policy for India*, 216–71 (New Delhi: Oxford University Press).

Joshi, Vijay and I.M.D. Little. 1996. *India's Economic Reforms 1991–2001* (New York: Oxford University Press).

Kohli, Atul. 1990. *Democracy and Discontent: India's Growing Crisis of Governability* (New York: Cambridge University Press).

Lal, Deepak, Suman Bery and Devendra Kumar Pant. 2005. "Real Exchange Rate, Fiscal Deficits and Capital Flows: Erratum and Addendum," *Economic and Political Weekly* 40(16):1650–55.

IMF. 2005. *India: Staff Report for 2005, Article IV Consultation*. Washington, D.C.: International Monetary Fund.

MOF. 2006a. *Economic Survey, 2005–06*. New Delhi: Ministry of Finance.

———. 2006b. *Indian Public Finance Statistics, 2006*. New Delhi: Ministry of Finance.

———. 2004. *Central Government Subsidies in India: A Report*. New Delhi: Government of India Press.

Musgrave, R. A. 1959. *The Theory of Public Finance* (New York: McGraw-Hill).

NCMP. 2004. *National Common Minimum Programme of the Government of India*. New Delhi: Government of India Press.

Oliveira, Jesus. 2001. "Economic Effects of Origin and Destination Principle for Value-Added Taxes." Working Paper, School of Business and Public Management, George Washington University.

Olson, Mancur. 1986. "Toward a More General Theory of Governmental Structure," *American Economic Review* 76(2):120–25.

Planning Commission. 2006. "Towards Faster and More Inclusive Growth: An Approach to the 11th Five Year Plan." New Delhi: Government of India.

Rajaraman, Indira. 2006. "Intergovernmental Finance and Policy Coordination: Implications of the Report of the Twelfth Finance Commission," in Peter Heller and Govinda Rao, eds., *Sustainable Fiscal Policy for India*, 8–43 (New Delhi: Oxford University Press).

Rakshit, Mihir. 2005. "Some Analytics and Empirics of Fiscal Restructuring in India" *Economic and Political Weekly* (July 2):3440–49.

Rangarajan, C. and D. K. Srivastava. 2005. "Fiscal Deficits and Government Debt: Implications for Growth and Stabilisation," *Economic and Political Weekly* (July 2):2919–33.

Rao, M. Govinda. 2000. "Tax Reform in India: Achievements and Challenges," *Asia-Pacific Development Journal* 7(2):59–74.

Rao, M. Govinda and Kavita Rao. 2006. "Trends and Issues in Tax Policy and Reform in India." *India Policy Forum.* Washington, D.C.: Brookings Institution.

Rao, M. Govinda and Nirvikar Singh. 2005. *Political Economy of Federalism in India* (New Delhi: Oxford University Press).

RBI. 2006a. *Macroeconomic and Monetary Developments 2005–06.* Mumbai: Reserve Bank of India.

———. 2006b. *Report of the Committee on Fuller Capital Account Convertibility.* Mumbai: Reserve Bank of India.

———. 2006c. *Annual Report 2005–06.* Mumbai: Reserve Bank of India.

———. 2007. *Handbook of Statistics on the Indian Economy.* Mumbai: Reserve Bank of India.

———. 2008. *Macroeconomic and Monetary Developments, Third Quarter Review, 2007–08.*

Rogoff, Kenneth. 2004. "Globalization and Global Disinflation," in *Monetary Policy and Uncertainty: Adapting to a Changing Economy. A Symposium* (Kansas City: Federal Reserve Bank).

———. 2006a. "Impact of Globalization of Monetary Policy," in *Monetary Policy and Uncertainty: Adapting to a Changing Economy. A Symposium* (Kansas City: Federal Reserve Bank).

———. 2006b. "The Globalization of Monetary Policy." Paper presented at the Arthur Okun Memorial Lectures, Department of Economics, Yale University, October 3–4.

Rudolph, Lloyd I. and Susanne H. Rudolph. 1987. *In Pursuit of Lakshmi: The Political Economy of the Indian State* (Chicago: University of Chicago Press).

Shome, Parthasarathi. 2002. *India's Fiscal Matters* (New Delhi: Oxford University Press).

Singh, Nirvikar. 2006. "State Finances in India: A Case for Systemic Reform," in S. Narayan, ed., *Documenting Reform: Case Studies from India*, 56–86 (New Delhi: Macmillan India).

Singh, Nivikar and T. N. Srinivasan. 2005. "Exchange Rates, Deficits and Capital Flows." *Economic and Political Weekly*, August 13, 2005: 2196–7.

———. 2006a. "Federalism and Economic Development in India—An Assessment." Paper presented at the Stanford University SCID Pan Asia Conference, June 1–3.

———. 2006b. "Indian Federalism, Economic Reform and Globalization," in Jessica S. Wallack and T. N. Srinivasan, eds., *Federalism and Economic Reform: International Perspectives*, 301–63 (New York: Cambridge University Press).

———. 2006c. "Fiscal Policy in India: Lessons and Priorities," in Peter Heller and Govinda Rao, eds., *Sustainable Fiscal Policy for India*, 383–439 (New Delhi: Oxford University Press).

Srinivasan, T. N. 1993. "Demand Deficiency and Indian Industrial Development," in M. Datta-Chaudhuri and T. N. Krishnan, eds., *Development and Change: Essays in Honor of K. N. Raj, Pranab Bardhan*, 246–63 (New Delhi: Oxford University Press).

———. 2002. "India's Fiscal Situation: Is Crisis Ahead?," in Anne O. Krueger, ed., *Economic Policy Reforms and the Indian Economy*, 47–79 (Chicago: University of Chicago Press).

Srinivasan, T. N. and Suresh Tendulkar. 2003. *Reintegrating India with the World Economy* (Washington, D.C.: Institute for International Economics; and New Delhi: Oxford University Press).

TFC. 2004. Report of the Twelfth Finance Commission (2005–10), November, 2004: http://fincomindia.nic.in/Report of 12th Finance Commision/index.html

Wallack, Jessica and T. N. Srinivasan, eds. 2006. *Federalism and Economic Reform: International Perspectives* (New York: Cambridge University Press).

World Bank. 1982. *World Development Report.* Washington, D.C.: World Bank.

———. 1990. *India: Trends, Issues and Options*, Vol. II, Report No. 8360-IN. (Washington, D.C.: World Bank).

———. 1993. *World Development Report.* Washington, D.C.: World Bank.

———. 2000. *India: Policies to Reduce Poverty and Accelerate Sustainable Development*, Report no. 19471-IN. Washington, D.C.: World Bank.

———. 2004. *Doing Business in 2005: India Regional Profile.* Washington, D.C.: World Bank. Available at http://rru.worldbank.org/doingbusiness (accessed 23 May 2005).

———. 2005a. *World Development Indicators.* Washington, D.C.: World Bank.

———. 2005b. *State Fiscal Reforms in India: Progress and Prospects* (*A World Bank Report*). New Delhi: Macmillan India.

———. 2006. *World Development Indicators.* Washington, D.C.: World Bank.

COMMENT

M. Govinda Rao

INTRODUCTION

The existing edifice of fiscal management in India was erected to accommodate a heavy industry–based, public sector–dominated, import-substituting industrialization strategy. This now has to be transformed to deal with a more liberalized and open economy's requirements. Despite considerable progress during the last decade and a half, much remains to be done to transform fiscal policies and institutions of fiscal management to meet the requirement of a market economy, and T. N. Srinivasan's chapter on the unfinished fiscal reforms is timely. The chapter provides a fresh perspective on organizational, operational, and managerial aspects of India's fiscal management within the context of Indian fiscal federalism. The paper covers important issues of fiscal policy reform, particularly (a) reforms related to the achievement of fiscal consolidation toward a stable and sustainable fiscal policy, and (b) tax and expenditure reforms to achieve macroeconomic goals and to achieve the greater efficiency in resource allocation necessary for accelerating the GDP growth rate to 8 percent per year. After a detailed assessment of recent fiscal reforms, the paper identifies further areas of reform in both policies and institutions to achieve fiscal consolidation.

My own thinking on reforms in policies and institutions has been shaped from the perspective of calibrating coordinated fiscal policy within the framework of fiscal federalism. This is necessary to achieve fiscal consolidation to promote growth and macroeconomic stability, avoid a pro-cyclical policy stance, enable improved standards of physical and social infrastructure, and minimize distortions to meet the challenges of globalization and ensure a common market unfettered by fiscal and regulatory impediments in the federation. Not surprisingly, I am in near total agreement with the chapter and therefore take issue only with some of the details and points of emphasis. In particular, in my view, the paper focuses more on stabilization aspects of fiscal policy and not enough on minimizing microlevel distortions. Second, whatever success was achieved in fiscal adjustment until 2003–4, including improvements in the initial years of reform, has been more due to creative accounting than to genuine effort. Third, much of the fiscal adjustment since 2003–4 has been due to improvement in tax administration, particularly the setting up of the information system, rather than to compression of expenditures. The focus of reforms in the 1990s was on the structure of the tax system. The inability to undertake expenditure reforms underlines political-economy constraints. Fourth, while, as emphasised in the paper, reforms should be calibrated within the framework of fiscal federalism, the institutional and policy details need to be discussed in greater detail.

ANALYSIS OF RECENT FISCAL TRENDS

The analysis of fiscal trends shows that there has been some success in fiscal adjustment in the initial years of reform. As a ratio of GDP, the fiscal deficit was reduced from 9.4 percent in 1991–92 to 6.4 percent 1996–97, but thereafter it increased steadily. The deficit level persisted at around 9 to 9.5 percent from 1998–99 to 2002–3. Subsequently, the situation has shown some improvement at both the central and state levels, and the combined deficit is estimated at 7.5 percent in 2005–6. Similarly, the combined revenue deficit that peaked in 2001–2 at 6.9 percent of GDP has been brought down to 3.1 percent in 2005–6.

In this fiscal-adjustment scenario, there are a number of notable features. First, the actual fiscal situation is worse than even the hesitant adjustment scenario painted above. There have been several attempts at creative accounting to show adjustments even when they were not achieved, and many of the improvements have been an illusion rather than a reality (Rao and Amar Nath 2000). Besides changes in practices and conventions, such as transferring the small-savings collections into a fund, treating the entire profits of the Reserve Bank of India as government revenue (which were used earlier to provide refinancing to financial institutions), and treating disinvestment proceeds as government revenue, the central government has been hiding a significant portion of its deficits in the public-sector accounts. The deficit in the oil-pool account is an example at the center, and the large deficit of the state electricity boards is an example at the state level. Discontinuation of lending to states, and yet showing that the deficit has remained at the same level (of 4.1) at the central level when, actually, it has slipped by 0.7 percent, is yet another case of concealing the deficit. While in 2004–5, the central deficit included the deficit incurred for lending to states, the practice was discontinued in the next year based on the recommendation of the Twelfth Finance Commission (TFC). It is time that measurement of deficits should be standardized and expanded to cover public-sector borrowing requirements (PSBR). Equally important is the need to have a detailed account of all contingent liabilities and evaluate the risk element in them.

Second, the progress in fiscal adjustment since 2001–2 is owing almost entirely to an increase in the buoyancy of central tax revenues, particularly direct taxes. This signifies three important things. First, the tax reforms based on the recommendation of the Tax Reforms Committee (TRC) (India 1991), with emphasis on broadening the base, reducing the rates, and reducing rate differentiation in direct taxes, helped to reform the structure. Thus, although, as Srinivasan argues, the progress in fiscal reforms in the 1990s was checkered, the edifice laid for a more scientific approach to tax reforms has helped. The report of the task force on direct and indirect taxes, and the report of the task force on the Fiscal Responsibility and Budget Management Act (FRBMA), which led to the building of the Tax Information Network (TIN), were built on the foundations laid by the TRC (India 2002, 2004). Second, the focus of the tax reforms adopted after the submission of the task force report was not on the structure of the tax system but on tax administration. In fact, the increase in buoyancy in the tax system since 2002–3 is attributable mainly to the TIN set up after 2002–3. Third, the progress in fiscal consolidation has been achieved mainly through an increase in the buoyancy of the tax system, and there was no progress in rationalizing expenditures. Despite much discussion and two white papers presented in the Parliament, one in 1995 and another in 2005, there has been hardly any attempt to compress subsidies. On the contrary, there has been a proliferation of expenditure schemes of doubtful usefulness, under compulsions of coalition politics.

Third, the fiscal trend until 2001–2 shows that, after some improvement in the initial years of reform, the situation actually deteriorated even more than what the fiscal deficit figures indicated. In fact, the proportion of revenue deficits in fiscal deficits in 2001–2 was 71 percent, much higher than in 1991–92 (45 percent). Indeed, since 2002–3, the consolidated fiscal situation has shown improvements, and both revenue and fiscal deficits have come down to 3.1 and 7.5 percent respectively.

Fourth, the reforms in the tax system in the 1990s were actually revenue decreasing. This is due to two important factors. First, there was no coordination between the reduction in external trade taxes and the rationalization in domestic trade taxes, as also in the tax reforms between the center and states. Normally, a reduction in an import duty is made up through at least partially loading on domestic trade taxes. As the sales tax was leviable by the states, the reduction in customs duty was not accompanied by sales-tax reforms. In fact, transforming the cascading-type sales tax to a destination-based value-added tax (VAT) is important in an open economy, to minimize distortions, but this reform did not take precedence. Even the present VAT reform is seen more as a measure to increase revenue productivity than as a way of enhancing competitiveness. Second, although emphasized by the TRC, the focus of reforms in the 1990s was on the structure of taxes and not on their administration. In contrast, the reforms since 2002–3 are invisible—mainly focused on instituting an information system through the TIN. The TIN has now been extended to about sixty cities in the country, and the income tax receipts will continue to show buoyancy as the scheme is expanded. It must also be stated that not much has been done so far to strengthen the information system in excise duties. Besides, it is necessary to make the appellate system effective to improve tax compliance.

What are the medium-term prospects of fiscal consolidation? A broadening and deepening of the tax administration reforms will continue the high buoyancy of the tax system. In fact, extending the reforms to excise duties could bring in significant dividends. At the state level, continuation of the reforms to evolve a destination-based VAT is likely to enhance revenue productivity. The unprecedented growth of the economy seen in the last three years has also favorably affected revenues, particularly in real estate and housing, including the more organized housing market as a result of the entry of several builders along with the rationalization of stamp duties. The revenue growth has been strong, as well, in the areas of motor vehicle taxation and excise duties from alcoholic products.

Political-economy factors threaten fiscal consolidation, however. The coalition government at the center has to meet competing demands from several constituents, and it cannot enforce discipline at the state level if the ruling party in the state is a pivotal member of the ruling coalition at the center. Coalition politics softens the budget constraints at both the central and state levels. Increased revenue growth creates a climate of complacency and can lead to further proliferation of schemes of doubtful utility. Despite legislating the Fiscal Responsibility and Budget Management Act (FRBMA), the center has already shown the way to escape discipline by shifting the target by a year from 2007–8 to 2008–9 and taking a "pause" in 2005–6. The demand from the Planning Commission to generate resources for the Eleventh Plan may create pressure to take further "pauses." Although most of the states have passed the Fiscal Responsibility Acts, the center has diluted its own stand and cannot morally enforce this on the states.

More serious risk comes from the appointment of the pay commission. Although state finances have improved considerably since 2003–4, and the fiscal restructuring targets set by the Twelfth Finance Commission for 2008–9 are likely to be achieved in 2006–7, the recommendations of the Sixth Pay Commission, when implemented, could derail the fiscal-adjustment process. The implementation of the Fifth Pay Commission recommendation worsened the revenue deficits of the central and state governments by over two percentage points of GDP.

An important source of risk for fiscal adjustment is in the changing nature of the polity itself. A coalition government at the center, regional parties in power in the states, and the latter playing pivotal roles in the central coalition, do not, in the aggregate, exactly create an environment conducive to either rule-based fiscal policy or fiscal discipline. The political environment affects both the magnitude of the fiscal-adjustment process and the nature of fiscal adjustment, which in turn have both macroeconomic and microeconomic implications.

The prevailing public debt profile (the composition of short-term debt), and availability of comfortable foreign exchange reserves, rule out any external payment crisis in the medium term. The fact that there has been a considerable improvement in the fiscal situation in the last couple of years strengthens this contention. Persistence of high levels of fiscal deficits, however, has had significant growth costs from all the three sources of growth: factor accumulation, resource-use efficiency, and technical progress. In addition to the impact of deficits, the effect of relative price distortions created by tax and expenditure policies, and the impact of fiscal impediments to mobility on economic growth, are equally important.

The issue of whether the persistent fiscal deficits have crowded out private investment continues to be debated in India. Clearly, preempting resources for the public sector involves opportunity costs, and these are certainly not negligible when the government uses borrowed resources to pay salaries, meet interest obligations, and provide subsidies. The "poor investment climate" story offered in the preceding chapter provides a reasonable explanation for the commercial banks' investments in government bonds in excess of statutory liquidity ratio (SLR) requirements. The important point is that the interest rate remained higher than the marginal efficiency of capital, and investment activity did not take place. Another explanation could be that with progressive liberalization of the financial sector, the corporate sector could meet its requirements from the international financial markets; but a perception of high risk by commercial banks could have resulted in these banks shying away from lending to the small-scale sector. Thus, even as commercial banks had excess liquidity and preferred to invest in government securities, the small-scale sector had to contract loans from the unorganized financial sector at very high interest rates. Not surprisingly, both output and employment in the small-manufacturing sector stagnated after the mid-1990s.

UNFINISHED REFORMS

Legislating fiscal discipline and targets is an important recent development in fiscal reform. Srinivasan's chapter takes the view that the FRBM Act as a commitment device has limited usefulness, as it does not take account of the fundamental problem of incentives arising from the common-pool problem. International experience with legislating fiscal discipline shows that these are neither necessary nor sufficient to bring about fiscal discipline, but they can be useful in the short and medium terms. Indian experience during the short period of its implementation substantiates this. Despite the compulsions of coalition politics, the consolidated fiscal deficit as a ratio of GDP has declined from 9.9 percent in 2001–2 to 7.5 percent in 2005–6 and the revenue deficit has been reduced from 7 percent to 3.1 percent during the same period.

I have long argued for calibrating coordinated fiscal reforms in Indian fiscal federalism, and therefore am in agreement with the approach adopted in the chapter. In fact, the need for the unfinished reform agenda to be calibrated in a coordinated manner is not merely confined to the intergovernmental fiscal arrangements but also to tax and expenditure policies and institutions. As argued earlier, the lack of coordination is one of the most important factors responsible for the decline in the tax revenue-to-GDP ratio during the 1990s.

A paradigm shift in tax policy is necessary to recognize that the tax bases of the central and state governments are interdependent. The principle of separation of tax bases followed in the constitutional assignment does not recognize that interdependence. It is desirable to provide concurrent tax powers to the center and the states with respect to both income and domestic consumption taxes. In the case of personal income tax, separation of tax powers between the center and the states based on whether the income is from the agricultural or the nonagricultural sector has been a major source of tax evasion. As agriculture is transformed into a business, it is important to levy the tax on incomes received from all the sources, both for reasons of neutrality and to minimize tax evasion. At the same time, both center and the states could be allowed to levy the tax with the latter piggybacking the levy on the central tax, subject to a ceiling rate. Similarly, it is important to unify multiple indirect taxes levied by the central and state governments into a single goods and services tax (GST), preferably with states piggybacking on the central levy for the two levels of government. The transition to such a concurrent tax system requires integrating the existing CENVAT and service taxes and extending the tax to the retail level, which would, inter alia, entail amendment of the Constitution. The states could piggyback on the levy.

The experience with TIN has shown the power of information in improving tax compliance. In fact, entrusting the task of building TIN to National Securities Depository Limited (NSDL) was an important step. In contrast, the information system for excise and customs entrusted to the National Informatics Centre (NIC), a public-sector firm, has failed in its task even to prevent excessive input tax credit being taken, which is one of the reasons for the stagnancy of revenue from the tax. Building a scientific information system for all taxes, sharing of information, and center-state coordination are extremely important. Improving tax administration, and particularly the information system, is the most important means to broaden the base, and, when achieved, further reduction in tax rates may be possible.

The reforms to broaden the base will have to continue, and the several exemptions and preferences prevailing at present will have to be contained. A recent addition to the long list of tax preferences, which threatens to erode the future tax base significantly, is the exemption given to Special Economic Zones (SEZs). The discretion and selectivity that was initially introduced to meet multiple objectives in a planned economy was later taken over by special-interest politics. This has to give way to rule-based taxation, both in structure and administration. Further, administered prices have continued in some sectors, such as petroleum, and there is a thin line between taxes and administered prices in public monopolies. It is also important to rationalize the tax system in order to avoid a disproportionate burden that is presently borne by some sectors and commodity groups. Notably, almost 40 percent of central excise duties and state sales taxes are borne by diesel and petrol, which creates a significant distortion.

As already mentioned, there has been very little reform on the expenditure side. Despite presenting two white papers on subsidies in the Parliament, there is little progress in containing explicit or implicit subsidies. Even nonpublic services provided by the government without a high degree of merit continue to be priced at very low rates. Considerable rationalization of government salary and pensions is also necessary. It is also necessary to disconnect the central pay scales from the pay scales of states. Here, for the purposes of accountability and to provide incentives, it may be necessary to create a district cadre of teachers and health workers.

The chapter rightly emphasizes that the root causes of endemic fiscal crises lie in the structure of fiscal federalism and the intergovernmental transfer system. A critical component of reform is to set hard budget constraints on the states, and this cannot be achieved unless the intergovernmental fiscal system is reformed. Indeed, centralized planning is the negation of federalism, and market-oriented reforms necessitate reform in intergovernmental fiscal policies as well as in institutions. Reforms will have to encompass changes in the assignment system, the transfer system, and intergovernmental fiscal institutions.

The chapter focuses on some important institutional restructuring. I am in agreement with Srinivasan on the need for the Fiscal Policy Review Council (FPRC), but this cannot be undertaken by the Inter-State Council. The Council will not be seen as neutral because it is a central government institution under the Union Home Ministry. This should be a permanent body with a professional secretariat, working as the institution for intergovernmental consultation, bargaining, and dispute resolution. A component of the FPRC should deal with the functions of the Finance Commissions. All transfers should be channeled though the Finance Commission. The Commission should deal with both plan and non-plan requirements of the states. The chairperson and members could be appointed for a period of five years. It would work as an agency not only recommending transfers but also monitoring them on a continuous basis. The recommendation that the Inter-State Council work as a body for negotiation is unworkable, mainly because it is an institution of the central government under the Union Home Ministry. As far as the Planning Commission is concerned, it should be converted into a fund for public investment to focus on physical infrastructure.

Finance Commissions should change their methodology. The present methodology fails to offset the fiscal disabilities of poorer states. Admittedly, the objective of the transfer system in any federation is not the equalization of incomes per se but the enablement of states to provide a given normative level of basic public services, so long as they raise revenues at comparable tax rates from the sources assigned to them. Offsetting fiscal disabilities will ensure a level playing field and enable them to exploit their developmental potential, and, in this sense, an equitable transfer system is a rare case in which equity and efficiency are not in conflict (Buchanan 1950; Boadway and Flatters 1982).

The methodology adopted by the Finance Commissions involves two basic problems. First, the "tyranny of the base year," that is, of taking base-year numbers of revenues and non-plan expenditures for projections, results in inequity. The states with low levels of expenditures are essentially the poorer states. Second, "fiscal dentistry"—the practice of filling in cavities between projected revenues and expenditures—causes the cavities to become larger in succeeding years. The situation is so bad that per-capita development expenditure in a state like Bihar is only 52 percent of the national average, and in Uttar Pradesh it is 56 percent. The TFC, which set out to equalize expenditures on basic education and health care, settled down to equalize only 15 percent of the former and 30 percent of the latter!

There are a variety of invisible transfers in Indian federalism arising from controls on prices (including interest rates) and output and from origin-based taxes, and these transfers are disequalizing (Rao 1997). With the progressive dismantling of the controlled-price regime, these implicit transfers will disappear, but at present they exist. Similarly, interstate tax exportation, implicit in the central sales tax, will vanish when a full fledged destination-based VAT comes into force; but until such time, the perverse transfer will continue and this should be taken into account in determining the overall transfers. There are many other reform issues on intergovernmental fiscal arrangements that are discussed in the literature (Rao and Singh 2005; Singh and Srinivasan 2006a,b).

CONCLUDING REMARKS

The challenges of globalization warrant structural reforms in the Indian fiscal system, and these reforms have to deal with both policies and institutions. The fiscal system in the country has evolved in the context of a planned development strategy in a closed economy. It will have to be restructured to meet the challenges of globalization. Achieving fiscal consolidation is of paramount importance, not only to ensure a stable macroeconomy but also to undertake further liberalization of capital-account transactions. The reforms should also help to create an enabling environment for the private sector. As regards tax system reform, there is a need for a paradigm shift. There is merit in providing concurrent tax powers to the center and the states on both income and domestic-trade taxes with clearly defined jurisdictions. This would help to evolve a comprehensive income tax, and an efficient goods and services tax, and help to achieve greater fiscal autonomy for states through a harmonized piggybacking mechanism with respect to both the taxes. Besides ensuring macroeconomic stability, the policy should ensure competitive levels of infrastructure, and the tax policy should generate revenues to compensate for the reduction in customs duties with minimum distortions. The reforms should not only deal with tax and expenditure needs but also help to create a healthy primary and secondary public-debt market.

Most important is the need to harden the budget constraints of subnational governments by reforming the intergovernmental fiscal system. The reforms in the intergovernmental fiscal system will have to deal with both policies and institutions. Intergovernmental coordination in the calibration of tax and expenditure policies is important. It is necessary also to provide a continuous monitoring system and a mechanism to resolve intergovernmental disputes. Srinivasan's chapter provides a clear road map for future fiscal reforms in many areas. It should be discussed extensively and should inform India's reform strategy.

REFERENCES

Boadway, Robin and Frank Flatters. 1982. *Equalization in a Federal State: An Economic Analysis* (Ottawa: Canadian Government Publishing Center).

Buchanan, J. M. 1950. "Federalism and Fiscal Equity," *American Economic Review* 40(4):421–32.

Heller, Peter and M. Govinda Rao. 2006. *Sustainable Fiscal Policy for India: An International Perspective* (New Delhi: Oxford University Press).

Rao, M. Govinda. 1997. "Invisible Transfers in Indian Federalism," *Public Finance/Finances Publiques* 52(3):299–316.

———. 2002. "Dynamics of Indian Federalism." Working Paper no. 150. Stanford Center for Economic Development.

Rao, M. Govinda and H. K. Amar Nath. 2000. "Fiscal Correction: Illusion and Reality," *Economic and Political Weekly* (August 5):2806–9.

Rao, M. Govinda and Nirvikar Singh. 2005. *Political Economy of Federalism in India* (New Delhi: Oxford University Press).

Singh, Nirvikar and T. N. Srinivasan. 2006a. "Indian Federalism, Economic Reform, and Globalization," in Jessica S. Wallack and T. N. Srinivasan, eds., *Federalism and Economic Reform: International Perspectives*, 301–63 (Cambridge: Cambridge University Press).

Singh, Nirvikar and T. N. Srinivasan. 2006b. "Fiscal Policy in India: Lessons and Priorities," in Peter Heller and Govinda Rao, eds., *A Sustainable Fiscal Policy for India: An International Perspective*, 383–439 (New Delhi: Oxford University Press).

CHAPTER 3

Reforming the Indian Electricity Supply Industry

Frank A. Wolak

1. INTRODUCTION

More than fifteen years of experience with electricity-industry restructuring in both industrialized and developing countries has demonstrated that success is extremely elusive. Even countries now offered as examples of successful restructuring processes have required significant regulatory intervention at some point during their development. The England and Wales electricity supply industry required several rounds of forced divestitures of generation capacity from the two dominant firms, and the original electricity-pool market design was abandoned and the New Electricity Trading Arrangements (NETA) implemented in early 2001. The Chilean electricity industry experienced shortages that required electricity curtailments for up to three hours per day from late 1998 until the middle of 1999. In response, a number of changes in the legal framework governing the operation of the Chilean electricity supply industry were implemented.[1]

Inadequate regulatory oversight has contributed to many of the recent wholesale electricity market failures. The California electricity crisis was due in large part to the failure of the Federal Energy Regulatory Commission (FERC), the United States wholesale market regulator, to enforce the Federal Power Act of 1930 during the summer of 2000. FERC's misguided attempt to implement "remedies" during late 2000 allowed a solvable problem to develop into a full-fledged financial crisis.[2] New Zealand experienced two sustained periods of extremely high spot prices during June to September of both 2001 and 2003. Immediately following the second event, the New Zealand government abandoned its "light-handed" approach to regulating the industry and formed a seven-member Electricity Commission to take over the governance functions for the market.

These successes and failures emphasize the essential role of a forward-looking regulatory process to intervene to correct market design flaws before they cause significant harm to consumers. Few developing countries have any experience with regulatory oversight before embarking on a restructuring program. Consequently, a major challenge to successful electricity industry restructuring is establishing a regulatory process that protects consumers from significant harm yet allows suppliers and retailers the opportunity to earn sufficient revenues to recover their production costs, including a reasonable return on their investment.

Many of the current problems in India's electricity supply industry are the direct result of an ineffective regulatory process. Only roughly 55 percent of electricity produced in India is billed, and slightly more than 40 percent is regularly paid for (DOE 2003). A large fraction of this shortfall is due to theft, what is often referred to as commercial or nontechnical line losses. For 2000–1, the average tariffs for the State Electricity Boards (SEBs) were set to recover less than 70 percent of the average cost of supplying electricity (Report of Expert Group 2001, p. 51). In many states, agricultural users are charged a small fraction of the cost of producing the electricity they consume, less than 1 cent per kWh (Dhume 1999). Attempts to raise these prices have been met with enormous political resistance.

Foreign investors have also shared the cost of this ineffective regulatory process. There are a number of examples of SEBs paying significantly less than the contract price to foreign investors for electricity produced from new generating facilities that these investors built under long-term supply contracts (Slater, 2003). Enron's $2.9 billion Dabhol plant is the best-known example of this phenomenon.

As the experiences of California and New Zealand demonstrate, short-term wholesale electricity markets can put enormous stress on the regulatory oversight process. Therefore, it is prudent for India to establish credible regulatory processes at both the state and federal levels before moving forward with further wholesale market restructuring. Besides limiting the risk of a wholesale market meltdown, this strategy has the potential to yield substantial short-term benefits without compromising the potential long-term benefits of establishing a national wholesale electricity market in India.

I first outline the initial conditions in the Indian electricity supply industry that argue in favor of establishing effective and credible regulatory processes at the state and federal levels before moving forward with further restructuring. I then describe the necessary conditions for an effective regulatory process and provide several recommendations for increasing the credibility of this regulatory process. I then summarize recent progress that has been made toward achieving this goal, particularly improvements that resulted from the Electricity Act of 2003. Finally, I propose a transition process for introducing wholesale competition in India, different from that proposed in the Electricity Act of 2003, which limits the stress that may be placed on state and federal regulatory processes.

My analysis of the current situation in the Indian electricity supply industry demonstrates that the potential benefits to the Indian economy from establishing an effective regulatory process swamp the short-term and medium-term benefits of introducing a competitive wholesale electricity market. The majority of the benefits from wholesale electricity competition can be captured without introducing many features that have led to the problems experienced in industrialized countries around the world. For example, Wolak (2003b) notes that the experience of many Latin American countries demonstrates that significant benefits from electricity industry restructuring can be captured without a bid-based spot market. Virtually all of the wholesale markets in Latin America use a cost-based spot market to maintain real-time system balance. The Latin American experience with electricity industry restructuring provides valuable lessons for designing a restructuring process for India that captures all sources of benefits that exceed their expected costs of implementation.

2. THE NEED FOR EFFECTIVE REGULATION IN THE INDIAN ELECTRICITY SUPPLY INDUSTRY

Initial conditions in the Indian electricity supply industry are not conducive to a successful restructuring process. In fact, it is difficult to imagine more adverse initial conditions. Tariffs are set significantly below the average cost of supplying power for all customer classes. This is particularly the case for agricultural users. Technical line losses are among the highest in world and theft of power is rampant. Consumption is unmetered for many agricultural users and is instead based on the water pump's horsepower rating, which encourages overuse and can allow theft to occur more easily (Dossani 2004). The transmission network has limited transfer capacity across regions of the country, which can often leave significant excess generation capacity in some parts of country that cannot be used to meet demand in other parts of the country (Lama and Kemal 2003). Private sector participation by foreign and domestic firms has declined substantially because of the much-publicized difficulties the SEBs have in fulfilling their payment obligations under long-term power purchase agreements. Recent statistics issued by the Ministry of Power demonstrate that all but 70 MW of approximately 5,700 MW of non-captive new generation capacity brought on line during 2004–5 is owned by the central government or a state government (Central Electricity Authority 2006, p. 57).

Commercial losses to the Indian electricity supply industry during 2001–2 were estimated to be equivalent to 1.5 percent of India's Gross Domestic Product (Report of Task Force 2004, p. 47). According the Ministry of Power, total subsidies for 2004–5, the latest year of data currently available, are roughly 25% lower than total subsidies for 2001–2. The rapid growth of the Indian economy has now made these subsidies slightly less than 1 percent of India's GDP. Although the financial conditions of several SEBs have improved in recent years, all but a few SEBs continue to post negative rates of return because retail tariffs are set below the average cost of supplying electricity and technical and commercial transmission and distribution losses continue to grow.

2.1 WHOLESALE COMPETITION VERSUS RATIONAL RETAIL MARKET POLICIES

The consensus view among academic observers is that the major source of benefits from introducing wholesale electricity competition is cost reduction that results from more efficient new capacity investment decisions.[3] During the former state-owned monopoly regime or privately owned geographic monopoly regime, these firms often pursued other objectives besides finding the least-cost technology necessary to meet a demand increase. The benefits associated with a more efficient dispatch of generation capacity because of competition to serve demand have turned out to be significantly smaller than was initially expected because of problems with the exercise of unilateral market power in the spot market.[4] In addition, it has turned out to be a significantly more difficult regulatory challenge to encourage active demand-side participation in the spot market, which has further enhanced the ability of suppliers to exercise unilateral market power in the spot market, and thereby limit the short-term gains associated with introducing a wholesale market.

Although it is extremely difficult to quantify the potential long-term gains associated with the formation of a wholesale electricity market, even the most aggressive, but plausible, estimate is that average retail electricity prices would fall by 5 percent. Because wholesale electricity prices account for slightly more than 50 percent of the retail price of electricity, this retail price reduction would require a fall in wholesale prices of approximately 10 percent.

The United Kingdom market is representative of the amount of time it might take to realize this price reduction. The restructuring process in England and Wales began in 1990, but it was almost ten years before tangible reductions in average wholesale electricity prices occurred as a result of substantial new entry and greater competition from existing capacity now owned by a substantially larger number of independent suppliers following several rounds of divestitures.

Considering the potential benefits of a competitive wholesale market and the amount of time necessary to realize these gains, the enormous costs associated with the existing electricity supply industry in India clearly demonstrate that introducing a competitive wholesale market in India should be a low priority. Eliminating the subsidies to electricity has the potential both to eliminate a significant burden on government revenues and to encourage more efficient electricity consumption decisions. The benefits from introducing wholesale electricity competition are, at best, a very small fraction of the benefits to the Indian economy from eliminating these subsidies and are likely to take at least ten years to realize. Consequently, the policy with the greatest expected benefits to the Indian economy is, by far, one that focuses on eliminating subsidies to the electricity supply industry as soon as possible.

The expected benefits to Indian consumers from this policy may be especially large because the existing subsidies to electricity consumption introduce a number of other costs. By artificially increasing both the demand for electricity and the growth in demand, these subsidies create secondary market harm in the form of overconsumption of groundwater by farmers because electricity used to pump groundwater typically has a zero marginal price. Charging farmers prices that reflect the cost of producing the electricity they consume for each kWh they consume would reduce the harm associated with overconsumption of groundwater.

Eliminating this enormous subsidy to electricity consumption would have the additional benefit of reducing the need to finance new generating facilities. A recent study by Filippini and Parchuari (2004) of the demand for electricity by urban Indian households, finds own-price elasticities for household electricity demand that are larger than those obtained for industrialized countries, although they are still less than one in absolute value. This study finds that for urban households, increasing the price of electricity by 10 percent should reduce the demand for electricity by approximately 5 percent. This study also found a positive income elasticity of demand, so that as household incomes increase, the demand for electricity should also increase. Moreover, if the Indian government's target of sustained GDP growth of 8 percent per year or more is realized, electricity demand should continue to increase, even at higher prices that contain no subsidies.

By reducing the rate of growth in demand for new generation capacity in the short-term as a result of the elimination of subsidies to electricity consumption, more scarce public funds could be devoted to investments in new transmission capacity to increase the interconnection capacity across regions of the country. This would allow the existing generation capacity to be used more efficiently by reducing the number of hours of the year when unused generation capacity cannot produce energy to be sold in neighboring regions because of insufficient transmission capacity.

Reducing the level of subsidies would also free up much-needed public funds to install meters and other technology necessary to measure final consumption. Setting a zero marginal price for electricity because of the lack metering technology imposes significant environmental damage. For the year 2004–5, 71.37 percent of India's electricity came from coal-fired generation facilities, 14.23 percent from hydroelectric facilities, 10.35 percent from natural gas–fired facilities, and the remainder from diesel, nuclear, wind, and other renewable energy sources (Central Electricity Authority 2006, p. 67). This technology mix implies that coal, a major contributor to greenhouse gas emissions, is the highest variable cost technology providing energy during many hours of the year. During the hours when coal is not the highest variable cost technology operating, other fossil fuel technologies are, such as diesel or natural gas–fired combustion turbines. This logic implies that the marginal private cost of producing an additional kWh of electricity is never close to zero (DOE 2003). Including the cost of greenhouse gas emissions in this calculation further increases the cost of an additional kWh. Pricing wholesale electricity closer to its marginal private cost of production would have significant environmental benefits in the form of reduced greenhouse gas emissions.

2.2 EXTENT OF FOREIGN PARTICIPATION IN THE INDIAN ELECTRICITY SECTOR

According to the Indian government, all of the SEBs are technically bankrupt, with cumulative losses totaling more than 220 billion rupees in 2004–5, down from 290 billion rupees in 2001–2.[5] Due to these financial difficulties and the failure of the SEBs to honor fully their payment obligations to investors, a large number of foreign-sponsored generation projects have been cancelled or delayed, and very few new projects have been initiated. According to the U.S. Energy Information Administration (EIA 2003):

> The $5 billion, 3,960-MW coal-fired Hirma Power Plant, was canceled by Mirant Corporation in December 2001.
>
> Electricite de France has quit the coal-fired 1072-MW Bhadrawati project in Maharashtra state.
>
> The 1,886-MW LNG-fired unit at Ennore, with an associated LNG import terminal, was canceled by CMS Energy in June 2001. CMS Energy also announced in October 2001 that it was pulling out of several smaller projects.
>
> India's National Thermal Power Company was planning a 2,000-MW LNG-fired plant at Pipavav, but the project was shelved in June 2001.
>
> Powergrid was planning a 1,320-MW coal-fired plant for Cuddalore, which was delayed indefinitely in early 2001.
>
> Cogentrix cancelled the 1,000-MW Mangalore coal-fired project in December 1999.
>
> South Korea's Daewoo Power and ABB Lummus cancelled plans for a 1,400-MW plant in Madhya Pradesh in August 2000.

According to the EIA, no major foreign-owned projects were launched during 2003. As noted earlier, only 70 MW of non-captive privately owned generation capacity came on line during 2004–5. The vast majority of privately owned generation capacity that has come on line over the past three years is captive generation capacity built to serve a nearby industrial facility. These captive generation facilities can, in most instances, sell surplus power to the bulk transmission grid. However, their financial viability depends on sales to captive customers.

The current financial condition of the SEBs and the financial condition of the international generation sector make further foreign investment in India for non-captive electricity needs extremely unlikely without significant progress toward improving the financial condition of the SEBs. This logic strengthens the argument in favor of delaying further restructuring of the Indian electricity supply industry and first developing an effective and credible regulatory process that charges prices that recover the total cost of producing electricity, including a return on the capital invested.

Immediate elimination of the enormous subsidies to agricultural users and smaller subsidies to residential users is politically impossible, but putting in place a regulatory structure to begin the process of reducing these subsidies to large customers in three to five years is feasible. That would also allow enough time to attract new foreign investment once the international generation sector recovers its financial footing. Although subsidies to some customers may remain, those subsidies should be means-tested and subject to maximum consumption levels. Section 5, below, discusses the current state of progress toward the goal of financial viability of the SEBs.

3. ESTABLISHING EFFECTIVE FEDERAL AND STATE REGULATORY PROCESSES

Foreign investors are unlikely to return to India unless they believe that long-term supply contracts signed to finance new generation facilities will be paid in full. Retail tariffs that recover the average cost of supplying electricity are an essential first-step toward increasing investor confidence in the industry. Unless the central government guarantees the revenue stream of all long-term supply contracts signed by SEBs with private investors, retail tariffs that cover the average cost of supplying electricity to final consumers are a necessary condition for private investors to enter into long-term supply contracts with the SEBs. Reducing the number of unmetered customers, technical line losses, and the amount of theft of power are all parts of an effective regulatory process. These actions would demonstrate a commitment on the part of the government to collect sufficient revenues from customers to pay for the electricity produced.

The Indian government already has a legal foundation for implementing effective and credible regulatory oversight through The Electricity Regulation Act of 1998. The 1998 Act established the State Electricity Regulatory Commissions (SERCs) to regulate retail rates. It also established the Central Electricity Regulatory Commission (CERC) as an independent statutory body with quasi-judicial powers. The CERC has a mandate to implement national tariff policy and regulate interstate power sales, to advise the central government on the formulation of tariff policy, and to promote competition and efficiency in the electricity sector. The

Electricity Act of 2003 has strengthened several aspects of this legal foundation. This is discussed in Section 5.

Significant government presence in the Indian electricity supply industry complicates the process of establishing an effective and credible regulatory process. There is a large academic literature documenting the incentive problems associated with government ownership of infrastructure industries (see Vickers and Yarrow 1988). Some are unique to developing countries, but others are common to government ownership in general. For example, a recent U.S. Congressional Budget Office study (CBO, 1997) noted the following four sources of incentives for inefficient provision of electricity associated with government ownership:

1. Separation between revenues and costs
2. Reduced cost of capital to government-owned businesses
3. No independent oversight of rates
4. Inadequate maintenance of facilities

All four of these problems appear in the Indian electricity supply industry.

Separation between revenues and costs means that the revenues from the sales of electricity accrue to the government, whereas the costs of production are appropriated as part of the budgetary process. In contrast, a privately owned firm must earn revenues that at least cover its production costs (including a rate of return on capital invested commensurate with the risk borne by investors) or it will be unable to attract the capital necessary to undertake investment to maintain or expand its plant and equipment. More generally, this separation between revenues and costs implies that government funds can be used almost indefinitely to subsidize electricity consumption. The government's continuing failure to implement and enforce the tariffs necessary to recover the cost of supplying electricity is a prime example of this phenomenon.

The reduced cost of capital to government-owned businesses implies that other factors besides economics determine whether investments are made by a government-owned entity. Political factors can and do play a major role in determining the type of technology employed, and the timing and size of new construction.

No independent oversight of rates implies that the government has considerable freedom in using electricity prices to pursue non-economic ends, because it has no requirement to cover production costs or a market-determined rate of return on the initial investment with retail electricity prices. In particular, the government can set electricity prices sufficiently low to attract electricity intensive industries to certain locations. For example, in the Pacific Northwest of the United States, large government-owned hydroelectricity facilities producing very low priced electricity resulted in the location of a number of electricity intensive industries nearby. Indian farmers are the major beneficiaries of India's low electricity prices, although residential consumers throughout India also benefit from tariffs below the average cost supplying the electricity (Dossani 2004).

The CBO report drew attention to the problem of inadequate maintenance of facilities, by which it meant that, relative to privately owned electricity generation facilities, the government-owned facilities spent considerably less on maintenance than did investor-owned facilities. For example, over the ten-year period from 1986 to 1996, U.S. investor-owned utilities averaged maintenance expenditures that were approximately 7.2 percent of their revenues from electricity sales, whereas the federal government–owned facilities averaged maintenance expenditures that were approximately 4.5 percent of their revenues from electricity sales.[6] These relatively lower maintenance expenditures appear to have led to lower operating efficiency for the federal government–owned facilities. The CBO report compared the ratio of production to operable generating capacity for federal government and nonfederal government hydropower producers from 1991 to 1995. For the year 1995, this ratio for all federal capacity was 38.7 percent, whereas the average for nonfederal capacity was 51.4 percent. The U.S. government appears to be better able to raise funds for new construction than to do so for undertaking maintenance operations on their existing facilities.

For the past thirty years, the Indian electricity sector has persistently seen low capacity factors from its thermal generation facilities. A major contributor to the initially low capacity factors was inadequate maintenance of thermal generation facilities. As a result of comprehensive efforts to increase plant-level capacity factors—the percent of potential energy that a plant could produce annually that it actually did produce—the overall average Indian thermal plant capacity factor increased to 70 percent in 2001–2 (Lama and Kemal 2003, p. 9), from as low as 44 percent in 1980–81 (Dadhich 2002). Plant-level capacity factors have continued to increase in recent years. The all-India average capacity factor for coal-fired facilities was 74.5 percent for 2004–5 (Central Electricity Authority 2006, p. 136).

Government ownership also makes it easier for customers to rationalize not paying their bills on time, or not paying at all. In most industrialized countries, customers unable to pay prices that reflect the full cost of the electricity are offered subsidized rates which are financed either from general governmental revenues or through higher prices paid by other customers. However, the extent of these subsidies is nowhere near the level it is in India. One task for CERC is to introduce national standards for means testing urban and rural households before they are able to consume at a subsidized rate. This is a typical function of the regulatory process in the United States. For example, California has the California Alternative Rates for Energy (CARE) program which provides a 20 percent discount on electricity bills to households of various combinations of sizes and income levels. This discount is funded through a rate surcharge on all other customers.

The CERC and SERCs should not avoid the difficult decision of determining which customers must pay prices that cover the average cost of supplying electricity and which customers must pay higher prices to subsidize those consumers who find it difficult to pay an unsubsidized price. Rationalizing prices may be at odds with the government's goal of increasing access to electricity in rural areas of the country. However, the fact that subsidies to electricity consumption are close to 1.5 percent of GDP demonstrates that too many consumers receive subsidies. Until retail prices can be increased to cover total production costs, further investment in new generation capacity using government funds would be imprudent. Given the current financial condition of the SEBs, additional private funding for new investment is extremely unlikely to materialize.

In most markets in industrialized countries, when a customer receives a subsidized rate there are restrictions on that customer's consumption. For example, in some markets customers receive subsidized rates in exchange for having a maximum amount they can withdraw from the distribution network during certain time intervals. For example, the maximum amount of energy a customer may be able to withdraw from the network during any given hour could be set at 5 kWh, and their monthly demand might not be allowed to exceed 250 kWh, or a penalty rate would be applied to all consumption above that level. These programs are designed to provide the customer with a subsistence level of electricity at a subsidized rate. If the customer would like to consume beyond that monthly level, he or she would have to switch to a tariff designed to recover the retailer's average cost of supply. The logic behind this arrangement is simple and compelling: there must be a downside to obtaining a subsidized rate or else customers will have little incentive to pay rates that recover the full cost of producing the electricity. While this model of subsidized rates for a subsistence level of electricity works for urban households, it must be altered to address the tariff structure in the agricultural sector.

Farmers could be endowed with a subsistence monthly consumption level at a subsidized price. They then could be charged at the marginal cost of additional electricity for any consumption above that level and be paid at this marginal price for any reductions in their monthly consumption relative to this baseline amount. For example, the farmer could be given the right to buy 100 kWh each month at 1 cent/kWh, but any consumption beyond that amount could be paid for at a price of 10 cents/kWh, which reflects the SEB's forward-looking marginal cost of supplying additional electricity. If a farmer consumed less than 100 kWh, then he or she would be paid 10 cents/kWh for the difference between 100 kWh and the farmer's actual consumption. The amount the farmer is entitled to purchase at this subsidized rate could decline over time, or the level of the subsidized price could increase over time, to phase out subsidies to agricultural users.

Dossani and Ranganathan (2003) present empirical evidence suggesting that needs-tested agricultural subsidies have the potential to reduce the aggregate amount of subsidies paid. The authors surveyed the willingness to pay for electricity by agricultural users in Andhra Pradesh in the year 2000. They found a surprising degree of heterogeneity across farmers in what they considered to be an "acceptable increase" in the price of electricity. Dossani and Ranganathan argue that greater discriminatory pricing of electricity to farmers by, for example, means-testing subsidies, would raise the amount of revenue collected by approximately 20 percent.

They also examined two quality dimensions for rural electricity supply that could justify higher prices. The first is rostering, which means supplying power in intervals rather than continuously throughout the day. In Andhra Pradesh, rural power is supplied in two blocks, of six and three hours, for a total of nine hours per day. This practice is not favored by some farmers as it can increase their total consumption of electricity. Some farmers waste water because of the need to re-water land only partially watered during the initial period of permissible electricity use during the day. Based on their survey results, Dossani and Raganathan (2003) argue that rostering results in an excess of usage of power of approximately 15 percent on average.

They also consider the costs of pump motor burnout because of voltage fluctuations and other power quality issues. The survey respondents reported an average of 1.59 pumpset burnouts per year attributable to power quality issues. Based on their survey results, Dossani and Raganathan (2003) argue that the net result of (a) eliminating pumpset burnout through higher quality supply, (b) increasing average prices by 50 percent for pumpsets exceeding 15 horsepower, and (c) eliminating rostering, would imply a 25 percent reduction in the level of subsidies.

There are a number of minimal requirements that the CERC must impose on all SEBs to begin the process of improving their financial condition. First, all SEBs should submit plans to install meters for 100 percent of their customers, including all agricultural customers, as soon as possible. All SEBs should be required to submit plans for reducing the extent of technical and commercial transmission and distribution losses as soon as possible. The CERC and SERCs should set clear standards for disconnecting all classes of customers that do not pay their bills. These rules should also include terms and conditions for customers to regain their connections if they are able to pay overdue bills. The CERC and the SERCs should work together to formulate a transition plan to raise electricity rates to the levels necessary recover the going-forward cost of supplying electricity. This does not mean that all subsidies would be eliminated, only that average prices to all customers would rise enough so that SEBs would regain their financial solvency.

To correct the mistaken perception that electricity is plentiful, the CERC should implement a national tariff policy requiring all customers, regardless of how poor they are, to pay a positive marginal price for electricity. Having a meter should be a precondition for a customer to receive service. For customers that are currently unmetered, CERC and the relevant SERC should set a date for terminating unmetered service. With the requirement that all new customers have metered service and an end date for unmetered access, the CERC and relevant SERC could be certain that all customers have metered access by some future date.

One way to transition a customer that currently pays a zero marginal price to a metered price is to set a sufficiently low marginal price so that the customer's monthly bill does not significantly increase immediately as a result of the transition to metered service. Then the customer can be introduced to future marginal price increases on an ability-to-pay basis.

In order to prevent tampering with a customer's meter, the SEB must be able to charge the customer at a penalty rate if it can be determined that a customer's meter has been altered. For example, the customer's monthly bill would be some penalty rate times the customer's highest monthly consumption over the previous year. The SEB also should have the ability to charge penalties for late payment. Both the process used to determine if a meter has been tampered with and to assess the penalties due, as well as the process for determining the penalties for late or non-payment, should be approved and monitored by the relevant SERC. To ensure consistent standards across the country, the CERC should issue general guidelines for assessing these penalties—guidelines to which all SERCs must comply.

An effective regulatory process must balance the competing interests of the industry participants and Indian consumers. There are a number of ways to increase the effectiveness and credibility of the state-level regulatory process and to adapt the industry to changing market conditions. CERC should establish regulatory guidelines with which the SERCs in each state must comply. A national regulatory policy would increase the commitment of state regulators. Rather than having to shoulder the burden of enforcing politically unpopular decisions, such as universal metering, nonzero marginal prices, and penalties and disconnection for late payment and nonpayment, implementing these as national policies can increase the degree of acceptance for these policies at the state level.

Clearly, all Indian consumers should agree that if electricity is sold to the vast majority of customers for less than it costs to produce, this creates an unsustainable electricity supply industry. Problems arise when one customer or customer class finds a way to pay a lower price, without some corresponding restriction on their consumption behavior. This creates incentives for other customers to attempt to obtain these lower prices, which is why binding maximum consumption restrictions on customers receiving subsidized rates are necessary, as is an automatic phase out of subsidies to agricultural users.

3.1 NATURE OF THE COMMITMENT PROBLEM IN REGULATION

A regulatory process must trade off two competing goals. Specifically, it must have sufficient flexibility to adapt to the changing conditions in the industry, and yet, at the same time, it must possess features that allow it to commit credibly to honoring previous commitments. The electricity industry requires extremely long-lived investments in generation, transmission, and distribution assets. Privately owned firms will not make the investments necessary for the long-term viability of the industry unless they believe that the regulator and government are willing to commit to allowing the firm the opportunity to earn a return on investment commensurate with the level of risk taken on by investors. For example, if prospective investors feel that the regulatory environment is unstable, they will decline to make investments that may be profitable under a more stable regulatory regime. They may also be willing to pay less for the same asset under an unstable regulatory regime than a stable regulatory regime. Another aspect of regulatory uncertainty is fuel cost uncertainty. The regulator must commit to allow spot electricity prices to increase to reflect increases in fuel costs, or else this will create another source of uncertainty that dulls the incentive for private firms to invest. Even in industrialized countries, an important aspect of electricity market design is building in mechanisms that allow market prices to move with production costs. The need to assure investors that they will have every opportunity to earn an adequate return on their investment underscores the importance of a comprehensive national regulatory policy managed by CERC and implemented at the state level by the various SERCs.

There are a variety of ways for the regulatory process to solve these commitment problems. For example, under the U.S. regulatory process, firms are, by law, allowed the opportunity to recover their production costs as well as a "fair rate of return" on their current "used and useful" capital stock. Under the U.S. regulatory process the firm's current "used and useful" capital stock is referred to as its ratebase. There are well-defined administrative processes for determining the regulated firm's ratebase as a function of its past investments. All of the firm's investment decisions are subject to a "reasonableness or prudence review" by the regulatory body. This review determines whether these investment expenses were reasonable in light of the best forecast of the future level of demand in the industry. If these investment expenditures are prudently incurred, then they enter the firm's ratebase, and the firm is allowed the opportunity to earn the regulated rate of return on its ratebase in the current period so long as these assets remain "used and useful."

This requirement means that the assets are actually used by the firm to produce its output and that they are useful for this activity, implying that it is reasonable to employ them, given the current technology, for electricity production. This commits future regulatory commissions to honor the investment decisions (if they were deemed prudent by previous regulatory commissions) that are actually employed in the production process. The current regulatory body is charged with setting the "fair rate of return" on these investment expenditures. This rate of return must, by law, then be applied to the firm's ratebase, which depends on all prudently incurred past and present investment expenditures currently used in production. Because the regulated rate of return must be applied to the entire ratebase in determining the firm's revenue requirements, the regulatory body commits to allowing the firm to earn this return on all previous used and useful investment expenditures. This is one example of how to build commitment into the regulatory process.

The CERC should establish national guidelines for computing the ratebase values for all capital equipment owned or operated by federal and state governments and private investors not covered by power purchase agreements. This should be part of a general process led by the CERC to establish general accounting standards for all entities regulated at the state and national level. Topics for standardization include common methods for dealing with accounts receivable and accounts payable, as well as investment expenditures and depreciation schedules for capital equipment. Power purchase agreements between generation unit owners and electricity retailers are an important source of accounts receivable and payable, respectively. The CERC should implement a national policy that requires the SERC to commit to raise sufficient revenues through the rate-making process to recover the payments due under the terms of these contracts in a timely manner. Standardization of accounting practices can make it much easier for the CERC to monitor the economic performance of the SEBs. In addition, standardization of accounting practices can also allow the implementation of yardstick regulation approaches to compensating SEBs for their economic performance.

It is important to emphasize that the ratebase value of a piece of capital equipment need not equal its historical cost or its replacement cost. Some of the capital stock in the Indian electricity supply industry is likely to be of considerably less value than the historical cost less accumulated depreciation expenses. CERC should establish national policies for determining the useful life of generation assets. It should also establish realistic depreciation expense schedules to recover the replacement costs of these projects.

The CERC document, "Final Regulations for Terms and Conditions for Electricity Tariff for the Five-Year Period Beginning April 1, 2004," contains pronouncements consistent with many of these required reforms.[7] Although this document lays out a framework for determining the costs of supplying electricity in a consistent manner, the more difficult problem remains one of ensuring that actual tariffs are set sufficiently high, to recover these costs and that SEBs receive sufficient revenues to recover the full cost of producing the energy consumed.

3.2 CHARACTERISTICS OF AN APPROPRIATE REGULATORY PROCESS

There are several rules governing the regulatory process that make solving the commitment problem much more straightforward. The first is a requirement of due process, ensuring that the regulatory process be carried out according to some set of established rules and principles. One of the most important established principles is the respect for precedent, that the logic of past decisions will be respected in making future decisions unless there is significant evidence that this logic was faulty. The U.S. regulatory process has a long history of honoring precedent. Because of this, market participants can be confident that past decisions will be respected and that future decisions will be made in a manner consistent with prior logic, unless there is significant evidence that the previous logic was flawed or inconsistent with current laws.

In order to determine if the prior logic is invalid, and that previous decisions based on that logic should be given a lower weight, the regulatory body must have the ability to gather information from market participants. The regulator should therefore be able to compel market participants to provide all of the information it requires to make that determination. A minimum requirement in this regard is annual financial balance sheet information. The regulatory body should also be able to request and receive periodically other information it deems necessary to reach a decision.

Supplemental data requests should be subject to a regulatory burden test. Compliance with the regulatory process should not be excessively burdensome to the firms involved, in the sense that the expected benefits associated with requiring the regulated entity to compile and submit data should be commensurate with the benefits expected to accrue to the regulatory process from having this information available. It cannot be emphasized enough that the quality of the regulatory process depends crucially on the quality of the data made available to the regulator. For this reason, the CERC should establish national standards for data release to the CERC and the SERCs. The CERC should set standards on how this information is reported to it and the SERCs. For example, the CERC could set standards for electronic submission which would significantly reduce the cost of data analysis for regulatory decision making.

The commitment problem may be difficult for a regulatory body to solve because of the external pressures it faces from market participants or the government. This implies that the agency's budget should be determined independently of any actions it might take, and all of its decision makers should be immune to influence by the government or market participants for predetermined terms of office. The requirement for a budget sufficient to accomplish its duties should be contained in the enabling legislation, which would prevent the government from cutting the agency's budget in the future if it makes decisions contrary to the government's wishes. Crucial to guaranteeing independence is ensuring that the regulatory agency's budget cannot be affected by current decisions that it makes and that the government cannot overturn the regulatory commission's decision except through legislative action or by judicial review.

The option for judicial review of decisions made by the regulatory body is particularly important, because another major requirement for solving the regulatory commitment problem is accountability of the regulatory body for the implications of its decisions. Endowing a regulatory body with the ability to set prices and service quality standards and to implement regulatory rule changes gives it an enormous amount of discretionary power. Without an accompanying obligation to do this is in a responsible manner that respects the legal rights of all parties involved and the precedents that exist from previous decisions, there is considerable leeway for opportunistic behavior by the regulatory body. By requiring the regulatory body to be accountable, in the sense of providing market participants with the opportunity to request a judicial review of regulatory decisions, the likelihood that the regulatory body will implement policies that violate previous regulatory commitments will be limited. The enabling legislation for the regulatory body should, therefore, provide it with a mission statement and general guidelines for its operation. This enabling legislation then would form the legal foundation for any attempt to overturn or modify a decision made by a regulatory body through judicial review.

This judicial review should focus on determining whether standard administrative processes and procedures were followed in reaching a decision, rather than reviewing the regulator's technical analysis and judgments. For example, in the United States, the regulatory body is required to follow a well-defined administrative process in reaching a decision. In particular, the basis for any decision it makes must be based on facts and opinions presented during a formal quasi-legal process. If a party to the decision believes that due process was violated in reaching a decision or that a decision is inconsistent with the legislation governing the regulatory process, then it can appeal the decision to the relevant court.

The early experience of the U.S. regulatory process provides insight on the role of judicial review. During the early stages of the regulation of electric utilities, natural gas pipelines, and other network industries, there were a large number of judicial reviews of decisions made by the newly created regulatory bodies. However, as a large body of legal precedent from these judicial reviews and from previous regulatory decisions developed, the number of major judicial reviews declined significantly.

Transparency of the regulatory process further increases its ability to balance the competing goals of honoring previous regulatory commitments against the flexibility to respond to changing industry conditions. A regulatory process is transparent if there is a single entity that makes the final decision and if there is a clear record of how this decision is made. It is essential that the regulatory body have the right to make the final decision on pricing, service quality, and market rule changes. A process where the regulatory body makes recommendations that must then be ultimately decided by another decision-making body introduces unnecessary uncertainty into the regulatory process and creates additional incentives for market participants or the government to attempt to distort the process. The full responsibility for decision making should reside with a single entity, subject to the opportunity for judicial review of its decisions, as discussed below.

Transparency has several dimensions. The first is that a written record of all information provided by market participants to the regulatory body must be provided to all other market participants. All decisions made by the regulatory body must be issued in written form and must take account of the written evidence or oral evidence (that is subsequently transcribed) entered into the regulatory proceedings. Decisions must address the issues presented by market participants by weighing the relative merits of the arguments made for and against the decision under consideration. Because of the risk of judicial review, it is unacceptable for the regulatory body to disregard sound economic or legal analysis of an issue in favor of a position with no explanation of the reasons behind it. This is what it means to satisfy the due process requirement.

The credibility of the regulatory body would also be severely undermined if market participants thought that it was possible to influence the regulatory outcome through secret meetings with members of the regulatory body or through other nonpublic forms of interaction.

In the United States, virtually all regulatory bodies prohibit nonpublic meetings between their members and staff and market participants that involve discussions of the issues currently under consideration by the regulatory body within a certain time period of the initiation of the formal decision-making process. This ex parte communication rule increases the perceived transparency of the regulatory process, because market participants can be confident that from a certain time forward all information conveyed to the regulatory body relevant to the decision-making process will be made in a public forum.

Another important aspect of an accountable and transparent regulatory process is open access to the proceedings. A permissive standard should be applied to the process of determining whether or not an individual, firm or government agency is allowed to submit evidence to a regulatory proceeding. If an individual is sufficiently interested in the issue to the take the time to submit written evidence or an oral argument on an issue, then this level of interest should be sufficient to allow participation in the regulatory proceeding. The process of soliciting input from all interested parties, even though these parties are very likely to argue positions that favor their financial interests, is extremely valuable when the regulatory body is attempting to formulate a new policy to adapt to changing circumstances in the industry.

In many regulatory proceedings in the United States and abroad, the regulatory body will post what is referred to as a notice of proposed rulemaking (NOPR). This document will lay out the specific issues that the regulatory body plans to address and solicit input from all interested parties on how it should formulate these proposed rules for regulating the industry. Interveners will then file comments on the regulatory body's initial NOPR after some time lag. Often independent academic commentators submit comments in order to assist the regulatory process with an unbiased analysis of the issue. Then the regulatory body will analyze these comments and issue its final ruling. This decision addresses comments it has received on the NOPR and provides a foundation for the final decision which respects legal precedents and other regulatory decisions. This information gathering process is an essential aspect of the "due process" associated with any major regulatory decision. Strict adherence to this information solicitation and information processing function before implementing any major regulatory policy change limits the ability of subsequent judicial review to overturn the regulatory body's initial decision for failure to adhere to the standards of due process.

Transparency of the regulatory process in India is crucial to achieving the dual goals of raising average tariffs to a level necessary to recover the forward-looking costs of production and reducing the level of technical and commercial losses to levels commensurate with those in industrialized countries. Achieving these two goals will require a national regulatory policy coordinated by CERC and implemented by SERC along with the full support of the federal- and state-level governments. Rather than attempting this on a state-by-state basis, a superior strategy is for CERC to lead a nationwide, highly visible commitment to more rational electricity pricing. Without such a policy, it is difficult see how foreign investors will ever again make significant generation investments in India (absent ironclad guarantees from the central government).

3.3 IMPLEMENTING A CREDIBLE REGULATORY PROCESS IN INDIA

The primary goal of regulation is to serve the interests of the citizens of the country or state in their role as consumers. It is not in the long-term interests of consumers for the regulator to set prices that do not allow suppliers ample opportunities to earn an adequate return on their investment. This implies that the regulatory body must recognize that its actions to protect consumers in the short run can increase the long-run costs of serving consumers, so in that sense the regulatory body must also be concerned with the interests of producers. The government may also use the regulatory process to pursue social goals, such as increasing the fraction of households with access to electricity.

Although a regulated firm or a consumer will certainly disagree with a regulatory decision that adversely affects its financial interests, if the firm or consumer can be convinced that the decision serves the best interests of all citizens of India, it will be less likely to attempt to undermine the implementation of a regulatory decision. This logic implies that particularly during the early stages of the restructuring process, the regulatory body must be a consensus builder that oversees the operation of the firms it regulates, rather than an additional layer of managerial oversight for the day-to-day operation of the firms. Because the major goal of the regulatory process in India over the next five years should be the difficult task of putting the SEBs on firm financial footing and reducing both technical and commercial line losses, consensus building is an extremely important task for the national and state regulators.

The regulatory process is far too complex for a single individual, or even a small number of individuals, to understand all of the details. There should instead be a permanent staff of experts in power systems engineering, economics, and law to assist the regulatory decision-making body. The staff would provide an institutional memory and expertise that is not possible in a regulatory process that relies very heavily on members of the decision-making body appointed to fixed terms for its expertise and institutional memory. Having a permanent staff with an institutional memory also increases the likelihood that the regulatory process will respect due process and precedent. Given the suspected overstaffing at many SEBs, there should be many qualified individuals available for staff positions at the state and federal levels.

Relative to the size of the industries that they oversee, the CERC and a number of the SERCs appear to be understaffed relative to what would be necessary to regulate in an effective and credible manner. The regulatory body should have a permanent professional staff of lawyers, engineers, and regulatory economists. Depending on their workloads, members of the regulatory decision-making body may require their own self-appointed assistants to interact with the permanent staff of their regulatory body.

For comparison, the California Public Utilities Commission (CPUC) employs approximately 850 staff, with half of these devoted to electricity regulation issues. FERC, the national wholesale energy market regulator, employs roughly 1,300 staff with an annual budget of approximately $200 million.

All successful regulatory bodies in the United States at both the state and the federal levels have the structure of a permanent staff of experts and a decision-making body composed of elected or appointed commissioners serving fixed terms. The staff have a strong interest in preserving the value of their expertise and will therefore be a strong force for respecting precedents and formal process. The major administrative work of the regulatory body is done by the staff.

The usual solution to an understaffing problem is for the regulatory agency to obtain partial or full funding from the entities that it regulates. In the United States, for example, the FERC collects fees from the entities it regulates to pay a significant fraction of its budget, although it can also receive funding from the U.S. government. The CPUC operates in a similar manner by collecting fees from customers of the entities that it regulates, but the State of California determines its final budget.

4. TRANSITION TO A NATIONAL WHOLESALE ELECTRICITY MARKET

A necessary condition to proceed with a national wholesale market is that the SEBs set tariffs that recover the full cost of supplying customers and ensure that technical and commercial line losses are close to those obtained in the median industrialized country. There are a number of other steps that can be taken in the meantime. The SEBs and the national Central Electricity Authority should be required by the CERC and relevant SERCs to create separate financial accounts to allow the CERC and SERC to break down the cost of retail electricity into the four basic components: (1) wholesale power, (2) transmission services, (3) distribution services, and (4) retailing services.

The SEBs should be encouraged to form separate corporatized entities that are allowed the opportunity by both CERC and SERC to earn the appropriate, regulated rate of return on their assets. Implementing uniform accounting standards across all entities in the electricity supply industry is an essential precondition to financial separation of the SEBs. Consistent methodologies for computing profits and losses across each segment of the industry for each of the SEBs and the Central Electricity Authority will greatly increase the information value of the financial data produced by these different entities.

By accumulating experience with the operation of the regulatory process, the CERC and the SERCs can increase the credibility of the regulatory process and its ability to respond to changing conditions in the industry. Credibility often comes from demonstrating that the industry can function according to the rules set out by the regulatory process without external government intervention.

4.1 SEPARATE PRICES FOR EACH SERVICE

An important step in this process is establishing separate component prices for retail electricity. For example, CERC should establish national guidelines for pricing wholesale power from generation facilities by fuel type. Similar guidelines should be adopted for transmission services, distribution services, and electricity retailing. Economic logic dictates that distribution costs should vary with the geography and population density of the customers served, although transmission services could be priced on a regional basis.

CERC should set guidelines for computing the regulated price retail price for each customer so that the price is equal to the sum of the component prices. The standard calculation runs as follows:

$$\text{P(retail)} = \text{P(wholesale)} + \text{P(Transmission \& System Operation)} + \text{P(Distribution)} + \text{P(supply)}$$

where P(x) is the price of service x. Separately regulated prices for generation, transmission and grid operation, distribution, and electricity supply serve two purposes.

First, they increase the transparency of the price-setting processes to final consumers. With a detailed breakdown of each component of the delivered price of electricity, it is possible for parties sympathetic to raising the retail price of electricity to the level necessary to cover the going-forward cost of all segments of the industry to make their case. These entities can compare the four cost components across states and over time.

Second, separate prices are essential to initiating further restructuring. Potential purchasers of generation assets must know the price that they will receive for electricity produced from these facilities as well as the regulatory mechanism that will be used to set these prices. Similar logic applies to the prices that are set for grid operation and transmission services and the prices set for local distribution and electricity supply.

This equation allows sufficient flexibility to allow different retail prices for different customer classes depending on the cross-customer variation in any of the component prices. For example, the price in one region may be higher because the local distribution price is higher in that region. Setting separate prices for each component of the retail electricity price and requiring that each entity recover its going-forward production costs from sales at these prices will begin the process of establishing a credible and transparent regulatory process for all segments of the industry.

The pricing scheme described above separates the pricing of what are usually considered monopoly services—transmission, system operation and distribution—from what are usually considered potentially competitive services—generation and supply. This scheme will make it easier to introduce competition into the segments of the industry where it is considered feasible. As the transition to competition begins, it may be necessary to raise the prices paid for monopoly services to attract new investment into these segments of the industry in order to improve the efficiency of the competitive generation market. Credibility to honor commitments to pay for new investment could be handled through a ratebase mechanism similar to the one described earlier.

Based on whatever the CERC and the relevant SERC establish as the ratebase value of the SEB's transmission assets, the regulatory process would then determine the price paid for transmission services and system operation by including an appropriate rate of return on this ratebase. In this same way, the distribution company's assets could be valued and placed in the ratebase to determine its revenue requirements in the regulatory price-setting process.

With a stable regulatory environment that sets prices for wholesale electricity, transmission services, distribution services, and electricity retailing that allow the SEBs to earn a rate of return on their entire ratebase, the process of introducing a national wholesale market can then move forward. A regulated industry structure where consumers pay for the vast majority of the power they consume, in which technical line losses are in line with international standards, and in which the revenues recovered from consumers are sufficient to pay the full costs of supplying electricity would be an environment very attractive to foreign investors. Moreover, a time series of regulated prices for various services purchased or provided by the SEBs would make it earlier for these prospective investors to value specific components of a SEB's business.

4.2 THE BENEFITS OF A FEDERAL SYSTEM

India's federal structure could be extremely beneficial to improving the efficiency of these state-level regulatory processes. All twenty-eight states in India have signed a Memorandum of Understanding (MOU) or Memorandum of Agreement (MOA) with the central government to undertake reforms. Although the geography of India is quite varied, similar technologies are employed for producing, transmitting, and distributing electricity throughout the country. Consequently, there is a major role for cross-state benchmarking of the performance of all or most aspects of the electricity supply industry. For example, comparisons of the heat rates, operating and maintenance costs, outage rates, capacity factors, and even pollutant-emissions rates across similar thermal units would provide valuable information to all SERCs that set regulated wholesale electricity prices. The CERC could serve as a central clearinghouse for all relevant financial and technical data necessary to set regulated wholesale electricity prices for generating facilities.

A similar approach could be used to collect information on the costs of transmission network construction and operation throughout India. CERC could issue guidelines on how the various entities should submit cost and technical information on their transmission network, and this information could be shared for the purposes of rate-setting among the various SERCs. This process could also be employed to set the prices for distribution services and electricity retailing.

There are a number of statistical methods for measuring productive efficiency that could be employed to measure magnitudes more rigorously. These methods have been used as part of the distribution regulatory process in the Nordic market, and recently recommendations have been made to implement these procedures in the South American countries. Estache, Rossi, and Ruzzier (2004) recommend using such methods to compute measures of firm-level productive efficiency to compare across countries and firms as part of the process of regulating the price of distribution services in South America. While a strict application of these measures to the case of India may not be possible, given problems with data availability, consistent measures of firm-level financial performance and productive efficiency can be very useful for increasing the incentives for efficient production.

For example, through a process coordinated by the CERC, the relevant state-level regulatory commissions could devise methods for compensating firms based on their productive efficiency relative to other similar firms from other parts of the country. These measures could then be used to devise high-powered incentives for efficient production. At a minimum, these measures could simply be compiled by the CERC and made publicly available, with the hope that public disclosure would provide incentives for those at the bottom of the productive efficiency ranking to take steps to improve their standing.

5. THE ELECTRICITY ACT OF 2003 AND PROGRESS TOWARD A CREDIBLE REGULATORY PROCESS

The stated objective of the Electricity Act of 2003 is to "introduce competition, protect consumer's interests and provide power for all."[8] As the previous sections have shown, the current conditions in the Indian electricity supply industry make it very unlikely that introducing competition will serve consumers' interests or is the best possible way to provide power for all. However, a number of provisions of the Electricity Act of 2003 do further the goal of establishing a credible regulatory process and a financially viable industry. The purpose of this section is to highlight the positive aspects of the Electricity Act of 2003 and to explain why the provisions of the Act that deal with introducing wholesale competition should not be implemented at this time.

5.1 BENEFICIAL FEATURES OF THE ELECTRICITY ACT

The provisions of the Electricity Act of 2003 most likely to help establish a firm foundation for further industry restructuring are: (1) mandatory SERCs for all states, (2) mandatory metering and stringent penalties for theft of electricity, and (3) the Accelerated Power Development and Reform Programme (APDRP).

According to the Ministry of Power, currently twenty-two states have either constituted or begun the process of constituting a SERC. Of these states, eighteen have issued tariff orders. The Ministry of Power website lists the current status of the process of establishing SERCs in the twenty-eight states. Although not part of the Electricity Act of 2003, all states have securitized their outstanding debts to Central Public Sector Undertakings (CPSUs) using standardized long-term bonds created by the central government. These are all positive steps toward implementing a standardized and more transparent regulatory process with financial separation of the four stages of electricity supply.

There has also been considerable progress in installing metering technology. The Ministry of Power states that 96 percent of the 11 kV distribution network feeders have a meter as of March 2006 versus 81 percent in 2000, and 92 percent of customer-level distribution points have meters versus 77.6 in 2000.[9] Five states have enacted antitheft legislation, and five have taken regulatory action to increase revenue collection and reduce commercial losses. Although many states experienced increasing average transmission and commercial (AT&C) losses from 2001–2 to 2004–5, the last year of data available, several states experienced declines in AT&C losses over this time period. However, none of these utilities have achieved AT&C losses close to the desired 10 percent level (close to what exists in developed countries) and many have experienced levels many times higher.

Average countrywide AT&C losses are approximately 35 percent, which suggests that a more comprehensive state and national effort is necessary to bring these AT&C losses down.[10]

The APDRP is a positive step toward reducing AT&C losses. It has two components: (1) an investment component that provides funds for strengthening and upgrading the subtransmission and distribution networks and installing meters at the 11 kV level and customer level, and (2) an incentive component equivalent to 50 percent of the actual cash loss reduction provided to the SEBs in the form of a grant. Under the investment component, central government funds are provided for 50 percent of the cost of the project in the form of a 50 percent grant and a 50 percent loan. For some states 100 percent of cost is provided by the central government. Priority for this funding is given to those states that are making the most progress toward implementing distribution reforms. For the incentive component, the year 2000–1 is the base year for the calculation of loss reduction payments in subsequent years. Unfortunately, the central budget outlay for these incentive payments has been significantly smaller than the amount of incentive payments actually made in 2002–3 and 2003–4. For both of these years the budget outlay was 35 billion rupees, but only 20.29 billion rupees were disbursed in 2002–3 and 28.59 billion rupees in 2003–4. In addition, the vast majority of these disbursements were concentrated in a relatively small number of states.

Although the experience with the APDRP is encouraging, moving forward with some of the other provisions of the Electricity Act of 2003 at this time could impose significant long-term harm on the India economy. In particular, the Act reduces the barriers to entry for captive electricity generation units and allows these entities to sell surplus energy using open access to the transmission and distribution network. The Act also encourages energy trading. The major problem with all of these provisions is that they limit the potential beneficiaries of competition in electricity supply to those entities able to construct captive electricity generation units. It is difficult to see how small industrial and commercial consumers and residential consumers will benefit from these provisions. It is more likely that any costs that the larger entities would prefer not to bear will be passed on to these customers, because they do not have the option to construct a captive generation unit and sell surplus power to escape these costs. The long-term implication of this policy is likely to be that all large customers that are able to pay for captive facilities will exit the system, leaving the SEBs to serve only the smaller customers that are collectively more costly to serve and less likely to pay. This process of losing the best customers to the competitive sector could severely hinder the process of improving the financial solvency of the SEBs.

The endpoint of this two-tiered policy would be a higher quality electricity supply with limited redundancy from the bulk transmission network for the large customers able to construct captive generation facilities, and a significantly less reliable supply from the central government and state-owned system to all other customers. In addition, because the large customers would be receiving supply from nearby generation units, there would be little impetus to build out the transmission network to allow more efficient use of India's existing generation resources. The ultimate mix and location of generation units in India would result in a substantially higher average cost of supply for the country because investment decisions for a large fraction of new generation capacity would be made to serve a single large customer rather than customers throughout the entire country. In short, these provisions of the Electricity Act of 2003 might benefit large customers in the short term, but they are very likely to harm small customers in the short and long term and may even eventually harm large customers. A more prudent policy is not to proceed with these provisions of the Act until the preconditions described in the following section are met.

6. A COST-BENEFIT TEST FOR FURTHER RESTRUCTURING

As discussed earlier, the major benefits from introducing a national wholesale electricity market are likely to be realized over the long term. As has been emphasized by the experience of California and a number of other industrialized countries, bid-based spot markets for electricity have a significant downside in terms of the potential to impose significant harm on consumers. Consequently, any decision to move forward with further restructuring should consider this potential downside.

The amount of metering and information technology infrastructure currently in the Indian transmission and distribution grid would make it very difficult to operate a real-time spot market for even a small amount of electricity without significant up-front investments and a time delay sufficient to implement this new technology. Implementing such a scheme would require real-time metering technology throughout the transmission grid to verify whether or not generators and loads actually honored their spot-market obligations in real time. A sophisticated settlement software is necessary to determine the hourly amounts paid to each market participant for fulfilling their real-time obligations and the amounts collected from each major load-serving entity for their real time electricity consumption. In addition, this settlement mechanism must give all market participants very strong incentives to honor their commitments in real-time because the amount of electricity supplied to the grid must equal the amount consumed at each instant in time.

The operation of an electricity spot market similar to those that currently exist in industrial countries also requires the construction of bidding protocols and market-making software, as well as the ability of all generation-owning and load-serving entities to communicate with the system operator in real time in order to translate commitments won in the spot market into the physical supply and consumption of electricity as rapidly as possible. In this regard, it is useful to note that the start-up cost associated with establishing the California electricity market was $250 million. The start-up cost for a national short-term electricity market in India may not be as high because of lower labor costs, but these costs are still likely to be significant.

It is important to emphasize that putting in place any sort of bid-based real-time or near-real-time market for energy and/or ancillary services, no matter how small, will still require a significant fraction of these up-front costs. For example, an imbalance energy market, where generators and loads buy and sell energy to make up deviations from their day-ahead or long-term contractual obligations, will require similar levels of start-up costs. Even if less than 5 percent of all energy consumed is traded in this market, significant start-up costs must still be incurred. Real-time metering technology is necessary to monitor real-time consumption and production of energy for compliance with the independent system operator's (ISO's) dispatch instructions. Market-making software is needed to take bids to supply imbalance energy from available generating units in real time in order to set the price for imbalance energy during each time interval.

Settlement software will also be necessary to determine payments and charges to generators and load-serving entities for their purchases and sale of real-time deviations from their contractual obligations. Price-based or non-price-based mechanisms must be in place to allocate in real time scarce transmission capacity to generators wishing to supply more or less energy or load-serving entities wishing to consume more or less energy.

Finally, the balance between electricity supply and demand must be maintained at all times and the ISO must carry sufficient reserve capacity to respond to unforeseen contingencies within the bulk transmission grid and unexpected generating unit outages.

The initial conditions in the Indian electricity supply industry differ in many important dimensions from those in the electricity supply industries of industrialized countries around the world at the time they began the restructuring process. As a general rule, in all of these countries, the price of retail electricity was thought to be high as a result of prices set to recover the embedded cost of poor past investment decisions made by the government-owned monopoly supplier. Inefficiencies in the dispatch process were also thought to increase the price of retail electricity further. Policymakers felt that privatization and the introduction of competition would impose market discipline on the investment behavior of the electricity generation sector. The prevailing view was that political concerns such as energy independence, support for a domestic coal industry, or promotion of renewable energy sources had led to these very costly investment decisions in the past. Given the growing demand for electricity in these countries, providing clear economic signals for new investment in generating capacity was an important policy goal. A major concern expressed in a 1981 study by the United Kingdom Monopolies and Mergers Commission (MMC) was that the pre-privatization market structure did not provide the proper signals for constructing the optimal amount and type of new generation capacity in a timely manner (Armstrong, Cowan, and Vickers 1994, p. 291). In California, a traditionally high-price electricity state, the promise of lower prices for all consumers was the major impetus for the state's recent restructuring efforts. Historically, high electricity prices in California were thought by many observers to be the direct result of poor past investment decisions by the state's regulated utilities.

In all countries, competition to supply electricity from existing plants was seen as a way to provide strong incentives for minimum cost operation of existing facilities. Consequently, restructuring efforts in all industrialized countries were aimed at reducing the retail price of electricity and stimulating the appropriate technology mix and quantity of new investment in generating capacity. Many of the reasons for introducing any sort of spot market for electricity (day-ahead, hour-ahead, or real-time) are not as relevant to India as they were for the other countries of the world that have restructured their electricity supply industry.

6.1 INTERMEDIATE PATH TO WHOLESALE COMPETITION

This does not mean that an intermediate path does not exist that still preserves the option to move forward with a bid-based spot market. This section presents such a proposal. This strategy avoids the significant up-front costs of a spot market but does not give up the opportunity to capture a large fraction of the potential benefits from privatization and the introduction of wholesale competition.

The primary goal of this approach to realizing the benefits of wholesale competition is to develop a forward market for electricity where private investors can sell obligations to supply electricity that can be used to finance new generation capacity investments. Problems with unilateral market power in short-term wholesale markets have proven extremely difficult for developed countries to solve, and many of them have a long history with regulation and competition policy, something that India does not have. Fortunately, market power problems are unlikely to arise in the market for long-term financial contracts that start to make deliveries more than two years into the future because there are few barriers to entry at this time horizon in advance of delivery.

Because all suppliers are going to need to buy and sell deviations from their final day-ahead schedules or longer-term energy schedules, a real-time price must be set. This can be accomplished by the former vertically integrated monopolist operating a real-time imbalance market using cost-based bids. All suppliers must file their costs with the ISO and after they are validated by the ISO they are made publicly available to all market participants. The ISO then dispatches all units based on these costs, which also produces locational marginal prices (LMPs) at all nodes in the network. It is not essential that suppliers be paid or pay their LMP for deviations from their final energy schedules. Retailers and large consumers could also be charged prices aggregated over larger geographic areas.

Initially there is little need to divest capacity from the incumbent SEBs and the CEA. It is more important for the regulator to focus on obtaining reliable start-up, no–load, and variable costs for all units in the control area. The goal of this cost-based dispatch for imbalances in real time is to establish a transparent mechanism that all market participants can use to assess the costs and benefits of using this imbalance mechanism. New entrants can factor expected imbalance costs into their willingness to supply energy though long-term contracts at specific locations in the transmission network. Cost-based dispatch also avoids most of the problems associated with a transmission network that cannot support a competitive wholesale spot market, an initial condition that exists in India. Setting LMPs using cost-based bids will provide useful information to the ISO about the benefits of transmission upgrades in the network and is an important input into the long-term process of constructing an economically reliable transmission network.

Once this dispatch process has been established, the process of opening the wholesale market to consumers can begin. This should be demand-driven. By this I mean that to the extent that large consumers are willing to subject themselves to the hourly spot price as their default price, the wholesale market should grow.

This market structure implies two types of consumers. The first type of consumer are those that are negawatt suppliers—the demand-side equivalent of privately owned generation owners. These noncore customers must purchase all of their demand at either the hourly spot price or at a forward contract price that they have managed to negotiate with some electricity supplier. In order for this to occur, these customers must have hourly meters installed. Consequently, a necessary condition for a customer to become non-core is an interval meter at their location.

The second type of consumer are those who wish to remain with their monopoly retailer. The monopoly retailer for their geographic area must manage the spot-price risk associated with serving these captive or core customers. Hourly meters are not necessary to serve these core customers. However, meters to record their monthly consumption should be installed on the customer's premises. Devices that allow these customers to benefit from responding to prices that vary with changes in real-time system conditions should be encouraged. The regulator should provide incentives to the retailer serving these customers to set retail prices that vary with system conditions.

The difference between the negawatt suppliers or noncore customers and captive or core customers is that the former group can shop around to any supplier for a better forward contract price for their electricity needs, but can never return to being a captive consumer. Because the negawatt suppliers cannot return to their default provider, in exchange for the opportunity to pay a lower price, they face the risk that there will not be enough new capacity to meet their demand. This will give them incentives to enter into forward contracts that can be used to finance new investments.

In order to set the retail price that the monopoly retailers must pay for wholesale electricity, the state regulator can run periodic auctions for standardized contracts for electricity supply. The SEBs will then be required to buy a pre-specified fraction of their load obligations in these markets. These standardized forward contracts should be sold far enough in advance of delivery to allow the greatest possible participation by new entrants.

SEBs should be required to purchase a minimum fraction of their annual energy requirements for serving their core customers from these auctions over, say, the next six years. Figure 3.1 gives a sample time path of these forward energy requirements. Let *QF* denote a forecast of the SEB's demand for the coming year prepared by the SERC that regulates it. The SEB would be required to purchase at least $f_1 \times QF$ MWh of energy from these auctions for the coming year ($t = 0$ to $t = 1$), $f_2 \times QF$ MWh of energy during the following year ($t = 1$ to $t = 2$). The required quantities that must be purchased for delivery in years three to six are the values of f_i for ($i = 3,4,5,6$) times *QF*, respectively. These forward contracting requirements for the SEBs could be enforced through a penalty scheme administered by the SERC that respects national guidelines set by CERC.

These forward contracting requirements would move forward in time according to the same pattern given in Figure 3.1. For example, suppose

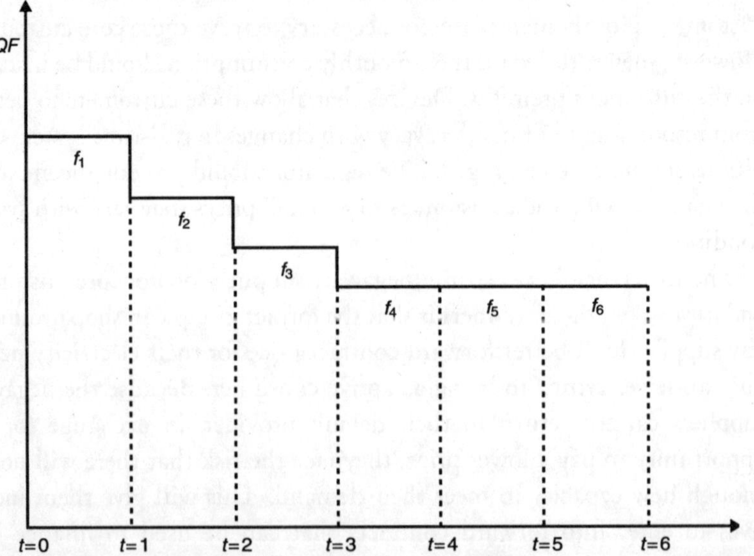

Figure 3.1 Time Path of SEB Forward Contract Obligations

that at some start date the SEB had met its forward contracting requirements for the coming six years given the forecast value of its demand for that year. Then at the end of the first year, period $t = 0$ to $t = 1$ would be reset to the following year and the SERC would provide the SEB with a value of QF for this year. This value of QF and the fractions given in Figure 3.1 would then set the forward contracting requirements for this SEB for the next six years. Forward market requirements for the next six-year time horizon would be updated each year in this manner using any pattern of f_i ($i = 1, \ldots, 6$) for the coming six years.

To allow new entrants to obtain the funding necessary to undertake investments in new generation capacity, different delivery requirements could be placed on forward contracts with longer times to delivery. For example, in order to sell a forward contract for delivery in the next three years, the SERC could require that the seller show that this financial commitment is backed up by a generating facility capable of delivering the contracted amount of energy.

Forward contracts for delivery four to six years into the future can be purely financial commitments, in the sense that there is no requirement to demonstrate physical deliverability of the electricity in order to sell the product. However, there should be a requirement to convert this financial commitment to one that is backed by a physical resource if the time to delivery for an outstanding contract is three years or less. This demonstration would first involve showing that an existing plant or a new plant under construction can provide the energy sold.

For new plants, there would be additional steps in the validation process to ensure the plant will actually be able to produce the energy sold by the delivery date. This process would be overseen by the SERC, according to national guidelines set by the CERC. The SERC should also have the authority to impose penalties for failure to meet the various deadlines for project completion. For example, the SERC could require the owner of the proposed new plant to place money in an escrow account at the start of the project to make sure that the company can pay any potential penalties.

If a supplier sells a commitment to a given quantity of energy to be delivered five years in the future to a specific geographic region of India, and if the supplier does not buy this commitment back in a future auction within the following two years, it would have to demonstrate to the SERC that it has the physical capacity to actually provide electricity to that location within three years according to a process administered by the SERC according to national guidelines set by the CERC.

This flexibility for purely financial trading of forward commitments four to six years in the future will provide new entrants with the freedom to sell forward energy commitments that have the option to turn into physical commitments. With such a forward financial commitment one would expect that a supplier could obtain the construction permits and financing for a new generation facility. If the firm is unable to get the new construction started within two to three years of selling the forward financial commitment, then the supplier has the option to sell this obligation back in a subsequent annual or monthly auction. However, assuming the buyer of the original contract never sells its financial obligation to consume energy, it is still guaranteed delivery of energy at the contracted price in the initial contract.

There are many different ways that these auctions could be structured depending on how much flexibility the auction designer would like to give to generation-unit owners and load-serving entities to express their willingness to supply and demand electricity over the next six years. All generation firms could be allowed to bid very flexible price-quantity pairs of energy over the six-year time horizon. The retailers could then submit willingness to purchase price-quantity pairs over this same horizon, and market-clearing prices and quantities or pay-as bid prices and quantities at each location could be determined by maximizing the sum of producer and consumer surplus over all geographic regions and time periods. Such an extremely high-dimensional strategy space for generation unit owners and SEBs provides these entities with the maximum flexibility to express their costs and willingness to consume in the bids they submit. However, this high-dimensional strategy space also has the downside that it provides each generation unit owner with a large number of bid parameters to use to attempt to raise market prices.

The State of New Jersey Basic Generation Supply (BGS) auctions provide a useful model for this process. Each year the New Jersey Public Bureau of Public Utilities (NJBPU) runs a three-year-ahead auction for roughly one-third of the default load obligations of the electricity retailers that are under its jurisdiction. This mechanism has several desirable features. First, it procures the energy required to serve the retailer's default load obligations far enough in advance that entrants can compete to supply this electricity. Second, it only procures one-third of default load obligation in a single year and in that sense spreads the price risk associated with high energy prices in any single year across at least three years. Third, it is run through an anonymous auction mechanism operated by the NJBPU, and therefore yields a single market-clearing price that is publicly observable and can be used in subsequent regulatory processes.

There are a number of details of the proposed auction mechanism that must be clarified before it can be implemented, but the basic idea of setting minimum annual sales quantities for federal and provincial suppliers and minimum annual purchase quantities for SEBs, both for periods of six years, should be a part of any auction design. The purely financial nature of distant year contracts and physical backing of near-to-delivery contracts is a second feature that should be part of any auction mechanism. As discussed above, as the time until delivery becomes smaller, a supplier would have to firm up the deliverability of the energy. Finally, some penalty mechanism enforcing the minimum sales requirements on suppliers and the minimum purchase requirements on SEBs should also be included in any auction design.

These forward market auctions could also be used to set the wholesale market revenue requirements for electricity retailers. Each year's auction market purchases would be used to set a portion of the retailer's annual wholesale market revenue requirements. For example, suppose the retailer purchased 500 MWh in year 0 for delivery in year 3 at a price of $20/MWh, 200 MWh in year 1 for delivery in year 3 at a price of $30/MWh and 100 MWh in year 2 for delivery in year 3 at a price of $10/MWh. Assuming that 800 MWh is the SERC's forecast of that SEB's demand in year 3, the total amount of revenue that this retailer would be permitted to recover from its customers for wholesale electricity purchases in year 3 would be equal to (500 MWh) × ($20/MWh) + (200 MWh) × ($30/MWh) + (100 MWh) × ($10/MWh) + $17,000.

The SEB should be permitted to offer any number of tariffs to final consumers that they could choose among on a voluntary basis, as long as each of these tariffs is expected to cover the cost of supplying the energy sold under the tariff. Any retail revenues to cover wholesale energy purchases to serve final consumers in excess of this magnitude would be returned to these customers in a lump sum payment. However, if as a result of energy trading activity or innovative retail tariffs the firm was able to reduce its wholesale energy purchase costs below this level, it would be able to keep 100 percent of the cost reductions in higher profits. Conversely, if these trading activities increased total wholesale energy purchase costs beyond this level, then the firm would be required to make up the difference in reduced payments to its shareholders.

Alternatively, the SERC could set the SEB's average wholesale price equal to its portfolio-average forward-contract costs for the coming year. In this case, the average wholesale price implicit in the retail tariffs would be equal to \$21.25/MWh = \$17,000/800 MWh. This mechanism may provide incentives for the retailer to increase it sales, because its average wholesale price is fixed, but not its total wholesale revenues. Depending on the values set for the f_1 given in Figure 3.1, this mechanism could set wholesale revenue requirements too high or too low. If f_1 is set too low and the SEB has not purchased enough forward contracts to hedge the price risk associated with its spot-market purchases, it could be exposed to a potentially very large spot-market obligation to meet its contractual obligations to retail customers. However, setting f_1 too high creates the potential for the opposite problem. By requiring the firm to purchase too much energy at too high a price, the SEB's retail price will be set too high. Consequently, in setting the value of f_i for each year, the SERC must balance these two competing goals. However, one point seems clear from this discussion: setting $f_1 = 1$, or requiring 100 percent of expected load to be hedged on a year-ahead basis seems to err on the side of setting prices too high. On the other hand, being overly dependent on the short-term market could exacerbate future supply shortfalls. For this reason, the value of f_i should certainly be above 0.90.

The combination of a cost-based imbalance energy market and an anonymous auction-based market for long-term contracts should create strong incentives for private sector participation in the wholesale market—assuming, of course, that retail prices are sufficient to provide the revenues necessary to cover all of the SEB's production costs. Moreover, it is unlikely that there will be significant market power problems in these long-term contract markets if the vast majority of purchases are made far enough in advance of delivery to allow new entrants to compete with firms that own existing generation capacity.

Because the imbalance market is cost-based, suppliers have less of an incentive to delay their electricity sales until the real-time market and there is less need for many of the up-front infrastructure and software investments described earlier that are necessary to operate a bid-based real-time market. Wholesale competition will instead focus on the market that has the greatest potential to be extremely competitive—the market for new generation capacity.

An additional benefit of a cost-based imbalance market is that it is substantially more straightforward to forecast imbalance market exposure relative to a bid-based market. Market participants need not predict the bidding behavior of other market participants or the impact of this bidding behavior on imbalance energy prices. Instead, all market participants can forecast these prices using the publicly available cost data and load forecasts obtained from the SERC. This greater transparency in imbalance-market exposure reduces the risk associated with selling a forward financial contract for electricity, which increases the competitiveness of the market for forward financial contracts.

7. CONCLUSION

The current financial condition of the Indian electricity supply industry implies that further restructuring is unlikely to benefit the Indian economy over the next five years. The level of subsidies to electricity consumption, primarily to agricultural consumers and residential and small business consumers, are too large for market forces to have much of an impact on the financial condition of the industry. This chapter argues that the benefits to the India economy from reducing these subsidies and returning the SEBs to financial solvency are enormous and easily swamp very optimistic estimates of the benefits from introducing nationwide wholesale competition along with a bid-based spot electricity market.

The solution to the current crisis in the Indian electricity supply industry is establishing the initial conditions necessary for a successful restructuring process as quickly as possible. One of the major lessons from industry restructuring processes around the world over the past fifteen years is that there are significant risks of failure and potentially enormous costs to consumers if it occurs. One way to increase the likelihood of success is by establishing an effective and credible regulatory process at the national and state levels that corrects small flaws before they develop into large and extremely costly disasters.

This chapter outlines a strategy for implementing such a process. Recommendations are also given for reducing the size of the subsidies to electricity consumption and for improving the efficiency of the retail rate-setting process, both of which should help to return the SEBs to financial solvency. In addition, a strategy is outlined for introducing wholesale competition in a manner that recognizes the initial conditions in the Indian electricity supply industry yet still has a high probability of realizing the vast majority of benefits of electricity industry restructuring.

NOTES

1. Fischer and Galetovic (2001) discuss this incident and the regulatory response to it.

2. Wolak (2003a) provides a comprehensive diagnosis of the causes of and cures for the California electricity crisis.

3. See Joskow (1997) for a discussion of this point.

4. Joskow (2003) discusses the unanticipated difficulties encountered in introducing short-term wholesale electricity markets around the world. Wolak (2003b) discusses the unique challenges faced by Latin American countries.

5. See "State Wise Commercial Losess of Power Utilities," available at http://www.apdrp.com/apdrp/projects/pdf/State_wise_Commercial_Losses_of_power_utilities.pdf

6. These numbers do not control for differences in the technology mix of government-owned versus privately owned generation facilities, although it is unclear whether, after controlling for differences in technology mix, this difference in maintenance expenditures as a percent of revenues would be larger or smaller.

7. Available from http://www.cercind.gov.in/28032004/finalregulations_terms&condition.pdf

8. Ministry of Power website, http://powermin.nic.in/indian_electricity_scenario/reforms_introduction.htm

9. Ministry of Power website, http://powermin.nic.in/projects/project_under_apdrp.htm

10. PDRP website, http://www.apdrp.com/apdrp/projects/pdf/AT&C_Loss_of_Power_Utilities.pdf

REFERENCES

Armstrong, Mark, Simon Cowan, and John Vickers. 1994. *Regulatory Reform: Economic Analysis and British Experience* (Cambridge, MA: MIT Press).

CBO. 1997. *Should the Federal Government Sell Electricity?* The Congress of the United States, Congressional Budget Office, November.

Central Electricity Authority. 2006. "All India Electricity Statistics: General Review 2006," Government of India, March.

Dadhich, Pradeep Kumar. 2002. "India Power Sector," available at http://www.fe.doe.gov/international/indiaover.html

DOE. 2003. "An Energy Overview of India," U.S. Department Energy, (http://www.fe.doe.gov/international/indiover.html)

Dhume, Sadanand. 1999. "Crossed Wires," *Far Eastern Economic Review* (August 12): 40–41.

Dossani, Rafiq. 2004. "Reorganization of the Power Distribution Sector in India," *Energy Policy* 32:1277–89.

Dossani, Rafig, and V. Ranganathan. 2003. "Farmers' Willingness to Pay for Power in India: Conceptual Issues, Survey Results, and Implications for Pricing," Stanford Institute for International Studies Discussion Paper, July.

EIA. 2003. "India: Country Review," U.S. Energy Information Administration, http://www.eia.doe.gov/emeu/cabs/india.hmtl

Estache, A., M. A. Rossi, and C. A. Ruzzier. 2004. "The Case for International Coordination of Electricity Regulation: Evidence from the Measurement of Efficiency in South America," *Journal of Regulatory Economics* 25(3):271–95.

Filippini, Massimo and Shonali Pachauri. 2004. "Elasticities of Electricity Demand in Urban Indian Households," *Energy Policy* 31:429–36.

Fischer, Ronald and Alexander Galetovic. 2001. "Regulatory Governance and Chile's 1998–1999 Electricity Shortage," World Bank Policy Research Working Paper no. 2704, November.

Haldea, Gajendra. 2001. "Whither Electricity Reforms?" *Economic and Political Weekly* (April 28).

Joskow, Paul. 1997. "Restructuring, Competition and Regulatory Reform in the U.S. Electricity Sector," *Journal of Economic Perspectives* 11(3):119–39.

———. 2003. "The Difficult Transition to Competitive Electricity Markets in the U.S." (May 2003), available at http://econ-www.mit.edu/faculty/index.htm?prof_id ? pjoskow)

Lama, M. P. and A. R. Kemal. 2003. "Power Sector Reforms in India and Pakistan: Scope for Cross-Border Trade in Power," working paper.

Report of the Expert Group. 2001. "Restructuring of SEBs," July.

Report of the Task Force. 2004. "Report on Power Sector Reform," March.

Slater, Joanna. 2003. "Slow Burn," *Far Eastern Economic* Review (August 21):19.

Vickers, John and George Yarrow. 1988. *Privatization: An Economic Analysis* (Cambridge, MA: MIT Press).

Wolak, Frank A. 2003a. "Diagnosing the California Electricity Crisis," *Electricity Journal*, August/September 2003:11–37.

Wolak, Frank A. 2003b. "Designing Competitive Wholesale Markets for Latin American Countries," Prepared for Stanford Center for International Development (SCID), Latin America Conference on Sector Reform, November. (Available at http://www.stanford.edu/~wolak)

COMMENT

Jessica Wallack

Frank Wolak's chapter is hard to disagree with. His main point is absolutely correct: India must address its distribution problems before thinking about moving to a competitive market. Many Indian policymakers would also agree with him; there is a lot of sympathy within India for a measured transition path to competitive markets. Former Minister of Power Prabhakar Prabhu's 2001 comment sums up an attitude that is still salient today: "I don't think the situation in India is ripe for a spot market. . . . In India, where markets are not perfect, a concept like spot market will put markets in a spot."[1] The 2006 Central Electricity Regulatory Commission (CERC) staff paper on developing a trading market emphasizes many of the same reasons for caution as those in this chapter, also citing international experience.[2]

Wolak's caution about introducing a spot market is also timely. The policy has been slow to move, but is gathering momentum. The idea of a market entered into official discussions in 2001, with the introduction of the Electricity Act of 2001 into Parliament. The bill became the Electricity Act of 2003. The Act described a new philosophy for price discovery but ultimately passed the responsibility for determining the structure of the market to the National Electricity Policy (NEP). When completed, the 2005 NEP assigned the responsibility to the CERC, and the CERC discussion paper for public comment was posted online in 2006. Most of the power generated today is locked up in long-term supply contracts, and states' intransigence in implementing open access for their portions of the transmission grid hampers even the bilateral trading that goes on today.

Nevertheless, the market is on the horizon and interest groups are forming. The little power that is traded today is extremely expensive.[3] Distribution utilities that anticipate lower prices from a competitive market (the ideal world) are lining up behind policies to create this market. New entrants into power generation also see the benefits of power markets as the means to provide access to larger groups of buyers. Private utilities are even offering to advise in setting up the market—an obvious conflict of interest if they expect to participate in the power market.

That said, I would like to extend Wolak's discussion in two directions.[4] First, the distribution-sector reform and regulatory strengthening that Wolak suggests are not enough to overcome the gap between the electricity supplied and that demanded. The shortfall in generation capacity, exacerbated by weak transmission links between the regions, will not be solved by demand-side management motivated by higher prices and stricter controls on theft. The distribution sector's financial ruin (in large part due to politicized price setting) does contribute to the problem by limiting private investors' incentives to invest in new capacity, but it is not the only constraint on private investment.

Second, while distribution-sector reform is important, the bigger question is why it has not been done faster. Politicians, bureaucrats, and outside experts alike have long emphasized the need to reform the distribution sector and develop the regulatory independence to support sustainable distribution. Why does India still have a distribution sector that is mostly public, mostly bankrupt, overseen by mostly politicized regulators? I argue that the federal division of jurisdiction is behind the recalcitrance.

Given that India is unlikely to become a unitary country, or to alter its constitution significantly to accommodate electricity-sector reform needs, I suggest some ways to make the best of the institutional setting.

A VERY REAL SHORTFALL, TODAY AND TOMORROW

Much of the Indian policy debate focuses on the "shortage" of electricity. The gap between electricity demand and supply at peak times has been roughly 11–12 percent higher than the power available over the past five years. The base load demand has been about 8 percent higher than the power available.[5] The capital city, Delhi, suffered weeks of rolling blackouts in August of 2006, as the temperature increased and various plants across North and Eastern India closed due to a lack of gas for fuel, flooding, and desilting work.

Wolak argues that this shortfall would be eliminated if prices were set to recover the cost of electricity. Distribution-sector reform would essentially solve the capacity constraint by motivating people to conserve energy. This emphasis on conservation is hard to reconcile with the fact that India's power consumption, at 435 kWh per capita, is less than 5 percent of the high-income country average consumption, and only about a quarter of the average per-capita consumption in middle-income countries.[6] Nearly half of all rural households do not have electricity. The remaining villages without electricity will take thirty-seven years to electrify at the average annual pace of village electrification over the past ten years.[7] Overall, India's economic production is not as energy-intensive as most other developing countries, and is particularly modest in comparison to China.[8]

More investment in generation will be needed in addition to managing demand through distribution reforms.

DISTRIBUTION-SECTOR REFORM ALONE WILL NOT ATTRACT INVESTMENT

Distribution-sector reform will do little to improve the public investment record. Public capacity addition should be relatively immune to the state of the distribution sector so long as the public enterprises have a loose budget constraint, but it has not kept up with targets. Barely half of the capacity scheduled to be added during the Ninth Plan (1997–01) was actually added.[9] The Tenth Plan's (2002–7) capacity addition has been slipping farther and farther from targets. The most recent estimates suggest that only 82 percent of the planned addition would be possible even on a "best effort" basis.[10]

Union Power Secretary R. V. Shahi set a target for capacity growth in 2002, for example, stating that: "To support 9 percent economic growth, capacity addition in the power sector will have to be on the order of at least 10,000 MW each year in the next five years and 11,000–12,000 every year in the subsequent five years."[11] Actual capacity addition between the 2002 and 2005 fiscal years was about half that.[12]

Nor is a sound distribution sector enough to attract more private capacity addition. As Wolak mentioned, the private sector has been reticent to make up the public shortfall and the marginal addition has been in captive power. Expectations have long outpaced the reality of private participation. About 17,000 MW of privately operated thermal generation capacity power was expected in the Ninth Plan. About 5,000 MW was actually added. Actual addition of hydro power was 86 MW, compared to an anticipated 550 MW. The private power capacity added as of 2006, about 7,500 MW from thirty-nine private power plants commissioned since 1991, is not much more than the goal for the Tenth Plan alone.

Distribution sector reform will go a long way toward matching reality to expectations, but it is not the only constraint on investment: fuel supply, transmission capacity, and clearances also affect the decisions to site and invest in a plant. These additional distortions also affect the gains from moving to a market with private investment. So long as these remain politicized, investment decisions will not necessarily be more efficient than public-sector decision making.

Private investors in India's power sector not only need to worry about how they will sell their electricity, but also how they will generate it. Domestic coal, natural gas, and naptha supplies are effectively controlled by public-sector monopolies and a web of complex pricing rules.

Gas prices, in particular, seem to be a matter of policy more than of markets. The regime is currently under discussion, but it does not look like these will be market-based. "Our task is to set a floor as well as a ceiling price and then let the market decide," a senior petroleum ministry official said at the time.[13] For investors in power plants, the ambiguity may swing in their favor so long as the demand for more power capacity addition remains politically salient, but the rival gas producers lobby is also politically powerful. In any case, hedging against policy fluctuation creates an entirely different risk than hedging against market fluctuations.

Transmission capacity is also a constraint. Transmission, long neglected by past public investment plans, provides little capacity for sharing power between regions, or for absorbing new capacity should it be built. The Ministry of Power's targets for building interregional capacity are ambitious, but unrealistic in light of past progress. Interregional capacity stood at 9,450 MW as of the end of 2005, with a target of 16,450 MW by the end of Tenth Plan in 2007, and about 37,150 MW by the end of Eleventh Plan.[14] The pace of transmission augmentation has increased, and current capacity is nearly double what it was in 2003–4, but clearly there is a long way to go.

Cost-based dispatch, as discussed by Wolak, would provide signals for where to invest in transmission networks. But land acquisition and state acquiescence remain significant risk factors that may deter investment in transmission lines.

Plants must acquire land, which always provokes a demonstration in which state officials and national Members of Parliament often become involved. Land acquisition has been one of the primary reasons cited in the delays in public investment projects; private projects are unlikely to be much different.[15] Environmental clearances, especially for coastal plants (one way of making it easier to import coal) have also held up some of the largest public projects. India's new ultra-mega-power-plant initiative advertises its attention to "tying up" clearances to potential investors almost as much as it touts the fuel-supply contracts and power purchase agreements built into the projects being offered.

The distribution-sector reform and regulatory strengthening that Wolak encourages are necessary but not sufficient conditions for solving India's power needs or attracting private investment in capacity.

WHY HASN'T DISTRIBUTION-SECTOR REFORM HAPPENED?

Distribution-sector reform has two components: restructuring of state electricity boards, and depoliticization of consumer pricing. Both have been discussed for over a decade, and some actions have been taken. Both are state-level political and regulatory decisions that the central government could influence to some extent.[16]

Central and state governments have agreed in several official statements that distribution-sector reform is essential. A 1996 summit between the Prime Minister and state chief ministers produced a Common Minimum Action Plan for Power that provided for establishing regulatory commissions and rationalizing retail tariffs. All officials committed to charging at least some nominal price for agricultural power, and ensuring that no sector paid less than 50 percent of the average cost of supply. The participants agreed on performance indicators for the state utilities. In 2001, a similar summit produced an agreement that commercially viable distribution would be necessary for sustainable investment in generation and transmission.

The 2005 National Electricity Policy emphasizes commercial viability. The Rajiv Gandhi Grameen Vidhyutikaran Yojana (RGGVY) rural electrification program, begun in 2005, mandates that electricity be paid for. And the Prime Minister's 2005 Independence Day speech notes that "[Indians] need to get used to paying a reasonable price for electricity just as we do for petroleum products. Through this we can ensure supply of electricity in the right quantity at the right time and of right quality."

States did seem to be heeding the call for pricing reform in the early 2000s. Andhra Pradesh increased tariffs by an average of 20 percent in

2000 (reduced to a 15 percent increase a few days later after public protest), and a 2002 ERC order created incentives for farmers to install meters and more efficient irrigation pumps. Punjab's six-year record of free power for agriculture ended in September 2002. Tamil Nadu proposed a tariff revision to increase the price for agriculture in 2003. Madhya Pradesh and Kerala did increase tariffs, especially for agriculture and domestic sectors, in 2002. The more recent record shows some reversals (discussed below), however, and pricing remains far below the cost of supplies.

Rhetoric aside, several features of India's federalism make further distribution and regulatory reform unlikely. First, the central government lacks the means to effectively pressure state governments to make decisions that are not locally politically popular. State parties often wield key positions in central-government coalitions, limiting the federal government's willingness to act as stern coordinator.[17] Various fiscal incentives such as the Accelerated Power Development and Reform Program (APDRP) have had some success in encouraging reduction of theft and installation of consumer meters, but other potential levers have not been used. The central government has threatened to cut power supply from its generating plants to states that do not pay their bills, but the cuts never last long. The Ministry of Power has, but does not use, the discretion to allocate some of the central government–generated power to reward reforming states.

The saga of state electricity board unbundling, one of the reforms Wolak recommends in his paper, provides a telling example of states' ability to defy central-government initiatives. The Electricity Act of 2003 mandated that all states separate their State Electricity Boards in generation, transmission, and distribution utilities by June 2004. This deadline has been extended at least twice, and some states still have not finished unbundling the integrated utilities.[18]

Second, central-government regulators also lack the institutional basis for coordinating state regulators to collectively impose more reasonable electricity pricing. The Electricity Act of 2003 gave the CERC more power to coordinate state ERCs than it had before (it had none), but the Act still says that the appropriate commission shall only be "guided by" the CERC. More importantly, both regulators are also separately beholden to politicians at their level of government, with obvious effects on the potential for interaction among regulators.

The CERC has only tenuous independence from politics. It has had the power to rule on tariff setting only since 1998, and the level of detail included in the Government's Tariff Policy of 2005 seemed to indicate that politicians were taking that power back. The Power Ministry's efforts to amend the bill that became the Electricity Act of 2003 to say that the CERC and SERCs would be have to act "in conformity to" rather than be "guided by" the Ministry's policy directions, were unsuccessful; but the commission still does not have an independent budget and requires government approval to create new posts.[19] The chairmanship of CERC was vacant from 2000–2, until the recently retired secretary of the Ministry of Power, A. K. Basu, was appointed Chair.

The SERCs' independence is hard to gauge, but the available evidence is not promising. ERCs are funded from the state government general funds. Abraham (2003) finds that many ERCs have gotten less than 70 percent of the budget proposed to them, some as low as 17–38 percent of the budget. Even where budgets have been disbursed in full and on time, the threat of reducing funding reduces autonomy. The ERCs also have limited authority to request data from state utilities. Only four states' utilities filed the required annual revenue data to regulators on time in 2006. Finally, Sections 107/108 of the Electricity Act say that governments "may issue directions to the concerned RC on "matters of public interest," with public interest to be defined by the concerned government.

Third, states have little incentive to be the first movers on something as unpopular as increasing electricity prices. States seem to be competing in the opposite direction, in part driven by electoral pressures. India's staggered elections mean that most states will see a neighboring state having elections in any given year, and that there are near-constant referendums on any party with a presence in more than one state. The 2004 wave of price reductions for agricultural power is illustrative. Andhra Pradesh's newly elected government, having campaigned on a platform appealing to rural voters, provided free power for farmers after the May 2004 elections. Tamil Nadu (with national elections in sight) followed the move in June. The Maharashtra government reduced power prices in July, just before October elections.[20]

The competitive price reductions occur outside of election periods as well. Punjab followed with free power for all farmers in September 2005, reverting to its early practice after a three-and-a-half-year policy of charging for agricultural power. Elections were not on the horizon until 2007. Neighboring Rajasthan was forced to lower its agricultural-power prices soon afterwards, under pressure from constituents who explicitly pointed to Punjab as an example.

WHAT TO DO?

India's electricity sector is likely to remain federal for the foreseeable future. The discussion above suggests two ways to mitigate the complications that concurrent responsibility creates: hold simultaneous elections for all states, and use a federal act of parliament to override the states' legal provisions for political oversight of regulators. These changes may be no more politically palatable than distribution reform and price increases.

Another approach would be to try to shift state governments' incentives to undertake distribution reform by enabling state policymakers to connect better service with higher prices. Wolak's chapter cites surveys demonstrating peoples' willingness to pay for more reliable electricity, and the record of generator ownership supports this point. State politicians cannot currently take advantage of this willingness to pay, however, because they cannot commit to providing reliable supply in exchange for higher prices. Their ability to supply electricity reliably depends on the condition of the intrastate grid, as well as on the allocations from the central grid and on the ability of the regional (multistate) load dispatch center to maintain grid discipline. The central government could enable state politicians to meet citizen demand for power by funding and providing technical support for upgrades of the state grids, as well as by allocating power to support reforms.

Any state distribution reforms or pricing changes that did emerge from the new political equilibrium could very well be a model for national policies. Some states are already demonstrating innovative reforms. Distribution franchisees seem to have improved revenue collection and service to consumers in parts of Assam, Karnataka, Orissa, Nagaland, and West Bengal. Gujarat's new rural-power policy, in which the electricity for irrigation pumps is separated from that for household use and provided predictably for part of the day, seems to be a popular way to reduce the fiscal drain and manage peak demand.

My comments have highlighted some of the problems that federalism creates for electricity-sector reform, but the potential for experimentation is one of the benefits. West Bengal's law was a model for national legislation on power theft. State utilities have also created innovative ways to encourage consumer-to-consumer policing. One of Delhi's distribution companies, for example, published the list of loss rates at its substations so that communities would be aware of their neighbors' theft. Further supporting federalism as a laboratory for experimentation may be the strongest way to encourage national improvements.

NOTES

1. Quote from 2001 interview discussing the introduction of the bill that eventually became the Electricity Act of 2003 into Parliamentary discussion. The same interview also emphasized the importance of reforming the distribution sector. "The Will to Implement is More Important than the Bill," *Business Today* September 30, 2001.

2. CERC (2006). "Development of A Common Platform for Trading Electricity," *Staff Paper*. July 2006. Available at www.cercind.org. Accessed October 10, 2006. Their conclusion that the only reason to launch a market would be to "send the tight signal to investors and consumers about transparent market development" also echoes Frank's discussion of the benefits of electricity markets for encouraging efficient investment.

3. According to CERC (2006), traded power is more expensive than the unscheduled interchange fees for over-drawing power from the national grid. This is difficult to explain.

4. These comments draw on research presented in Wallack, Jessica, and N.K. Singh (2007). "Federalism and Reform: The Case of India's Electricity Sector. *Mimeo.*

5. Government of India, Ministry of Power (various years). *Annual Report.* New Delhi: Ministry of Power.

6. Energy Information Administration (2004). *International Energy Annual 2004.* Table 6.2 The Ministry of Power reports per capita consumption closer to 600 kwh per capita, but this is still a fraction of the power consumed in higher-income countries.

7. Wallack, Jessica and N. K. Singh (2007). "India's Infrastructure Gap and Why it Matters," *Mimeo.*

8. EIA (2004). Ibid. See table E.1g World Energy Intensity—Total Primary Energy Consumption per Dollar of Gross Domestic Product.

9. 21,000 MW of capacity addition, compared to the 40,000 MW targeted.

10. Reported in "Power ministry steps up monitoring of ongoing projects," Energylineindia.com December 10, 2006.

11. Shahi, R. V. (2006). *Indian Power Sector: Challenge and Response.* New Delhi: Excel Publishers. Chapter 1. Shahi does acknowledge that "policy initiatives, commensurate systems and procedures and suitable monitoring mechanisms will all have to be put in place to meet this challenge."

12. Based on Ministry of Power Annual Reports, capacity addition includes utilities, railways, and non-utilities (captive) power. The National Electricity Policy of 2005 reiterates the goal, aiming to fully meet demand and overcome peaking shortages with plants operating at 85% of installed capacity.

13. "Government in a Bind on Gas Pricing Formula," *Hindustan Times*, Tuesday, August 22, 2006.

14. Ministry of Power (2006). *Annual Report 2006–7*.

15. Ministry of Statistics and Program Implementation, Government of India, "Project Implementation Status Reports," various years. Available at http://mospi.gov.in/mospi_pi_status_report.htm

16. The constitution designates electricity as a concurrent subject, which means that State Legislative Assemblies can make laws with respect to electricity as long as these do not conflict with a Central Act. The de facto division of authority has left distribution and intra-state transmission in state hands, and interstate transmission and some generation capacity in federal hands.

17. Central government policymakers are also far from united about the means to strengthen the distribution sector. The change in government in 2004 immediately brought calls to amend the Electricity Act of 2003, over the protests of senior officials in the Ministry of Power.

18. Power Ministry officials stated that no further extension would be given as each extension was granted.

19. Parliamentary debate reported by Prayas (2005). "India Power Reforms Update, v. 11—December 2005."

20. The state government only consulted the ERC in August about the change. When the ERC forced the government to pay the SEB in cash for issuing zero bills for farmers, the government paid the cash but the SEB paid half of it back as "advance repayment of Government of Maharashtra loans." Prayas, 2004, v. 9, 2005, 10.

REFERENCE

Abraham, P. 2003. *Focus on Distribution*. New Delhi: Suryakumari Abraham Memorial Foundation.

CHAPTER 4

The Indian Software Industry and Its Prospects

Ashish Arora[1]

1. INTRODUCTION

India's emergence as a major exporter of software services in less than a decade and a half has excited debate about the causes of its success and ignited hopes for similar success in other industries. The subsequent growth of exports of other business services appears to validate the belief of some observers (including myself) that India's software success could have broader benefits for the Indian economy.

Despite this, there is a perennial undercurrent of concern about the prospects of the Indian software industry. The causes for concern are not difficult to find. Wages for software professionals have consistently risen year after year, and employee attrition remains a persistent problem for companies. Indian exports continue to be mostly services with a modest technology content, and there is little evidence of successful product development. Add to these the ever-present possibility of China (or Eastern Europe or the Philippines) emerging as a potent rival, and there is much to be concerned about.

In this chapter, I shall briefly describe the growth and evolution of the software industry. Next, I shall identify the major factors that contributed to its success, and some possible ones that were not as important. The prospects of the industry are discussed next, and in this context I shall summarize the available evidence on the extent to which India and Indian firms are participating in software innovation. This will lead to an assessment of whether the industry has and can provide higher value-added products and services. Finally, I shall comment on the direct and indirect impacts of the industry on the Indian economy.

2. THE SOFTWARE VALUE CHAIN AND INDIAN EXPORTS

As is by now well known, software production and exports from India have grown rapidly, particularly since the early 1990s. The most often used source, the Indian software industry association, NASSCOM, estimates that software service exports (including the categories of engineering services and R&D, and software products) in 2005 were about $13 billion.

In 1996, the time when I first became interested in the Indian software sector, this seemed fantastic, in the original sense of the word. At that time, Indian exports were barely $1 billion, and though the future looked bright, a number of concerns were already being bruited about by knowledgeable observers and industry participants themselves. These included the shortage of skilled workers ("software professionals"), the terribly deficient physical infrastructure, potential competition from China and the Philippines, the development of automated tools that would substitute for the lower end of software services provided by India, and the apparent unwillingness or inability of Indian software firms to move beyond leveraging access to lower-cost workers. Together, this potent mix of forces was seen as threatening the future of the industry. The prescriptions for the malaise were also clear: firms had to "move up the value chain" by developing proprietary products, and by providing more technology-intensive services. *Innovation* was the watchword, and implicitly, most understood this to refer to new technologies or new products.

For the most part, the prescriptions have not been followed. The shortage of workers is said to loom as large as ever, the infrastructure has improved only modestly, and there are few Indian software products on the world markets. And yet, exports have increased about thirteen-fold, and an entirely new sector of related business services, with revenues of about $4.5 billion, has emerged. The domestic software market has also grown, albeit more slowly, and the size of the Indian software industry is over $20 billion. This growth has enabled the industry to overtake Brazil, whose industry was of comparable size in 2001, but in 2005, at $10–12 billion, is substantially smaller.

To comprehend this astonishing story, we need to take a detour to understand the software sector itself.[2] Contrary to popular belief, software products such as word-processing software, accounting software, and email software are not the dominant part of the industry. Rather, the bulk of the value added, and the bulk of employment, in software is generated in customizing these products, maintaining them, adding functionality, and making these products work with existing products already in use. Some, but not all, of this activity is performed by firms classified as software firms. Software-using firms, which include the vast preponderance of all firms of any size in advanced economies, are responsible for a substantial part, as well.

One can distinguish three sets of value-adding activities in software. First, there are design and development activities, which encompass all of what one would traditionally define as software products, such as word processors, operating systems, enterprise software such as Enterprise Resource Planning (ERP) and business intelligence software, as well as middleware software products, such as some transaction-processing middleware and enterprise application integration. The total value of production in the software product industry was about $61 billion in 1997, employing about 240 thousand.[3] Firms that operate in this value chain include all of the well-recognized names that are traditionally regarded as "software" firms, including Microsoft, Adobe, Oracle, and SAS.[4]

Quantitatively more significant is the set of firms involved in custom programming and software analysis and design for clients, including the custom development of software products (also called "bespoke software products"). The total value created by these firms was about $115 billion in 1997 and total employment was about 1 million, indicating that both revenue and employment are greater than that in the packaged software industry.[5]

The third set of actors involved in software is the users themselves. Even if one confines oneself to the activity of professional programmers and software designers employed by IT-using firms (and ignores programming activities performed by others in IT-using organizations), the monetary value of this user-based activity, though difficult to estimate precisely, is very significant. Occupation data from the United States indicates that over two-thirds of software professionals do not work for IT firms but instead work for IT-using industries. Data from the Bureau of Labor Statistics (BLS) for 2001 indicate that about 3.8 million people were working in computer- and software-related occupations (including hardware designers, programmers, systems analysts, software architects, and computer scientists), of which 72,000 worked in the computer equipment industry, about 1 million worked in the computer and software services sector, with the remaining 2.8 million working in the rest of the economy. Figure 4.1, which shows the intensity of software occupations by state for the United States, reflects this. Employment in software related

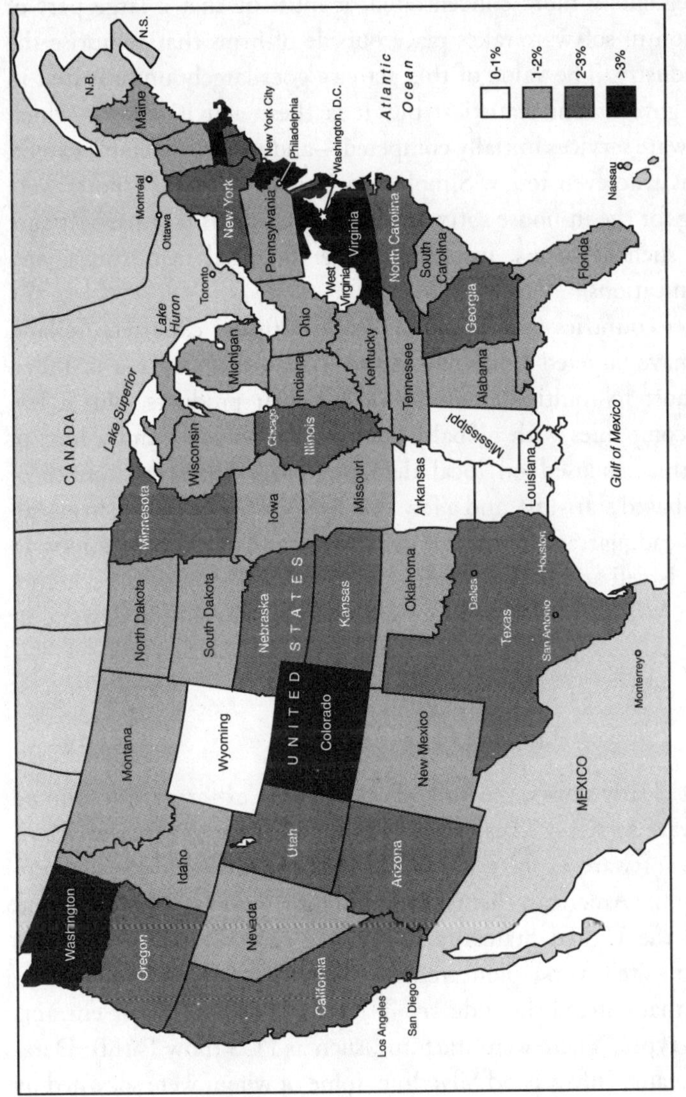

Figure 4.1 U.S. Software Employment as a Share of Total Employment by State, 2001

Source: BLS, 2001.

occupations is geographically dispersed, rarely exceeding 3 percent of employment, but also rarely below 1 percent.

To summarize, software as an activity is widespread, roughly proportional to overall economic activity in a region. Since the leading software firms are regionally more concentrated, it must be that a large part of value creation in software takes place outside of firms that comprise the software industry. The value of this activity goes largely unmeasured in traditional government statistics, but it is these activities with which Indian software services initially competed—and to a considerable extent, this remains true even today. Simply put, Indian software exports were substituting for the in-house software activities of firms that use software intensively, such as banks, insurance, other financial institutions, and telecommunications.

Two other countries that have emerged as software exporters, Ireland and Israel, have targeted a different segment than that targeted in India. Ireland is host to multinationals localizing their products, plus a few innovative companies with globally competitive products and a host of tiny companies focused on local demand. Israel boasts a number of technology-based start-ups, and a few that have grown into large firms, all now with headquarters in the United States and R&D operations in Israel. Both Israeli and Irish software exports stumbled after the dot-com bubble burst in 2000–1 and their growth appears to have been slower ever since.

3. A BRIEF HISTORY

As Table 4.1 clearly shows, the bulk of the software exports are accounted for by software services. These are a mixture of different types of activities. Indian software exports started as Indian firms "rented out" programmers to the American clients, by sending them to work for the client, typically in the United States itself. Athreye (2005b) claims that this model of "on-site" work, pioneered by TCS, was rapidly emulated by other firms that entered the industry in the early 1980s.[6] These entrants were of two types. There were start-ups, such as PCS (now Patni), Datamatics, and, later, Infosys and Silverline, some of whom were spawned by incumbents. The second type of entrants consisted of existing firms diversifying into software, including computer hardware firms, such as HCL and Wipro, as well as firms with large in-house data-processing and

Table 4.1 Indian IT Industry-Sector-wise Break-up

USD Billion	FY 2004	FY 2005	FY 2006E
IT Services	**10.4**	**13.5**	**17.5**
-Exports	7.3	10.0	13.2
-Domestic	3.1	3.5	4.3
ITES-BPO	**3.4**	**5.2**	**7.2**
-Exports	3.1	4.6	6.3
-Domestic	0.3	0.6	0.9
Engineering Services and R&D, Software Products	**2.9**	**3.9**	**4.8**
-Exports	2.5	3.1	3.9
-Domestic	0.4	0.7	0.9
Total Software and Services Revenues	**16.7**	**22.6**	**29.5**
Of which, exports are	*12.9*	*17.7*	*23.4*
Hardware	**5.0**	**5.9**	**6.9**
Total IT Industry (including Hardware)	**21.6**	**28.4**	**36.3**

Source: Nasscom (IT factsheet), www.nasscom.org (accessed 18 September 2006).

system-integration capabilities, such as Larsen & Toubro. Others, such as BFL, Sonata, Satyam, and Birla Horizons began as divisions of industrial groups.

U.S.-based start-ups, such as Mastech (now IGate), Information Management Resources (IMR), Syntel, and CBSL (now Covansys), following in the footsteps of companies like Patni and Datamatics, were started by entrepreneurs of Indian origin.[7] They used their India operations much in the way that Indian software export firms did, to tap a large pool of relatively cheap but skilled workers. For understandable reasons, they were slower in developing management capability in India. Perhaps as a result, these firms have not ascended to the very top tier of Indian companies. Nonetheless, being U.S. headquartered, they played an important role in legitimizing the use of Indian programmers by U.S. firms when the Indian industry was young.[8]

Early export projects involved jobs such as rewriting code to migrate applications from mainframes to the then newly emerging client-server platforms. Coincidently, Indian programmers had acquired a degree of expertise in this due to IBM's departure from India in the late 1970s, which then required that existing computer applications used in India be transferred to other platforms such as Wang, Unisys, and DEC. Naturally, in the course of moving applications, the applications were sometimes enhanced and new functionality was added, a task that also fell to the Indian software firms. Other services included maintaining such applications, sometimes called legacy applications, while the client changed over to new systems and new applications. Later, data-conversion projects, such as the well known Y2K projects, emerged. But a substantial business consisted of simply providing temporary programmers for whatever the client needed to be done.

Most of the clients were user firms, and most of the jobs involved systems that these firms needed to run their businesses. Software firms, especially firms developing software products, outsourced more sparingly, and were more likely to simply "rent" Indian programmers for tasks such as testing.

The success of the serendipitously discovered business strategy of sending small teams of programmers overseas to service the client is not surprising, at least in hindsight. Indian firms were short of capital, infrastructure, and management. But far more important was that even in the early 1990s, Brand India was anything but that. Clients in America had to be cajoled to entrust their technology systems, least of all to a country that was until recently among the poorest in the world. It took time and an initial round of successful projects before American firms were comfortable having the projects performed in India, and managed by the Indian supplier.

Athreye (2005b) points out that Texas Instruments and COSL (part of Citibank) played an important role in pioneering the other part of the business strategy, namely, that of using India as a place to develop software, not merely to hire temporary programmers. Though infrastructure constraints imposed large fixed costs on outsourced software projects, there were offsetting factors. The twelve-hour time difference meant that investing in dedicated satellite links would enable hardware facilities lying idle in the United States to be used. Combined with the cost advantage in software salaries, this conferred enormous cost advantages to locating in India. The experience of COSL and TI had demonstrated that an Indian subsidiary could be a low-cost way for a large corporation to develop software for sale, or to provide for its in-house software needs. Software was developed at the Indian subsidiary and then installed on-site by teams of Indian software professionals. Even so, the projects were small, and rarely mission-critical or on the leading edge of the technology.[9] With time, firms such as Oracle were able to move responsibility for much more significant tasks to its Indian subsidiary. Dossani describes a similar evolution, but for a later date and on a more compressed time scale, for business services, which once again was pioneered by American multinationals such as GE and Agilent (Dossani 2006, p. 251, fig. 2).

Though multinationals pioneered the offshore model, their ability to leverage it was limited by their internal market and organizational exigencies. It was left to the domestic firms to develop and exploit more fully what was to become the offshore model—developing software for clients in India, managed by the Indian firm. Athreye (2005a) credits Satyam as pioneering this model among Indian firms in 1991. The model was adopted by leading domestic firms, though they were initially entrusted with autonomy by foreign customers only for fairly small, specific and noncritical tasks. Falling telecommunications costs, helped by the growth of the STPI scheme, meant that smaller firms could also profitably adopt this model.

The process was slow. As late as 1997, the median NASSCOM member firm had about seventy employees, and the largest had only 9,000. In a sample of over a hundred software firms in 1997 (with a median size of two hundred employees, and thus nearly three times larger than the typical Indian software firm), the average size of the "most important" export project undertaken by the firm in the previous year was 510 man-months, whereas the median size was only about 150 man-months (Arora et al. 2001). Using the sample average revenue per year per employee of $24,000, this implies the dollar value of these projects as not much greater than $100,000. Over time, more important and complicated tasks were moved to India. Currently, projects often exceed $1 million, and the leading firms have signed deals for multi-year projects, each worth hundreds of millions! (See also Table 4.9.)

Offshore development was substantially cheaper, although few American firms were willing to say so openly amid concerns about alienating their own workers and facilitating their lobbying for more work permits for Indian programmers.[10] But if cheap programmers were all that mattered, the Indian software industry would not have seen quite as many domestic firms, for many customers were large enough to profitably set up Indian subsidiaries. Instead, they outsourced to Indian suppliers because it appears that the latter were better at recruiting and managing Indian programmers, and in particular, appear to have become more skilled at "ramping up and ramping down"—putting together large teams at relatively short notice, and redeploying them when the project is done. They were also better able to cope with the high levels of turnover that the frothy IT markets of the late 1990s created. Simply put, Indian firms were better at managing software projects executed in India for overseas clients, using low-cost and inexperienced developers and managers.

Since the foregoing point is often ignored, it bears repeating. Indian firms proved to be better at exploiting the larger supply of talented but young and inexperienced software developers that India had to offer. As service providers operating in a tight labor market with employee turnover rates approaching 40 percent at times, Indian software firms invested in processes that helped them cope. They learned how to manage globally distributed software projects where part of the project team was located overseas while others were located half a world away. The big surge in CMM certification (Capability Maturity Model) with one Indian firm after another touting its CMM level 5 certification, at a time when scarcely a handful of U.S. firms could do so, reflects these investments. However, the drive for CMM certification did not so much create this ability at managing software projects as certify it. Many observers have inferred from such certification that Indian firms produced high-quality software. Interpreted broadly, this is correct. However, CMM is principally about managing software development, not about the quality of the software code produced. Not surprisingly, the available empirical evidence suggests that CMM certification primarily benefited a firm by allowing it to take on larger projects, not to charge higher prices (Arora and Asundi 1999). In other words, it enabled firms to grow more rapidly.

The evidence also suggests that larger firms earn higher revenues per worker, and in this sense, are more productive.[11] Using NASSCOM member firms as the basis, firms in the third quartile of size earned revenues of Rs. 0.62 million per employee in 1994 and Rs. 0.95 million per employee in 1999. The revenue per employee in millions of rupees for the median firm was 0.33 and 0.49 respectively for the two years, or about one half that for firms in the third quartile. This superior software development management capability has stood the leading Indian firms in good stead over the past decade, even as competition from foreign and domestic competitors has intensified. As I shall argue below, this also has important implications for their future strategies and prospects.

4. EXPLAINING SOFTWARE SUCCESS

4.1 HUMAN CAPITAL AND COMPARATIVE ADVANTAGE

The main contours of the argument must be evident from the foregoing discussion. At its base is the simple concept of comparative advantage: India was relatively abundant in the factor in which software is relatively abundant, or, in plain English, software depends heavily on software developers, and India had many people willing (and able) to develop software for less.

Since this argument is widely accepted, at least in its simpler form of absolute advantage, I shall not dwell on it. Wages for Indian software professionals were much lower than those of their counterparts in developed countries. Though they have risen over time, they remain lower (although the precise magnitude of the difference is unclear), in no small measure because the typical software professional in the United States has much greater experience.[12]

But this is not a sufficient explanation. How did a poor country like India become so well endowed with human capital? What of other countries, with similar endowments, that perhaps ought also to have succeeded but did not? Why was this latent advantage not adequately exploited by established software firms or large users in the United States and elsewhere?

India is not well endowed with human capital by most measures. Barely 50 percent of the population is literate, and, normalized by population, the stocks of scientific and technical personnel are modest—well below countries in East Asia. It is merely that India is (or, more precisely, was during the relevant period) well endowed with human capital relative to its economic needs. Or, more provocatively, during the 1970s and 1980s, India found itself with more engineers than its stagnant domestic economy could employ on attractive terms. Many of them emigrated to America, where they rose to middle management positions in large firms.[13]

When the big surge in IT demand came in the early 1990s, these emigrants were well positioned to broker the small initial contracts with Indian software firms, or as Kapur (2002) dubs it, act as "reputational intermediaries." Some, as we have already noted, became entrepreneurs, leading the on-site model of software service exports. In more recent years, there has been a greater return flow to India, chiefly to pursue more niche, technology-intensive activities. However, Kapur and McHale (2005) conclude that the return flow is as yet small. Foreign direct investment from the Indian diaspora is only 5 percent of its Chinese counterpart, and National Science Foundation longitudinal data on Ph.D.s indicate return rates below 10 percent.

Initial software exports from India relied upon software developers, who had gained experience in the domestic market or by working on overseas projects. As well, talented developers and managers were hired away from other domestic sectors. However, experienced managers and developers were often snared by multinationals in India or employers overseas. The surge in exports has been fueled by young and inexperienced engineering graduates. Over the last decade and a half, Indian engineering baccalaureate capacity has increased dramatically. This expansion has sustained the growth of Indian software exports. Sharply rising wages would have choked the growth in the industry but for the remarkable expansion in engineering education. Though the fruits of this expansion are frequently touted in discussions of the number of engineers that India graduates, the fuller account is worthwhile for what it teaches us about the process of economic growth and development.

Much of what Indian software exports consist of does not require an engineering background, yet software exports from India rely very heavily on engineering graduates. A survey of over one hundred Indian software firms in 1997 indicate that 80 percent of the software professionals employed had engineering degrees, while 12 percent only had diplomas from private training institutes (Arora et al. 2001). In interviews, few firms admitted to hiring non-engineers, principally for the signal it might send to potential customers and recruits. The CEO of a leading firm I interviewed in 1997 conceded that he hired only engineering graduates from the best possible schools, not because their training was relevant, but because these students tended to be smart and their backgrounds were useful in signaling quality to potential customers. Insofar as software developers had to be sent to the United States, an engineering degree was especially valuable in getting temporary work-permits, an artifact of the way in which U.S. visa laws operate.

Table 4.2 below shows that in 1985, roughly the time when software exports begin, Indian colleges graduated about 45,000 engineers of all types. By 2004, the *capacity* had increased to nearly tenfold to 440,000. The actual number graduated was smaller, both because of the inherent lags and because the entire capacity was not utilized. Our estimates suggest that the actual number of engineers graduated in 2004, which reflect capacity in 2000, was likely closer to 160,000–180,000 (Arora and Bagde 2006). These figures do not reflect the large number of non-engineers who acquire computer training and skills in using relevant tools at non–degree granting institutes such as NIIT and Aptech.

Almost all of the increase in engineering baccalaureate capacity was in IT-relevant fields of engineering, and, more importantly, was in private colleges that do not receive government subsidies. During the early 1990s,

Table 4.2 Sanctioned Engineering Baccalaureate Capacity in India, 1951–2004

Year	Population in Millions	Engineering College Capacity	Engineering College Capacity Per Million of Population
1951	361	4,788	13
1985	765	45,136	59
1995	928	105,000	113
2004	1,086	439,689	405

Source: Arora and Bagde (2006), based on data from The Ministry of Human Resources Development, AICTE, NTMIS.

the increase was also regionally concentrated. These trends are closely related. Table 4.3 shows the sanctioned intake capacity (for undergraduate engineering degree programs) by state. We see a large interstate variation in capacity. In fact, Andhra Pradesh, Karnataka, Maharashtra, and Tamil Nadu accounted for about three-quarters of the national capacity in 1987, as compared to 29 percent of the population, and, even in 2003, accounted for just under two-thirds of the capacity. The bulk of the interregional variation is due to non-granted engineering colleges.

In 1981, almost all engineering college capacity was in government-aided colleges. Constraints on public budgets and regulatory constraints on capacity expansion by existing colleges meant that new private (i.e., not publicly funded) colleges became the main source of growth (see Arora and Bagde 2006, for more details). Karnataka was among the first state to

Table 4.3 Sanctioned Intake Capacity in Undergraduate Technical Institutions, in '00s

Year	AP	Delhi	GJ	HR	KA	KL	MP	MH	OA	PN	RJ	TN	UP	WB
1990	58	9	33	5	170	27	17	192	11	5	11	92	31	23
1991	55	10	33	6	180	28	19	199	11	5	11	92	32	23
1992	55	10	34	8	188	29	19	238	11	5	13	94	33	23
1993	55	11	36	8	172	30	19	256	11	11	14	118	33	23
1994	56	10	38	8	193	35	19	280	12	11	14	141	33	24
1995	80	13	44	9	202	45	32	309	12	19	14	185	37	25
1996	86	12	50	9	203	47	34	333	17	19	15	222	44	26
1997	130	13	54	33	238	49	48	344	33	22	15	238	49	26
1998	196	16	64	33	244	51	43	397	45	22	20	273	68	40
1999	241	21	73	47	262	67	71	429	62	22	27	366	85	45
2000	277	23	91	67	282	88	102	429	62	34	50	505	153	52
2001	440	30	106	86	356	113	109	446	88	44	63	655	213	62
2002	624	34	106	98	381	183	160	470	88	86	82	702	231	107
2003	658	35	103	101	389	199	194	475	107	107	115	707	242	107

AP: Andhra Pradesh, GJ: Gujarat, HR: Haryana, KA: Karnataka, KL: Kerala, MP: Madhya Pradesh, OA: Orissa, PN: Punjab, RJ: Rajasthan, TN: Tamil Nadu, UP: Uttar Pradesh, WB: West Bengal

Source: Arora and Bagde, 2006.

permit private-sector entry in undergraduate engineering education in 1957. Thereafter, one in 1962 and two in 1963 started their operation in the state. Then a large number of private colleges entered, beginning in 1979, with nine colleges opening in 1979 and eleven in 1980. The first private college started in 1977 in Andhra Pradesh and in 1983 in Maharashtra after the government introduced its policy permitting such colleges. Figure 4.2 shows that in 1987, the earliest year for which I was able to get data from the All India Council for Technical Education, the body responsible for sanctioning and accrediting engineering colleges in India, the share of private colleges (not funded by the government) in baccalaureate capacity in engineering varied across states. It was between 60 percent and 80 percent in states such as Karnataka, Maharashtra, Andhra Pradesh, and Tamil Nadu, and substantially smaller in other states. A very similar picture emerges if one examines only IT-relevant engineering fields, consistent with the observation that the initial interregional variation was due to differences in private engineering baccalaureate capacity, and that this capacity was mostly in the "hotter" IT-relevant fields.

It is noteworthy that the growth of engineering baccalaureate capacity in the IT hub states predates by some margin the period of rapid growth of the software industry. Although accurate figures for the early period

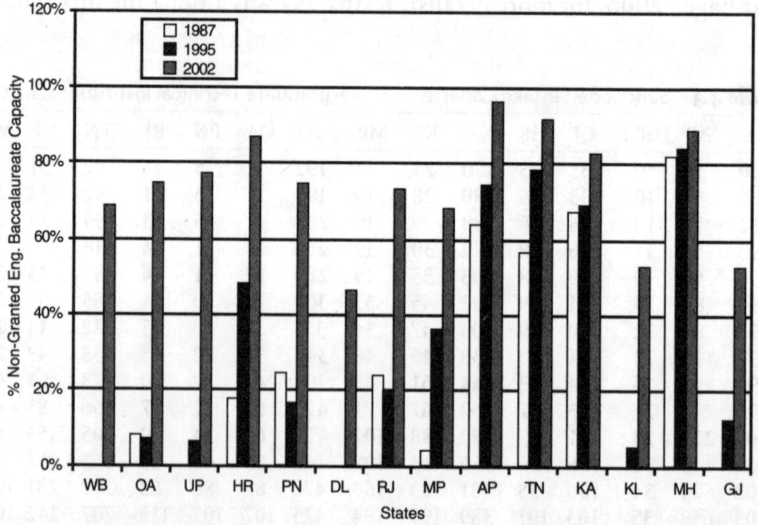

Figure 4.2 State Shares of Private Non-Granted College Education in Sanctioned Engineering Baccalaureate Programs, various years

Source: Author's calculations based on AICTE data on sanctioned capacity.

are unavailable, estimates suggest that software exports in 1985 were on the order of $25 million. Indeed, as late as 1990, software exports were a mere $128 million, employing fewer than 20,000, spread between Bangalore, Mumbai, Delhi, and Chennai. It is unlikely, therefore, that education policy changes were primarily intended to support software exports. Rather, it reflects differences in state policies regarding the entry of private colleges. By 1986, only six states had private colleges. Four of these, Andhra Pradesh, Karnataka, Maharashtra, and Tamil Nadu, accounted for the bulk of engineering college capacity in the entire country. As software exports grew, demand for engineering degrees also grew rapidly. Beginning in 1992, other states began to allow private self-financed institutions and, by 1999, all fourteen states studied by Arora and Bagde (2006) had allowed private engineering colleges.

It is only to be expected that education quality should have suffered greatly during this great expansion in capacity. Many of the new colleges are not up to the task of training engineers, and their graduates frequently need extended periods of training by employers before they can be put to work.[14] Thus far, large Indian firms have undertaken substantial investments in in-house training, in some cases spending 3–4 percent of revenues on training. Some, though not all, of this could be usefully provided in college itself. Future growth of software will require improvements in the quality of Indian colleges and universities. Given an acute shortage of Ph.D.s and good-quality postgraduate-level engineering teachers, this improvement will require investment as well as some thought.[15]

To sum up, the relative abundance in India of human capital is the result of a combination of its mediocre economic performance between 1955 and 1984, overinvestment in tertiary education in the 1950s and 1960s, and a market response by Indians willing to invest precious savings in an engineering degree for their children and by "entrepreneurs" who responded by starting new colleges.

Kapur (2002) and Srinivasan (2005) note, however, that this simple appeal to comparative advantage is an insufficient explanation. Many other countries had underemployed engineers and perhaps even the diaspora to broker the software export deals, and some even spoke English. For instance, the Philippines had 27 percent tertiary enrollment in 1991 compared to only 7 percent in India. Accenture had begun software development in the Philippines in the 1980s, and there are longstanding cultural links between the United States and the Philippines. Understandably, in 1997 many of the software firms I interviewed in India mentioned the

Philippines as a potential potent competitor, a fear that has not materialized. Interestingly enough, the Philippines is emerging as a business processing outsourcing (BPO) center, suggesting that the comparison is apt. Similarly, many countries in Eastern Europe have a large number of well-trained and poorly paid engineers and scientists, many of whom speak English well. Yet software exports from these countries are small. Russian software exports, though often technically very impressive, are barely over $1 billion.

4.2 PROTECTION—AND LEARNING FROM THE DOMESTIC MARKET

If simple comparative advantage is not enough, what are the missing pieces of the puzzle? The first potential one, which can be readily rejected, is a protected domestic market, which enabled firms to develop expertise that they could leverage for exports (cf. Dossani 2006). It is true that IBM's departure, and some fortuitous decisions to invest in Unix platforms, provided useful experience to Indian programmers. But, as I have argued above, Indian software exports, particularly early on, did not require deep technical skills. Rather, they relied upon a "reserve army of underemployed engineers" with the knowledge of software tools and a willingness to undertake tedious tasks. Protection undoubtedly helped produce the miserable economic performance that led to the "reserve army of underemployed engineers," but the irony here is self-evident. More to the point, the growth of software exports depended upon firm capabilities in recruiting, organizing teams, and maintaining service in the face of high rates of employee turnover.

Very few firms with substantial domestic experience were great export successes, with the possible exceptions of TCS and Wipro. Other early entrants such as Hindtron and CMC, which focused on the domestic market, remain domestic market–focused. The evidence from comparable developing countries provides little succor for the proponents of this view. Brazil had substantially protected its IT sector until the mid-1990s, and, unlike India, it had a very sophisticated banking, telecommunication, and government user sector. Though software production in Brazil was about $8–9 billion in 2002, only 10 percent of that is from exports. China, too, has an effectively protected market for software. Though more successful than Brazil in exports, it lags behind India by a substantial margin.

Undoubtedly, some firms acquired very sophisticated skills in the domestic market, but these skills were of little use in software exports, as illustrated in the following quote from the CEO of a subsidiary of a very large Indian engineering firm.

> [Our parent firm] has ES 9000s and IBM mainframes. It was the first firm to use IBM mainframes in India for a very long time . . . We have the most qualified experts on IBM mainframes. So as far as legacy maintenance on IBM mainframes is considered we know the technology inside out. . . . [But] technology is not such a critical factor as compared to understanding business practices. ". . . Domestic expertise may be useful in gaining technical expertise such as in coding and project management. *However, domestic and export projects are two different ball games.*" (Interview by author in Bombay, 1997; extracted from Arora et al. 2001. Emphasis added.)

Sometimes the argument in favor of protection or learning from the domestic market is accompanied by an emphasis on the role of domestic markets in helping develop software products. Indeed, firms such as Ramco, Sonata, and Mastek did initially focus on developing products for the domestic markets but had little export success.

Athreye's study of CITIL (now i-Flex), a Citibank subsidiary, indicates that the Indian market could provide a fruitful learning base for products (in this case, a back-end banking product) that could be successfully exported (Athreye 2005b). The study also makes clear, however, that this strategy depends on a number of concomitants for its success. In this case, Citibank's own internal use of the product (albeit in India and other developing country markets) provided important legitimization. Further, CITIL's strategy was to initially focus on other developing-country markets, particularly in the British Commonwealth, avoiding head-to-head competition with incumbent producers in developed countries, most of which were large, established firms. Only after succeeding in other export markets did CITIL enter the developed-country markets, and appears to have fared well in this attempt.

4.3 THE ROLE OF PUBLIC POLICY

The second candidate explanation is public policy. It is helpful, in this context, to distinguish between affirmative, sector-specific policies on the one hand, and all other policies. By the former I have in mind measures such as subsidies targeted to software exporters, or R&D investments in software. It could also include, as was true in Israel, investments in networking technologies and government procurement policies, motivated by national defense considerations, which propelled Israel into the forefront in security software and encryption technologies. In the latter category I include policies that generally improve the business climate.

Domestic and international economic liberalization, begun in 1984 and reinforced strongly in 1991, while broadly beneficial to all sectors, was especially helpful to the fledgling software industry in India, a point that Kapur (2002) argues with some force. I agree, and since this proposition is widely accepted, I shall not dwell on it. Surely providing an industry with tax incentives cannot hurt it (though it might hurt other industries), and neither can it hurt to relax onerous import restrictions and other types of regulations that strangled growth in other Indian industries. One might note that software was not very sensitive to a great deal of the pervasive regulation since it was not very capital intensive, the minimum scale of entry was small, obviating the need for bank finance, and it was not likely to be hampered by union activity. It did, however, benefit from the easing of trade and foreign-exchange regulations in 1991, whose timing coincided with the boom in international demand for IT skills. The element of luck, which often hovers in the background in such discussions, must firmly be brought to the forefront in this instance. Unquestionably, the reforms came at an opportune time, leaving India especially well positioned to benefit from the boom in global IT demand in the 1990s.

The role of affirmative sector-specific policies is harder to evaluate as neatly since there have been a plethora of such policies, varying in focus and detail over time. Though earlier accounts characterized the policy regime facing software as one of "benign neglect" (Arora et al. 2001), it is probably better described as inconsistent and ineffective. Athreye (2005a, table 8) details the various policy changes in import restrictions and export incentives. With the exception of telecommunication infrastructure, most of the many policies said to have aided software were not specific to software, and, in any case, were merely ameliorating bad existing policy. Hardware, the focus of much of policymaking efforts in the 1970s and 1980s, was showered by all these policies but with little to show for it.

Athreye (2005a) argues that during the crucial years of its development, the software industry flew "under the radar." The domestic market was small (and therefore there was little to be gained from protection) and as a service, it was naturally exempt from many of the laws and regulations that have stifled the growth of Indian manufacturing. Neither were the large investments in the 1960s and 1970s in science and engineering directed at software. Instead, the objective was to supply the manufacturing sector, whose slower-than-hoped-for growth resulted in the excess supply of engineers described earlier. In more recent years, of course, the software industry and its industry association, NASSCOM, have come to exercise substantial political influence and helped craft favorable public policies. But that is the consequence of its success, not its cause.

Balakrishnan (2006) makes the clearest case for targeted public policy. He notes that Bangalore was unusually well supplied with public-sector R&D institutions, including nine defense-related labs, which made it an attractive location for software firms, especially multinationals. Thus, he argues that India's software success testifies to the success of the government's "strategic intent."

> *Almost all private entrants, whether Indian or foreign, had started out in Bangalore* as this was seen as the locale most conducive, at least initially, to the success of an IT enterprise in India. Bangalore was India's science city, a deliberate construction of the policy of trying to establish an independent, world-class scientific foundation on Indian soil. By locating here, private entrepreneurs had access to scientists, engineers and management professionals who had honed their skills in the best technological environment in India, *almost exclusively created by the government*. (Balakrishnan 2006, p, 3870; emphasis added.)

Balakrishnan concludes the success of the software industry required a two-pronged effort.

> First, via long-term investment by the state in technical education and science and technology, with neither necessarily directed at the production of software. Subsequently, an incipient software industry with recognizably high export potential has been targeted via fiscal incentives and the provision of export-enabling infrastructure. *The emergence of a globally competitive Indian software industry serves as an interesting example of successful state intervention at a time when the model is largely out of fashion*. (Balkrishnan 2006, p. 3868; emphasis added.)

There are two observations to be made in response. First, although the presence of public-sector R&D labs may explain why Bangalore has emerged as an IT hub, it is not the only IT hub in India: there are five, roughly equally sized software clusters. Though Bangalore has attracted most of the hype, the data suggest that it has not been the only source of exports. Table 4.4 below presents data on software exports for the fourteen major Indian states over time. The data for 1996 and later comes from STPI figures. For earlier years, it is based on location of corporate headquarters and revenues for firms, gathered from NASSCOM and Dataquest. For TCS, which had software development activities in multiple regions, revenues were allocated to different locations based on company-provided estimates of employment by location. Table 4.4 shows quite clearly that Mumbai was where most of the initial software activities were located (indeed, Infosys was started in Mumbai and later moved to Bangalore). Other pioneers such as TCS, Patni, and Datamatics were Mumbai based as well. HCL was based in Delhi, as was another early leader, IIS Infotech. Furthermore, if one aggregates Delhi, UP and Haryana, which together make up the Delhi-Gurgaon-Noida cluster, exports produced are comparable to Karnataka between 1994 and 2000. Karnataka pulls away from the other clusters only after 2000, by which time the Indian software exports are already very sizable (over $8 billion by 2001).

Complementary evidence is provided by Table 4.5, which lists the location of NASSCOM member firms based on headquarters until 2001. Since most firms tended to be single-location firms, especially in the early years after formation, the location of the headquarters is a useful measure of activity. Table 4.5 paints the same picture as Table 4.4: until 2000 or so, Bangalore was not markedly more attractive a location than Mumbai or the Delhi cluster.

The second reason for doubting the claim that government science and technology investments explain why Bangalore emerged as a leading IT hub has to do with the nature of software exports. As I have stressed repeatedly, software exports, especially at the start, consisted of relatively simple activities or of programmers sent to America and elsewhere. Undoubtedly, some of them were hired away from the many public-sector labs, which proved to be a useful reservoir of skilled human capital. But that is it. The sophisticated capabilities resident in the public-sector labs were, for the most part, irrelevant to software success, with the exception of attracting firms such as TI and Motorola to locate there. Ironically enough, these capabilities and the multinational labs they attracted may explain why Bangalore is now acquiring a reputation for being the place to do product development and other R&D-intensive software activities.

Table 4.4 Indian Software Exports, by State, 1990–2003, for 14 Major Indian States (in Millions of Rupees at Constant Prices of 1993–94)

Year	KA	TN	MH	AP	DL	HA	UP	WB	OA	KL	MP	GJ	PN	RJ
1990	626	374	1,571	127	301	0	129	80	0	2	0	0	0	0
1991	1,189	489	1,774	158	430	0	188	94	0	6	0	0	0	0
1992	1,595	654	2,521	242	387	119	248	143	0	13	0	0	0	0
1993	2,235	1,124	3,836	277	986	170	385	251	3	17	0	2	0	0
1994	3,079	1,800	4,771	511	2,849	248	541	319	4	19	0	10	0	0
1995	4,386	2,725	5,321	857	3,459	458	770	410	9	29	0	12	0	0
1996	7,609	4,563	9,764	1,813	5,493	745	1,288	465	15	62	0	30	0	0
1997	12,630	7,502	12,751	2,127	9,458	1,442	1,644	743	28	196	0	40	0	0
1998	24,347	9,174	14,114	4,587	17,643	7,763	7,057	1,411	565	374	106	93	56	26
1999	29,158	13,171	13,703	7,037	26,027	6,448	8,255	2,434	726	442	239	183	99	99
2000	48,681	24,435	25,853	12,103	23,869	9,108	21,935	2,946	1,256	706	314	641	314	188
2001	71,786	36,465	37,866	18,052	14,215	17,923	15,451	4,363	1,545	909	544	754	433	278
2002	81,834	43,529	40,754	22,001	17,121	20,377	17,992	7,545	1,741	958	604	609	406	269
2003	107,598	44,925	54,921	28,152	19,412	27,732	19,689	8,874	1,803	1,212	693	782	1,009	277

Source: Arora and Bagde, 2006. See paper for details on data sources.

Table 4.5 Entry Dates and the Regional Location of Firms, 2001

Location	Pre-1980	1981–84	1985–91	1992–99	2000–1
Bangalore	3	3	19	50	15
Mumbai/Pune	9	11	32	63	8
(Pune)	(1)	(0)	(8)	(17)	(2)
Chennai	3	5	9	34	6
Delhi: of which	5	4	25	63	17
(Noida)		(1)	(6)	(18)	(4)
(Gurgaon)			(1)	(9)	(2)
Hyderabad/Secundrabad		1	6	29	8

NOTES: Computed from NASSCOM (2002) after excluding government departments, liaison offices and firms with missing data on years of establishment. (N = 449).
Source: Athreye (2005a), table 5, and my additions.

Unfortunately for the "public policy is the cause" explanation, this is taking place after the success of software exports.

Additional support is provided by the findings of Suma Athreye's survey of 205 software firms in 2002–3. In the survey, research links with universities and labs were ranked dead last among the factors that influenced their location decisions. Government financial incentives and the presence of other firms were also ranked very low among the factors that influenced the location decisions of firms (Athreye 2006).

Srinivasan (2006) rightly singles out telecommunication reforms and the creation of Software Technology Parks (STPs) as key pieces of the puzzle. Software firms needed to interact cheaply and easily with their clients, and to work upon systems remotely. Indeed, surveys done in 1997 by me, and more recently the survey by Athreye mentioned earlier, indicate that good transport and communications infrastructure is seen by firms as among the most important factors conditioning their performance.

Srinivasan's inference, however, that the initial phase of "body shopping" was a response to poor information infrastructure is off the mark. Some amount of physical proximity is inevitable. Outsourcing had, and continues to have, an important local component. One way of examining the tradability of IT services is to examine the extent to which they are clustered near local demand. If markets for IT services are local, then we should expect the entry decisions of IT services firms to depend in part upon the size of the local market. If markets are not local, then the composition of local demand should matter little: rather, suppliers should locate in low-cost regions. Using data from the U.S. Census County Business Patterns, Arora and Forman (2007) find that the elasticity of local supply to local demand characteristics is higher for programming and design (0.806) than for hosting (0.1899).

The importance of physical proximity will depend upon the nature of the service. Programming and design services involve tasks such as programming, and planning and designing information systems. These tasks require communication of detailed user requirements to the outsourcing firm in order to succeed. Hosting, on the other hand, involves the management and operation of computer and data-processing services for the client. After an initial set-up period, the requirements of such hosting services will be relatively static and will require relatively little coordination between the client and the service provider. Thus, ex ante we would expect that hosting activities may more easily be conducted at a distance than can other activities. Indeed, Arora and Forman (2007) find that outsourcing of programming and design services is much more sensitive to local supply conditions than hosting.

In other words, sending Indian programmers to their U.S. clients for part of the job is almost inevitable. In the Indian context, the body-shopping phase was essential for another important reason. Good telecommunications or not, outsourcing software development to India was not an easy sell in 1991, as the following comment by a founding member of NASSCOM (interviewed by Suma Athreye in 2005) indicates:

> When I was out there in 1991, the country was bankrupt. We had three governments in one year, an assassination of a prime minister, and we were hawking our gold. You know, selling overseas was not a piece of cake. . . . [I]f I have to present ten slides, the first eight had to be to sell India and the ninth one would say we do have an IT industry in India and unless the guy bought those nine slides, your tenth one about your company was meaningless. Because who are you anyway? Fifty people—its no big deal. So we were building up the [India] brand from day one. (Cited in Athreye and Hobday 2006)

An offer to send people over was undoubtedly more palatable to nervous American IT managers than an invitation to send the work over to India.

4.4 ENTREPRENEURSHIP AND OPENNESS

As the quote above also indicates, underlying this remarkable export success story is a perhaps even more remarkable story of Indian entrepreneurship. Even though the details of the entrepreneurial process are poorly understood, one may tentatively adduce two explanations for India's export success: entrepreneurship and openness.[16]

In an insightful article, Hausmann and Rodrik (2002) note that such market experiments appear to lie at the very heart of export successes from developing countries. They argue that in an uncertain world, figuring out where and how to exploit a certain type of resource abundance is not straightforward. For instance, Bangladesh's abundant supplies of cheap labor give it a comparative advantage in labor-intensive products as opposed to high-tech machinery. But labor-intensive manufactures vary from a range of textiles to diamond polishing. Even in textiles, where Bangladesh has focused, Bangladesh's exports to the United States are narrowly concentrated in men's cotton shirts and trousers and knitted hats. By contrast, Pakistan, with a similar resource endowment, exports bedsheets to the United States but few hats. This is not an isolated example. Hausman and Rodrik show that of the top twenty-five exports of each country, there are only six items in common. They find the same pattern for other pairs of comparable countries, such as Honduras and the Dominican Republic, and Taiwan and South Korea. They conclude that in most developing economies, "industrial success entails concentration in a relatively narrow range of activities."

Moreover, the precise product lines and activities that will eventually prove to be a success are very difficult to predict. An early, but unsuccessful, attempt to exploit India's comparative advantage in labor-intensive activities is illustrative. Patni Computer Systems, through its U.S. affiliate, Data Conversion, launched a project in the late 1970s for data entry as well as code embedding for commercial databases (now Lexus-Nexus). However, steep import duties on computer equipment imports, as well as union regulations, caused much of data-conversion work to be shifted to China and Taiwan and the project failed. Athreye (2005a) documents the many market experiments that Indian entrepreneurs engaged in, from developing products for the local (and, less frequently, the export) market to experimenting with different ways ("delivery models") for service exports.

Other countries also provide comparable examples. Breznitz (2005) shows that while it was evident that Israel's comparative advantage lay in R&D-intensive sectors, it was not at all clear in the beginning that software would emerge as a prominent industry. Indeed, the Office of Chief Scientist did not even include software in the technologies to which R&D subsidies would be provided until 1985. Multinationals demonstrated the viability of developing software in Ireland, but it was left to some indigenous firms to demonstrate that Irish firms could develop successful software products. As Hausman and Rodrik put it, "learning what one is good at producing," which may be key to the process of economic growth in follower countries, is not yet well understood. Economic experiments or entrepreneurship is the way such learning takes place.

For export success, information from outside the country, particularly from potential export markets, may be very important. This is reflected in the sources of firm formation in the software industry in Ireland, Israel and India. Of the thirty-eight Irish software companies for which Sands (2005) presents data, twenty-eight had one or more founders who worked abroad, and thirty-eight out of fifty-eight of the founders had worked abroad. Similarly, Arora, Gambardella, and Klepper (2005) present evidence that 40 percent of a sample of two hundred top managers of the leading Israeli software firms had earlier worked for an American company, and a third had their highest degree from a U.S. university. These percentages are markedly higher for managers in charge of finance or marketing, consistent with the idea that although Israeli entrepreneurs were technically proficient, they needed marketing and financial expertise from American managers to turn this into commercial success.

The importance of the "foreign connection" is evident in the Indian software industry as well. A number of successful software entrepreneurs in India had substantial overseas experience. For a sample of 530 firms that were members of NASSCOM in the year 2000, Athreye (2005a) finds that ninety-five (18 percent) were created by existing Indian firms diversifying into software, ninety-six (18 percent) were multinationals, forty-four were founded by expatriate Indians overseas, almost all located in the United States. There are 212 (40 percent) *de novo* start ups, 160 of which were founded by those who had worked for other software or hardware firms. It is likely that a very substantial fraction of these had worked overseas on software export projects. The foreign hand is even more visible if one confines attention to the leading exporters. Of the twenty leading exporters identified by NASSCOM, a quarter (five) were started by Indians living in America, and another 20 percent (four) are multinationals. Of the remaining firms, in virtually every case, the founders were educated or worked abroad. Since the NASSCOM list excludes leading exporters such as IBM, Accenture, HP, and Intelligroup on the one hand, and Kanbay, Cognizant, and Syntel, on the other, the share of multinational corporations and firms started by the Indian diaspora overseas is even higher.

Indian entrepreneurs were tested by the struggle to use inexperienced and newly minted engineers, to compete for export orders in the face of power shortages, bad roads, high employee turnover, and an initially indifferent government. To someone growing up in the India of the 1970s, where superior access to government favors passed for entrepreneurship, that such large numbers readily accepted the challenge is surprising enough, let alone that so many succeeded. However, this itself should provide comfort regarding the future prospects of the Indian economy.

5. THE PROSPECTS OF THE INDUSTRY

5.1 MOVING UP THE VALUE CHAIN: SOFTWARE PRODUCTS

Much ink has been spilled over whether Indian software exports are "low end" or not. For instance, many observers of the Indian software industry believe the growth of the Indian software industry was unsustainable unless firms began to invest in R&D to undertake sophisticated product development, because rising wages would undercut their existing cost advantages (e.g., Schware 1992; Heeks 1996). As one early observer put it:

> Onsite working increases the opportunities for a "brain drain" of talent, while offering programming services can become self-reinforcing with little skill being built up, so that the higher skills necessary for software innovation remain the preserve of developed countries. . . . [A]nd may also leave the Indian industry unable to move significantly to a different form of exports, such as package exports. (Quoted in Heeks 1998)

In this, they were in good company. Virtually every CEO I interviewed espoused such views. Industry leaders continue to hold to them even today, as the following quote attests.

> Indian software entrepreneurs would need to focus more on innovation of new IT products rather than on services or outsourcing if India had to be at the forefront of the IT revolution and transform itself into a software powerhouse, according to founder of Hotmail, Sabeer Bhatia. (*Economic Times*, July 15, 2005)

Such views are sometimes part of a broader mindset wherein progress in technology-intensive industries must necessarily take the form of moving up the technology ladder, to parallel (if not imitate) the activities undertaken in the rich countries. Indeed, policy makers in developing countries often point with pride to the technological accomplishments achieved in their countries, treating them as indicators of success. Considerable pride is staked on the formation of national champions and the ability to undertake high-tech projects and produce technically sophisticated products, regardless of their commercial feasibility. For the most part, as I show below, India has not produced technically sophisticated products and services, although there certainly are exceptions to which one can point. But Indian software growth appears none the worse for being behind the technological frontier, though a skeptic may contend that it is only a matter of time before wage growth exacts its revenge.

What then are the prospects for the Indian software industry and for Indian software firms? It is helpful to distinguish between two distinct ways in which one can "move up the value chain." First, one could produce software products. Products allow one to "write once and sell many times," the ultimate source of economies of scale. The reality is of course more complicated. Products, once written, have to be patched to take care of bugs and security flaws that inevitably creep in; they have to be upgraded to remain interoperable with other products; and they have to take on new functionality to keep up with the competition. Moreover, products have to be marketed, and, once sold, have to be installed and integrated with existing products. All of this takes software services. A comparison of the profit and loss statements for Oracle, the leading vendor for databases and other enterprise computing products, and TCS, is illuminating in this respect (see Appendix Table 4.1). Not only does Oracle expend substantial resources on services, its overall profit margins are not much different from those at TCS. The one major difference is that Oracle is about five times larger than TCS (or was, prior to its acquisition of PeopleSoft and JD Edwards).

Despite this, many of the leading Indian firms have tried to develop products, with limited success. The lack of success ought not to surprise anyone. Penny-pinching and risk-averse management habits ingrained while growing in an infrastructure- and capital-scarce and labor-abundant environment are unlikely to make for successful technology innovators. Development organizations geared to fulfill requirements laid down by clients are unlikely to be able to divine the needs of as yet unknown buyers of their product, nor are sales organizations used to answering RFQs best suited to sell a product for which the customer has not yet felt a need.[17]

Innovation, particularly technical innovation, will have to come from start-ups and other entrants. Some smaller incumbents, forced by the success of the market leaders, may also specialize and choose technology-intensive software services as their niche. In unpublished research, Athreye reports on a survey of 205 Indian software firms. Of these, only fifty-two firms, or about a quarter, reported any revenues from product and technical licensing, and thirty-nine of those fifty-two firms also earned some revenues in customized services. In other words, only thirteen, or around 6 percent, of the firms were focused on products. The average revenue earned through each activity for the group of firms that report licensing revenue is 34 percent from customization and 29 percent through product licensing, with an expected negative correlation. Athreye's data also suggest that entrepreneurial and spin-off firms are more likely to report licensing revenues, as opposed to firms that are part of business houses or are established firms.

Table 4.6 lists the leading software product producers with their associated product revenues (including domestic sales). Only i-flex, a Citibank spin-off, has achieved a measure of success. The other noteworthy point from the table is the virtual absence of the leading software firms. The two featured in the table, Infosys and TCS, have total revenues in excess of $2 billion, so that product sales account for 2–3 percent of total sales revenues.

Moreover, Indian firms are not alone in their failure to develop software products. The United States dominates the software product market to an astonishing degree. OECD data show that the United States continues to be the leader by a wide margin in the export of software products,

Table 4.6 Leading Software Product Companies and Software Product Revenues, $ Million.

	2004–5	2005–6
i-flex	122.3	157.7
Infosys	44.4	74.2
TCS	41.0	53.5
3i Infotech	26.9	40.6
Cranes	27.9	34.2
Ramco	25.8	32.9
Tally	47.7	28.5
Subex	13.1	24.4
Flextronics (earlier Hughes Software Systems)	14.8	23.8
Polaris	24.6	15.4
Total	**388.5**	**485.2**

Source: DataQuest Magazine, online site accessed 26 September 2006.

accounting for 21.7 percent of total software exports; but, in reality, it probably produces about a third of all software exports. The discrepancy results because the second leading exporter, Ireland, is mostly a value-added reseller of software products developed and designed in the United States by U.S. firms. North America also represents the largest share of packaged software sales, and this percentage has been increasing over time, from 47 percent in 1990 to 54 percent in 2001. Other than SAP, the German ERP producer, all the leading software product companies are American (see Arora, Forman, and Yoon 2007 for more details).

An important reason for American dominance is the importance of user-producer interactions, which are particularly salient for successful software product design. For example, the well known SABRE airline reservation system was an outgrowth of a chance encounter between R. Blair Smith of IBM's Santa Monica sales office with C. R. Smith, American Airlines' president, on a flight. This led the two companies to collaborate on developing SABRE (Campbell-Kelly 2003; Copeland and McKenney 1988). As long as the lead users, particularly for enterprise software, are American, the United States is likely to remain the center for product innovation in software.

Firms in other countries have succeeded typically when their products were targeted to niches where incumbent American firms had not entered, or where the products are deeply technical, such as design of chip components. Such was the case for security software, where Israeli firms such as Checkpoint, seized the opening. But even when firms from outside America successfully develop a product, the typical pattern is for those firms to move their commercial activities to the United States.[18] This is certainly true of the Israeli and Irish firms, which have tended to retain only research activities in their home countries. For instance, Checkpoint, an Israeli firm that pioneered software security products such as firewalls, is now an American company with mostly research activities located in Israel.

This suggests a more nuanced approach to thinking about the issue of software products. As discussed at the start of the paper, software products are typically used by firms to run their business processes such as accounting, sales and marketing, purchasing, and supply chains. For the most part, such software cannot be successfully developed and sold without a deep understanding of how these users run their businesses, and without the users having some ongoing relationships with the software vendor. Business software often is bundled with a set of business rules and assumptions about business processes that must be integrated with the existing business organization, its activities and its processes. Proximity between software developers and users is particularly important for this co-inventive activity to occur. At the very least, large users are unlikely to adopt a product that will become enmeshed in their business processes without considerable assurances of the support and maintenance of the products for the foreseeable future. Since the United States accounts for a substantial share of the software market and since most of the lead users, who play a very important role in a product's success, are American, it is difficult for a firm not substantially based in America to succeed in software product exports.

In turn, this raises two possibilities. First, firms outside the United States could develop products aimed at firms whose needs are different from American firms, as i-flex apparently did, or develop products that are not embedded in the business processes of users, as is the case for firewalls and anti-virus software. A second possibility is that firms could use India (or Israel or Ireland) as a base for doing product development and maintenance, while maintaining a substantial commercial presence in America. Indeed, this is the strategy that Texas Instrument pioneered, and many of the leading technology firms such as Motorola, Oracle, Cadence, Microsoft, Freescale and Intel have followed.

5.2 MOVING UP THE VALUE CHAIN: R&D AND ENGINEERING SERVICES

Thus, India could host technology-intensive software development by the subsidiaries of large multinationals, or by Indian firms developing technology that is not dependent on close proximity to customers, or Indian firms doing contract research for overseas clients. The evidence suggests that both are going on.

There is anecdotal evidence that even small firms are beginning to locate product development activities with a view to increasing the pace and reducing the cost of product development. There is also some anecdotal evidence that Indian firms may be increasingly performing R&D-intensive activities, especially in the semiconductor sector. Sasken and Mindtree are the prime examples of two Indian firms that are trying to develop proprietary technology, leveraging domain expertise and profits obtained by providing R&D services to clients.

Table 4.7 Leading Indian Engineering and R&D Service Companies

Company	Revenue (2005–6) $ Million	Growth (%)
HCL Technologies	222	40
TCS	196	62
Satyam	82	53
Rolta India	31	30
Quest	15	40
Neilsoft	8	40

Source: DQ estimates, converted from rupee values at $1 = Rs. 48.

Exports of R&D services are quite substantial. As shown in Table 4.1 earlier, exports of R&D and engineering services were projected to amount to about $5 billion. The exact nature of such services is hard to pin down. However, sales of embedded software, for instance software written for electronic devices such as mobile phones and printers, are a substantial category. Unlike software services for business processes, this category of exports is heavily dependent on technical and engineering expertise about relevant domains, such as electronics or automobiles. Table 4.7 lists the leading firms in providing R&D services. In addition, firms such as Persistent, IndusLogic and Aspire provide more generic product development services to clients. These are not small companies—Persistent employs over 2,000 people, and IndusLogic employs over 1,000 and has reported revenues of $30 million in 2005.

Patents statistics are another possible indicator of the extent to which India is being used as a place to do R&D. Arora, Forman, and Yoon (2007) use patent data to examine whether, in addition to software services, software inventive activity is globalizing. Though subject to a variety of caveats, the answer is no. There are, of course, significant limitations to the use of software patents as a measure of inventive activity. As Jaffe and Trajtenberg (2002) note, not all inventions meet the U.S. Patent and Trade Office (USPTO) criteria for patentability, and inventors must make an explicit decision to patent an invention, as opposed to relying on some other method of intellectual property protection. Both of these issues are particularly acute in the patenting of software. Another challenge is identifying software patents. In recent years, a number of authors have begun to use patent data to examine innovation in software (cf., Graham and Mowery 2003; Bessen and Hunt 2004; Allison et al. 2005; Thoma and Torrisi 2006; and Hall and MacGarvie 2006).

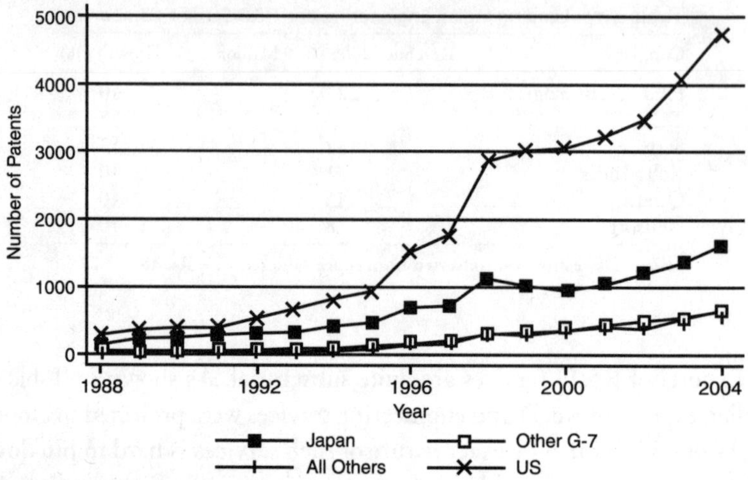

Figure 4.3 Software Patents at the U.S. Patent Office (Invented in United States and Other Countries)

Source: Arora, Foreman, and Yoon (2006) Based on USPTO Data.

Figure 4.3 shows that the United States also dominates software patenting and the difference between it and the rest of the world has become very pronounced over the last ten years.

In 2004, 4,695 software patents were issued to inventors in the United States, a larger number of patents than all other areas of the world combined (2,811). Moreover, patenting by U.S. inventors grew by nearly 20 percent per year, compared to 16.1 percent in Japan and 18.0 percent in other G-7 nations. These figures may reflect a "home country bias": U.S. firms may be more likely to patent in the U.S. market than foreign firms. However, these trends are very robust. Thoma and Torrisi (2006) examine the rate of software patenting in European patents and find very similar results: U.S. firms are responsible for the majority of software patenting activity, followed by Japanese firms, and then all others. Moreover, Thoma and Torrisi (2006) note that of the European patents in their database, 80.3 percent have also been granted by the USPTO and 73.8 percent have also been granted by the Japanese Patent Office.

Figure 4.3 shows the number of patents invented in the "underdog" countries, which includes India, along with the United States, Japan, and other G-7 countries. Of the "underdog" countries, Israel is the only one among them to have a significant number of U.S. patents. Israeli patenting activity increased from three in 1998 to a high of ninety in 2003. No other country has had more than twenty patents in any one year, though

Table 4.8 Patenting Activities of Leading Software Firms in India

Panel A: MNCs patents invented in India					Panel B: Indian SW patenting firms				
	2004–5		2005–6			2004–5		2005–6	
Company	Filed	Granted	Filed	Granted	Company	Filed	Granted	Filed	Granted
Microsoft	40	–	70	–	Infosys	–	–	20	–
Symantec	47	43	57	16	Ramco	16	–	16	–
ST Micro	62	32	37	14	TCS	16	5	13	4
Adobe	10	–	32*	–	Sasken	5	–	5	5
Freescale	10	–	16	4	Mindtree	1	–	2	–
Flextronics	2	1	4	1	Subex	–	–	2	–
Cadence	1	5	–	–					
Texas Instruments	35	10	–	–					

Source: DQ estimates.
All figures represent U.S. patents filed by the Indian R&D facilities of these MNCs in all fields, not just software patents.
*Adobe's patents represent the total number of patents filed since start of India operations.

the number of patents invented in India has risen slightly in recent years, from an average of 0.5 throughout the 1990s to sixteen in 2004.

A different way to ask the question is to look at the patenting activities of software firms, keeping in mind that their patents may well fall in areas that we do not classify as software. As panel A of Table 4.8 confirms, most of the inventive activity by software firms is by multinationals. However, as panel B shows, some Indian firms are filing for U.S. patents, as well. Given average pendencies of two years or more, patents granted in 2005 reflect applications in 2003.

Overall, the evidence suggests that in recent years, R&D and software-related innovation activities in India have grown, albeit from a small base. However, the quantitative significance of such activities is still small. Using India to develop software for sale in distant markets poses significant challenges. One major challenge to offshoring software product development work results from the difficulty of coordinating software development activity across a globally distributed team. As is well known, partitioning complicated software development projects across multiple team members is difficult, and often substantially increases the costs of software development (Brooks 1995). These problems may become still greater when attempting to manage such projects at a distance (Armstrong and Cole 2002; Olson and Olson 2000). Further, as Treffler (2005) notes, such contractual arrangements face many challenges, and India may be deficient in the institutional infrastructure for overcoming them.

5.3 MOVE UP THE VALUE CHAIN: MORE VALUABLE BUSINESS EXPERTISE

Supplying technology-intensive products and services is not the only way of moving up the value chain; providing organization capability–intensive services is another, and this is the route the leading Indian software firms will likely take. They may try to diversify into emerging niches without entrenched incumbents, as for instance TCS's forays into bio-informatics show. A select few may attempt to acquire the required hardware capability to become systems integrators, though that remains to be seen.

For the most part, however, the leading Indian software firms shall strive, quite sensibly, to become capable of executing large, complex, multi-year software development, implementation, and maintenance projects. In so doing, they will build upon their existing business units, which focus upon serving selected industries. Indeed, this sort of "vertical" focus is more prominently visible among Indian firms which entered later, and hence, are smaller, and also less successful at competing for large multi-year projects. Examples include Cognizant in health care, Polaris in banking, RMSI in geographical mapping and GIS, and Geometric Software in CAD software and services.

In bidding for large-scale projects, the established Indian firms will run up against established incumbents such as the global services division of IBM, Accenture, and EDS. The outcome of this impending clash is unclear, although the advantage must lie with the incumbents. Whereas the Indian firms perhaps have an advantage in terms of superior access to the Indian labor market, the latter have much greater demonstrated expertise in large projects in a wider range of end-user sectors, established relationships with customers, and global presence. The latter also appear to have realized the seriousness of the challenge and have begun to recruit heavily in India, for the software to be developed in India itself. For instance, IBM Global Services is believed to have over 40,000 employees in India. By themselves developing software in India, American (for they are almost all American) software service and solution providers hope to lower their costs, and thereby undercut the only significant advantage that Indian software firms are thought to enjoy.

Even so, Indian firms have become experts at a "global delivery" model of software services, wherein some of the work is done offshore and some done on-site, using the large number of talented but often poorly trained and inexperienced engineering graduates, a substantial fraction of whom will stay with the firm for a couple of years before moving on.[19] As already noted, operating under these conditions, Indian firms were forced to develop management practices to cope.

This business model, which Indian firms stumbled into, is something that their foreign competitors have yet to learn. There is no reason why they should not be able to do so, but the Indian firms have a head start. A recent news item noted that Accenture's market value is below that of TCS and Infosys, even though Accenture is substantially larger. Given Accenture's technical capabilities, this may reflect investor skepticism about its ability to be as cost-effective in software service delivery in a geographically distributed environment. On the other hand, the Indian firms will have to learn how to operate as global companies, with a multinational workforce, a task they have only recently, and timidly, embarked upon.[20]

As the Indian market grows, MNCs will start aggressively going after "local" business. For example, the ten-year deal between Accenture and Dabur for management of Dabur's IT needs, the Bank of India–HP deal for branch office computertization, $750-million Bharti-IBM deal, and both the mega–Reliance Infocomm telecom network and the Reliance retail-petrol-pump projects with IBM are clear indicators of what can happen in the Indian landscape. The lack of hardware and systems-integration capability are clearly a weak area. On the other hand, this is the flip side of the coin of comparative advantage. Indian firms have certain relative strengths, which imply corresponding relative weaknesses. Contrast that with the Chinese case where local business is almost exclusively the preserve of local firms, all of which are incredibly diversified (Tschang and Xue 2005), and none of which are internationally competitive.

Moreover, one should distinguish between the prospects of Indian firms and prospects for India as a location for software and IT. The latter prospect is surely brighter. Leading multinationals such as IBM, Accenture, and HP employ over 70,000 people in India. If Indian firms are indeed deficient in certain aspects of management, the multinationals could be the training ground for new managers and the seedbed for new startups.

A greater threat may perhaps come from the technology itself. Evangelists for service-oriented architectures, software components, utility computing, and so on paint a picture of a world where users will no longer have to invest in large in-house IT infrastructures. Instead, computing will be like a utility—a menu of services that organizations can use, varying the scope and scale according to need. More importantly, the tedious

Table 4.9 Examples of Large Contracts Obtained by Indian SW Firms

Date	Indian Firm	Client	Contract Type	Value (Million) (Period)
2006	Wipro	GM		$27–$300
Sep 2005	TCS	ABN	SW Dev	$260
Sep 2005	Infosys	ABN	SW Dev, maintenance	$140
Aug 2003	L&T	Motorola		$70–90 (3–5 yrs)
Aug 2003	Satyam	Certain Teed (U.S.)	Implement supply chain solution	$15 (9 months)
Jun 2003	HCL	Airbus	Embedded SW	–
April 2003	HCL	BT group (U.K.)	Business telemarketing, billing conferencing	$160 (5 yrs)
April 2003	Infosys	BT group (U.K.)	Second service provider for BPO services	– (5 yrs)
Mar 2003	Patni	Guardian Life (U.S.)	Gap analysis and implementation	$35 (7 yrs)
Mar 2003	Ramco-Boeing	Aloha Airlines (U.S.)	Technical services with main marketing by Boeing (50% of revenues for each)	–
Nov 2002	TCS & Wipro	Lehmann Bros.	IT outsourcing	$50–70
Jan 2002	TCS	GE medical	'Take or pay' model,	$100–120 (2 yrs)
July 2001	Wipro	Lattice Group (U.S.)	Outsourcing	$70 (3 yrs)

Based on Athreye, 2005a and author's additions.

business of maintaining and upgrading applications, and keeping up with changes in underlying computing platforms will become much less tedious: Information infrastructure providers such as IBM, HP, EMC, and others will take on this task for them. The market for third parties, such as TCS, Wipro, and Infosys, to customize, enhance, and maintain the existing software infrastructure will shrink quite dramatically.

That is, of course, if such a state comes to pass. Information technology has so often promised "automation" that would reduce demand for skilled (and expensive) workers only to deceive. A number of difficult problems, both technical and organizational, would have to be solved to achieve this state. Even if this state of bliss were realized, it would take a long time. Much like old soldiers, old code never dies but fades away, often very slowly.[21] Prognosticating about technology is best left to experts, but a reasonable guess is that for the next decade or so, demand for software services will keep growing. The growth in emerging markets, and especially the Indian economy, may provide an additional source of demand, which will surely be satisfied by Indian programmers, albeit perhaps working for a foreign company.

6. IMPLICATIONS FOR THE INDIAN ECONOMY

Impressive though the Indian software industry may be, its direct economic impact is small, though growing rapidly. Table 4.10 below shows that the total employment in IT Services is about 800,000, a miniscule fraction of the 340 million–strong workforce. Panagariya (2007) cites data that indicated business services (which include IT services) comprised only 1.1 percent of GDP in 2000. However, even as GDP has grown at a healthy clip since then, IT services have grown even faster. Data from the Ministry of Finance indicates that IT services accounted for 4 percent of GDP in 2004, which speaks to the astonishing growth of this sector.

Projections from the same source foretell of much greater future impact. The Economic Survey 2005 projects that value added in IT and in BPO services is expected to be 7 percent of GDP by 2008. Further, exports are expected to be around $60 billion by 2010, accounting for 35 percent of all Indian exports (MOF Economic Survey 2005, box 6.2). This projection appears to be based on an assumption that software export revenues will continue to grow at 30 percent per year, an assumption that appears optimistic. If that should come to pass, it would be astonishing for a sector which even today barely employs 1.2 million people, out of a labor force of well over 360 million.

Even more optimistic are the long-run projections, such as those from a study by the AIMA and BCG, cited by Srinivasan (2005), which projects that by 2020, remote service exports and in situ services to foreigners could lead to export revenues between $139 billion (if IT service exports grow by 10 percent between 2010 and 2020) and $365 billion (if exports grow by 20 percent), and additional employment of between 20 and 72 million. The employment projections appear to be the most suspect. As Panagariya (2007) notes in a broader context, this is unlikely to happen without substantial improvements in the physical infrastructure, particularly electricity and ground and air transport.

Bottlenecks in the supply of the required human capital may also prevent these optimistic projections from being fulfilled. Even non-IT

Table 4.10 Employment in the Indian Software and Services Sector

Sector	FY 2004	FY 2005	FY 2006
IT Services	614,000	741,000	878,000
ITES-BPO	253,000	316,000	415,000

Source: Nasscom (IT factsheet), www.nasscom.org (accessed 18 September 2006).

business services require college graduates at the very minimum, and barely 7 percent of the college-age population is actually enrolled in universities. India's output of masters and Ph.D. graduates is barely 3 percent that of the United States and more than 60 percent of postgraduate seats in engineering colleges are vacant. The consequent low output of postgraduates has serious implications for training future generations (World Bank 2000, annex 1, para. 23; cited in Kapur 2001). The mounting budget deficits of the public and private sector make it unlikely that large public investments in university education capacity are forthcoming.

However, as the Indian experience with engineering education has indicated, Indians are willing to invest in education when it yields an economic return, and Indian entrepreneurs are willing to supply it. I suspect a similar process has been going on at the pre-university level, in terms of both formal schooling and the informal "cram" schools and coaching classes. As with the private engineering colleges, the quality of teachers and of the education provided are uneven. Most private engineering colleges have virtually no research capability. Many even employ teachers with only a baccalaureate and limited expertise and teaching experience. On the other hand, the existing publicly funded schools and colleges are not much to write home about, with the exception of those at the very top. Moreover, one must avoid making the good the enemy of best: Compared to the alternative of relying solely upon publicly funded education (which even the Indian middle-class has not done, at least for pre-university education), private schools and colleges, even of uneven quality, are a Pareto improvement.

In this respect, Panagariya (2007) makes a number of sensible suggestions, including relaxing the regulation on the number of students that colleges can admit in various fields, the fees they can charge, and so on. The most important of his suggestions, to my mind, is relaxing the control of the University Grants Commission and encouraging decentralization of decision making and control. Here, again, the software industry experience is instructive. In 1990, only six states permitted private engineering colleges. Rising interstate competition pushed all the remaining nine states to allow private colleges by 1999. There is anecdotal evidence that suggests that in this, state governments were responding to middle-class demands. The broader point is that competition between states, for talent and for firms, is important and must be allowed freer reign. This will enable market forces to drive improvements in quality in education and will have broader benefits as well.

I am, however, not optimistic that the private engineering colleges will see that it is in their (short-run) interest to subsidize the production of masters and Ph.D. education. If, as appears to be happening, these private engineering colleges have to compete for students, some may decide to move up-market by hiring well qualified professors and paying them higher salaries. This may provide some incentive for investment by individuals in Ph.D.s. However, this mechanism, by itself will likely be insufficient. It will require government investment and ideally even some substantial investments by the leading IT firms operating in India.

But the excitement regarding India's software exports has never been about its employment-generation capability. Rather, it is an example of what is possible. In other words, it is the indirect and less quantifiable impacts that have always held the greatest attraction. As we concluded in Arora et al. (2001),

> [O]ur optimism about the beneficial impact of the Indian software industry on the Indian economy in the long run is not based entirely on the quantitative importance of the relatively smaller number of successes among software service exporters. We think that in the shadow of the much more prominent software services firms; we are finding firms developing a variety of new software products, components and technologies. [S]oftware service firms are exemplars of organizational forms and practices that are relatively new to India. A large number of software firms are *de novo* start-ups, indicating that the supply of entrepreneurial talent appears to be forthcoming when the opportunity arises, even in new and technology intensive sectors. . . . Top managers of the leading software firms have been profiled in the popular press in India and are viewed favourably by many Indians, particularly in comparison to traditional Indian business leaders. Further, this industry has pioneered equity stakes and stock options for employees in India, and many of these companies are star performers on the Indian stock market. Thus, unlike in the past, the fruits of the success of the industry have been shared far more broadly. The implications of the success of this industry, at a time of slow but far ranging changes in the Indian economy, can be immense and far-reaching. (Arora et al. 2001, p. 1287)

This faith appears to have been vindicated. Athreye (2005a) argues that the organizational capabilities developed by Indian software firms are generic in the sense of being applicable to sectors other than software.

This is true in areas such as engineering services, where leading software firms such as HCL and TCS have a substantial presence (see Table 4.7 above). This is also true in the more rapidly growing area of business process services. Indeed, some of the entrants into the BPO sector have been IT firms. Table 4.11 shows that of the leading BPO firms in India, two of the top five, and four of the top ten, are also leading software firms. These account for nearly a quarter of the employment of this group. The table also shows the diverse sources of firm entry, and how closely it mirrors the sources of firm entry into software—start-ups, spin-offs, business houses, and multinationals.

There are even more intangible, but no less important, impacts. Software made the "Brand India" a respected one, paving the way for other sectors. For instance, there is a small but growing set of firms that develop semiconductor technology and provide affiliated services. The Indian Software Association estimates that about two hundred semiconductor

Table 4.11 Leading BPO Firms in India

	Employees	% Voice	Start Year	Software	Origin
Genpact	26,000	20	1997		Spin-off (GE)
IBM Daksh	18,000	67	2000	Yes	
Wipro	16,000	86	2000	Yes	(Acquired Spectramind, a start-up)
WNS	10,000	30	1996		Start-up—Diaspora
Convergys	10,000		?		MNC
HCL BPO	10,000	70	2001	Yes	
Intelnet	9,500	60	2000		Start-up—HDFC
MphasiS	8,300	80	1999	Yes	Spin-off (Citibank)
Aegis	8,000	75	2004		Business House (Essar)
Sutherland	8,000		1986		MNC
Hinduja TMT	7,500	70	2001		Business House
ICICI OneSource	7,300	70	2001		
EYesL	7,300		1999		Start-up—Diaspora
Progeon (infosys)	7,000	18	2002	Yes	
24/7	7,000		2000		Start-up—Diaspora
TCS	5,000	15	?	Yes	
Eforce	3,200		1999		Start-up—Diaspora
vCustomer	3,000		1999		Start-up—Diaspora
Sitel India	3,000	73	2000		MNC
Transworks	2,235	78	1999		Business House (Birla)
GTL	1,700	90	1999		
Datamatics	1,125	0	1991	Yes	
Techbooks		0	1988		
eFunds					MNC

Source: The list of BPO firms and their size is from Dataquest magazine, the origins are based on information available from company websites.

companies currently operate a facility in India, and of these, about 60 percent are involved in chip design (the remainder do software development). The membership of the ISA itself consists of over a hundred firms, most of which are American firms in semiconductor design, manufacturing, and design tools and services. A fifth are firms headquartered in the United States with CEOs of Indian origin, and another fifth are Indian firms, including HCL, Wipro, and TCS. The success of software exports surely played a role in signaling the potential of India as a location for such activities. The software industry led the fight for regulatory reforms, in areas such as liberalizing access to the stock market and listing requirements. It also led the way in corporate governance, with their emphasis on transparency and ethical management.[22]

But perhaps the most important achievement of all is that software showed potential entrepreneurs what is possible with talent, luck, and hard work—that success is not reserved for those with connections or for those born to wealth (Kapur 2002). Hitherto, wealth was acquired by breaking laws or at least bending them to one's convenience; software was the first instance where wealth was created honestly and legally, and, more important, visibly so. Hitherto, commercial success had invited envy, cynicism, and even outright hostility; only rarely did it engender admiration. While envy and hostility are by no means gone, there is much more of admiration, and, more importantly, a desire for imitation.

Appendix Table 1 NASSCOM Top Indian IT Service Exporters, 2005–6

Name of Firm	Year Est.	Origin/Type of Firm	Notes
TCS	1968	Business house	Founder U.S. educated
Wipro	1980	Business house	
Infosys	1981	Spin-off (Patni)	
Satyam	1987	Business house	Founder U.S. educated
HCL	1991	Entrepreneur	
Patni	1978	Entrepreneur	Diaspora
i-flex	1989	Spawn (Citibank)	MNC spawned
Tech Mahindra	1988	Business house	
Perot Systems	1996	MNC	(earlier joint venture with HCL)
L&T Infotech	1996	Business House	
Polaris	1993	Entrepreneurial	
Hexaware	1989	Entrepreneurial	(Venture funded)
Mastek	1982	Entrepreneurial	
MphasiS BFL	1992	Spin-off (Citibank)	Diaspora
Siemens		MNC	

(continued)

Appendix Table 1 *continued*

Name of firm	Year Est.	Origin/Type of Firm	Notes
Genpact	1997	Spawn (GE)	MNC—Diaspora
IGate	1993	Entrepreneur (U.S. based)	Diaspora
Flextronics	1991	MNC	(Hughes Software)—Diaspora
NIIT	1981	Entrepreneur	HCL spawned
Covansys India	1985	Entrepreneur (U.S. based)	Diaspora (CBSL)
Accenture		MNC	
IBM India	1987	MNC	
Cognizant	1994	Spawn (Dunn & Bradstreet)	Diaspora
HP Globalsoft	1988	MNC	Digital Globalsoft
Syntel	1980	Entrepreneur (U.S. based)	Diaspora
Kanbay	1991	MNC	Diaspora founded

Appendix Table 2 Oracle and TCS Income Statements, 2004

Revenues	2004
New license	3,541
License updates	4,529
Software	*8,070*
Services	2,086
Total revenues	10,156
Operating Expenses	
License updates and product support	547
Sales & Market	2,136
Cost of services	1,770
R&D	1,278
G&A	561
Total Expenses	6,292
Net Income	2,681

Appendix Table 2.2 TCS Income Statement

Revenues	2004
Consultancy services	1,461
Sale of equipment and software licenses	*108*
Other revenues	13
Total revenues	**1,583**
Operating expenses:	
Selling, G&A expenses	314
Cost of services	760
Cost of equipment and software licenses	97
R&D	7
Net Income	**405**

NOTES

1. I gratefully acknowledge support from The Sloan Foundation and from Industry Canada. I am also grateful to Suma Athreye, Surendra Bagde, Chris Forman. Alfonso Gambardella, Steven Klepper, Anita Sands, and Salvo Torrisi, on whose work I have drawn in writing this paper. I am especially thankful to Dan Trefler and Someshwar Rao for helpful comments. They are not responsible for any deficiencies in this paper.

2. The next few paragraphs draw upon Arora, Foreman, and Yoon 2007.

3. Source: U.S. Bureau of Economic Analysis Input-Output Tables. This figure includes the total value of products made in NIPA industry 511200 (Software Publishers). 1997 is the latest benchmark year for the Input-Output tables. More recent years do not separate software producers from other information publishers.

4. Source: Bureau of Labor Statistics (BLS) data on the number of employees in software publishing industry; available at http://www.bls.gov/ces/home.htm

5. These calculations are based on total sales in custom computer programming services (NAICS 541511) and computer systems design services (NAICS 541512). This latter category may include activities outside of programming, such as IT systems design and integration. A conservative estimate of the value and employment of third-party custom programming services uses only NAICS 541511, and yields and estimate of $86,326.8 million and 522.3 thousand, respectively.

6. In addition to these firms that focused on software exports, there were others that served domestic users, most notable Computer Maintenance Corporation, or CMC. Responsible for maintaining computer systems after IBM left India, CMC developed the ability to develop and implement large and complex projects, especially for infrastructure systems. CMC also proved to be a good training ground for managers that would later be employed by other, private-sector firms. CMC is now part of TCS, a leading Indian software service firm.

7. Cognizant, the erstwhile joint venture of Dunn and Bradstreet and Satyam, is the latest in the line of U.S.-headquartered firms having the bulk of their operations in India, with an Indian emigrant as CEO.

8. IGate's founder and CEO, Sunil Wadhwani, in an interview with the author in 1997, noted that leading American IT service providers had until then tended to ignore the hinterland—smaller firms typically located outside the large urban areas, for whom a large in-house IT staff was economically not viable but who needed to adopt IT for their business operations (not their technical operations.) These were the customers that IGate targeted. It is unlikely that such customers would have been within the reach of Indian software firms when the latter were just beginning to export.

9. In Arora et al. 2001, we report on interviews with U.S. firms, which bear out this contention. "The managers at a leading electronics and telecom firm said they outsource work related to sophisticated but mature digital signal processing software to their Indian subsidiary. The telecom firms we interviewed outsourced domain related software maintenance or tool development for the maintenance or enhancement of existing applications. The manager at a value added telecom services firm said that they were outsourcing testing of their existing software and to some extent maintenance of their old UNIX based software. However, we did find . . . one exception: A leading computer manufacturer out sources mission critical device-driver software that is shipped directly from the Indian vendor for distribution."

10. Their behavior, however, clearly shows the importance of lower costs. Indian vendors routinely reported tough price negotiations. During the 1990s, Infosys gave up an existing GE account rather than lower its rates. Another North American company I interviewed in 1998, a leading telecommunication company, described a typical strategy. It had two of the leading Indian firms as suppliers which accounted for much of the outsourced work, and two "lower end" suppliers with smaller contracts, primarily to keep the price pressure on the main suppliers.

11. Possible economies of scale from more intensive utilization of workers or through the use of proprietary tools may also contribute to the higher labor productivity, as might differences in the capital stock employed.

12. Athreye (2005a) presents data that suggest that whereas U.S. salaries for a variety of software occupations such as programmer, project leader, quality assurance specialist, and systems designer increased by about 21 percent between 1995 and 1999, Indian salaries increased nearly twice as fast.

13. U.S. Census data analyzed by Kapur and McHale (2005) indicate that 77 percent of the Indian-born population in the United States in 2000 had college degrees, and 37 percent had a masters degree or higher!

14. It is also a tribute to the superior management capability of Indian firms that they were able to use such inexperienced and poorly trained (but bright) young men and women. In some sense, Indian firms embraced, out of necessity, the Taylorization of software services while their competitors were slower to do so.

15. A recent government initiative in which the IITs were tasked to develop video- and computer-based learning materials exemplifies the point. The NPTEL program, begun in 2003, has resulted in the creation of material for over a hundred courses, involving more than three hundred IIT faculty. Yet, there has been very little thought given to whether any of the intended beneficiaries, including the various engineering colleges thought to be suffering from a lack of qualified faculty, will use these materials, which are to be made available free to anyone. This type of "supply side"–oriented government programs, which contributed to the relative abundance of human capital in India in the first instance, does not auger well for the future.

16. The next few paragraphs draw upon Arora and Gambardella (2005).

17. Indeed, Infosys now spins off promising product development opportunities, as is the case of Onmobile, which develops mobile applications.

18. This pattern is evident in the case of Talisma, which is sells a customer relationship management product. Talisma was spun off from Aditi, an Indian software firm started by Pradeep Singh, an ex-Microsoft employee of Indian origin. In 1999, Talisma was incorporated in the United States; the founder resigned from the firm in 2003 and the financiers installed a new management team. For all intents and purposes, it is now an American firm.

19. Some idea of the importance of the last point can be gleaned from the recent move at Infosys, wherein the company's longstanding CFO, Mohandas Pai, moved to head the human resources function, a move that would be inconceivable in an American context.

20. Even Infosys, the most global of the Indian software firms, has only 3 percent of its employees who are not Indian nationals.

21. Bresnahan and Greenstein (1996), in a detailed study of client-servers, show that the diffusion of client-servers was slow and incomplete, and was the slowest when computers were used to run business processes. I conjecture that the spread of service-oriented architectures will encounter a similar fate.

22. A recent news story reports that Infosys fined a member of its board of directors for not following procedure in a trade involving the companies stock. See http://news.oneindia.in/2006/08/31/infosys-fines-director-breaching-code-conduct.html

REFERENCES

Adam B Jaffe and Manuel Trajtenberg; 2002. Patents, citations, and innovations a window on the knowledge economy, MIT Press, Cambridge, Mass.

Allison, John and Emerson Tiller. 2003. "Internet Business Method Patents," in Wesley M. Cohen and Steve A. Merrill, eds., *Patents in the Knowledge-Based Economy*, 259–75 (Washington, D.C.: National Academies Press).

Allison, John, Arti Rai, and Bhaven N. Sampat. 2005. University Software Ownership: Trends, Determinants, Issues. Working Paper, Columbia University.

Armstrong, D. J. and P. Cole. 2002. "Managing Distances and Differences in Geographically Distributed Work Groups," in Pamela J. Hinds and Sara Kiesler, eds., *Distributed Work*, 167–86 (Cambridge, MA: MIT Press).

Arora, Ashish, V. S. Arunachalam, V. S. Asundi, and R. Fernandes. 2001. The Indian software services industry.*Research Policy* 30(8): 1267-1287.

Arora, Ashish and Jai Asundi. 1999. "Quality Certification and the Economics of Contract Software Development: A Study of the Indian Software Industry." NBER working paper 7260. Arora, Ashish, V. S. Arunachalam, V. S. Asundi, and R. Fernandes. 2001. "The Indian Software Services Industry," *Research Policy* 30(8):1267–87.

Arora, Ashish and Surendrakumar Bagde. 2006. "The Indian Software Industry: the Human Capital Story." Working Paper, Heinz School of Public Policy & Management, Carnegie Mellon University.

Arora, Ashish and Chris Forman. 2007. "Proximity and IT Technology: How Local Are IT Services Markets." *Journal of Management Information Systems* 24(2):73–102.

Arora, Ashish, Chris Forman and Jiwoong Yoon. 2007. "Software," in Jeff Macher and David Mowery, eds., Running Faster to Keep Up: Prospering In Global Innovation Networks (Washington, D.C.: National Academies Press).

Arora, Ashish and Alfonso Gambardella. 2005. "The Globalization of the Software Industry: Perspectives and Opportunities for Developed and Developing Countries," In Adam Jaffe, Josh Lerner and Scott Stern, eds., *Innovation Policy and the Economy*, 1–32 (Cambridge, MA: MIT Press).

Arora, Ashish, Alfonso Gambardella and Steven Klepper, 2005, Organizational capabilities and the rise of the software industry in the emerging economies: Lessons from the history of some U.S. industries, in*From Underdogs to Tigers: The Rise and Growth of the Software Industry in Brazil, China, India, Ireland, and Israel* (eds.) Ashish Arora and Alfonso Gambardella, p. 171-206, Oxford: Oxford University Press.

Athreye, Suma. 2005a. "The Indian Software Industry," in Ashish Arora and Alfonso Gambardella, eds., *From Underdogs to Tigers: The Rise and Growth of the Software Industry in Brazil, China, India, Ireland, and Israel*, 7–40 (Oxford: Oxford University Press).

———. 2005b. "The Indian Software Industry and Its Evolving Service Capability," *Industrial and Corporate Change* 14(3):393–418.

———. 2006. "Entrepreneurship in the Indian Software Industry." Unpublished manuscript, Brunel University Business School.

Athreye, Suma and Mike Hobday. 2006. "Overcoming Development Adversity: Entrepreneurs Led Development in India." Unpublished manuscript.

Balakrishnan, Pulpure. 2006. "Benign Neglect or Strategic Intent? Contested Lineage of Indian Software Industry," *Economic and Political Weekly* (September 9): 3866–72.

Bessen, James and Robert M. Hunt. 2004. "An Empirical Look at Software Patents." Working Paper 03–17/R, *Research on Innovation.*

Bresnahan, Timothy and Shane Greenstein. 1996. "Technical Progress in Computing and in the Uses of Computers," *Brookings Papers on Economic Activity; Microeconomics*: 1–78.

Bresnitz, Dan. 2005. "The Israeli Software Industry," in Ashish Arora and Alfonso Gambardella, eds., *From Underdogs to Tigers: The Rise and Growth of the Software Industry in Brazil, China, India, Ireland, and Israel*, 72–99 (Oxford: Oxford University Press).

Brooks, Frederick. 1995. *The Mythical Man-Month: Essays on Software Engineering—20th Anniversary Edition* (Boston: Addison-Wesley).

Campbell-Kelly, Martin. 2003. *From Airline Reservations to Sonic the Hedgehog: A History of the Software Industry* (Cambridge, MA: MIT Press).

Copeland, Duncan G. and James L. McKenney. 1988. "Airline Reservations Systems: Lessons from History," *MIS Quarterly* 12(3):353–70.

D'Costa, Anthony. 2003. "Uneven and Combined Development: Understanding India's Software Exports," *World Development* 31(1):211–26.

Dossani, Rafiq. 2006. "Globalization and the Outsourcing of Services: The Impact of Indian Offshoring," in Susan M. Collins and Lael Brainard, eds., *Offshoring White-Collar Work* (Washington, D.C.: Brookings Institution Press).

General Accounting Office, United States. 2005. "U.S. and India Data on Offshoring Show Significant Differences." GAO Report GAO-06–116 (Washington, D.C.: GPO).

Graham, Stuart J. H. and David C. Mowery. 2003. "Intellectual Property Protection in the U.S. Software Industry," in W. M. Cohen and S. A. Merrill, eds., *Patents in the Knowledge-Based Economy*, 219–58 (Washington, D.C.: National Academies Press).

Hall, Bronwyn H. and Megan MacGarvie. 2006. "The Private Value of Software Patents." NBER working paper 12195.

Hausmann, R. and D. Rodrik. 2002. "Economic Development as Self Discovery," *Journal of Development Economics* 72:603–33.

Heeks, Richard. 1996. *India's Software Industry: State Policy, Liberalization and Industrial Development* (Delhi: Sage Publications).

———. 1998. "India's Uneven Software Exports." Working Paper, IDPM, University of Manchester.

Herbsleb, James D., Daniel J. Paulish, and Matthew Bass. 2005. "Global Software Development at Siemens: Experience from Nine Projects." International Conference on Software Engineering, St. Louis, MO.

Ilavarasan, P. Vigneswara. 2006. "R&D in Indian Software Industry," in Roli Varma, ed., *Managing Industrial Research Effectively*, 134–43 (Bangalore: ICFAI University Press).

Kapur, Devesh. 2001. "Diasporas and Technology Transfer," *Journal of Human Development* 2(2):265–86.

———. 2002. "The Causes and Consequences of India's IT Boom," *India Review* 1(2):91–110.

Kapur, Davesh and John McHale. 2005. "Sojourns and Software: Internationally Mobile Human Capital and High-Tech Industry Development in India, Ireland, and Israel," in Ashish Arora and Alfonso Gambardella, eds., *From Underdogs to Tigers: The Rise and Growth of the Software Industry in Brazil, China, India, Ireland, and Israel,* 236–74 (Oxford: Oxford University Press).

Olson, G. M. and J. S. Olson. 2000. "Distance Matters," *Human-Computer Interaction* 15(2&3):139–78.

Parthasarathy, Balaji and Yuko Aoyama. 2006. "From Software Services to R&D Services: Local Entrepreneurship in the Software Industry in Bangalore, India," *Environment and Planning* 38(7):1269–85.

Panagariya, Arvind. 2007. Why India Lags behind China and How It Can Bridge the Gap," *The World Economy* 30(2):229–48.

Sands, Anita. 2005. "The Irish Software Industry," in Ashish Arora and Alfonso Gambardella, eds., *From Underdogs to Tigers: The Rise and Growth of the Software Industry in Brazil, China, India, Ireland, and Israel,* 41–71 (Oxford: Oxford University Press).

Schware, Robert. 1992. "Software Industry Entry Strategies for Developing Countries: A 'Walking on Two Legs' Proposition," *World Development* 20(2):143–64. (New York: Pergamon Press).

Srinivasan, T. N. 2005. "Information-Technology-Enabled Services and India's Growth Prospects," in Susan M. Collins and Lael Brainard, eds., *Offshoring White-Collar Work,* 203–31 (Washington, D.C.: Brookings Institution Press).

Thoma, Grid and Salvatore Torrisi. 2006. "The Evolution of the Software Industry in Europe." Working Paper, CESPRI, Bocconi University.

Treffler, Dan. 2005. "Service Offshoring: Threats and Opportunities," in Susan M. Collins and Lael Brainard, eds., *Offshoring White-Collar Work,* 35–60 (Washington, D.C.: Brookings Institution Press).

Tschang, Ted and Lan Xue. 2005. "The Chinese Software Industry," in Ashish Arora and Alfonso Gambardella, eds., *From Underdogs to Tigers: The Rise and Growth of the Software Industry in Brazil, China, India, Ireland, and Israel,* 171–206 (Oxford: Oxford University Press).

COMMENT

Frank Levy

Several years ago, I had an email exchange with a Motorola engineer. A reporter had quoted my guess that while routine programming work was going offshore, the software architecture would stay here. The engineer introduced himself by saying that he had worked in the Peace Corps in Tibet and was sympathetic to developing countries' aspirations. Nonetheless, he thought that they posed a real threat to our scientific infrastructure. He said my distinction between programmers and software architects was based on a false analogy with the construction industry. In construction, bricklayers rarely became architects. But most software architects began as programmers, and so whatever tasks the Indian software industry was then doing, they would be competing with us at all levels soon enough.

Ashish Arora's excellent chapter argues that this threat to comparative advantage from the Indian software industry has been overstated. I find much of his argument convincing, but I don't think that the situation is quite as sanguine for the United States as he makes it sound. After briefly summarizing his argument, I will give a slightly different interpretation of his findings.

At the outset, every offshored activity must overcome the same cognitive limitation: all information is inherently ambiguous and we process information by imposing a context on it. When people don't share the same context, misunderstandings can arise. Every parent of a college-age child understands this: your child emails you describing the tattoos that he or she is going to get. You can pray that the child is joking, but you are by no means sure.

It was this context problem that Dick Murnane and I had in mind when we argued several years ago that the work most easily offshored was very similar to the work most easily computerized; in both kinds of work, the required information processing could be expressed in rules. Without rules, you are dealing with one special case after another. With rules, all cases can be processed with one standard operating procedure—and so you face the context problem only once, to learn that procedure.

Much professional work, by contrast, involves a series of special cases, where problems are solved through experience and tacit knowledge. At a minimum, this raises the bar for all new entrants to demonstrate that they can do the work.

Arora's excellent description of the global software industry shows the importance of both rule-based and what I have called professional work. Programming itself, of course, is a system of rules, and it is these rules—the fact that everyone studies from the same books—that helped India get into the game in the first place. Smita Srinivas, one of our Ph.D. students who recently joined the Columbia faculty, found that international standards for generic drugs helped India in a similar way to enter the pharmaceutical industry. But, as Arora points out, coding is a tool that is used in three main contexts:

- The design and development of shrink-wrapped products that we all use.
- The custom programming activities that create applications for specific customers.
- The general set of programming activities within user firms themselves.

As Arora explains, India has found it hard to break into the first and second segments. With respect to the shrink-wrapped segment, he argues that it is hard to develop innovative products from a distance where you cannot understand the potential user context. With respect to the custom-programming segment, he argues that it is hard to tailor good applications from a distance, where you cannot understand the day-to-day routines of the user organizations. Thus, up to this point, Indian firms have concentrated more on the third segment, leaving the others for the United States and preserving much of what we see as the U.S. comparative advantage. Based on this conclusion, the Motorola engineer had nothing to worry about.

In practice, however, these obstacles may be more temporary than Arora suggests. Japanese performance in the U.S. auto and electronic markets suggests that it is possible ultimately to understand new products that can sell in another country. To be sure, it requires organizations with employees located on both sides of the water. As the chapter describes, some Indian software entrepreneurs are already working in this way. In our own work on the Indian radiology industry, Indian firms have moved radiologists to London to get certified through the British system—something they largely cannot do here—and learn the details of the British industry in order to successfully bid for work. Beyond Indian firms per se, Arora also describes multinationals like IBM that can sell work in this country while doing much of the coding in India. As he notes, managing multination products is no easy job, but Indian firms have learned to do it out of necessity. Presumably other firms will learn, as well.

There is, in addition, a threat to comparative advantage that is implicit in the Motorola engineer's warning. If "simple" work increasingly gets sent offshore, there will ultimately be fewer entry-level positions. And if all software architects do begin as programmers, we will be cutting off the pipeline for future architects. In our radiologist work, both British and Singaporean senior radiologists have argued about the difficulty of training if simple cases begin to go offshore. Of course, if much of the simple work goes offshore, we will also be losing many of the so called "spin-off jobs" that make us value the comparative advantage in the first place.

Short-term trends in this area are full of noise—the rapid falloff of computer science majors at MIT has much to do with the dramatic buildup of these majors in the late 1990s when all students believed that they could be millionaires by age twenty-two. But it is clear that when a firm like Microsoft both expands its Indian presence and bemoans the limited number of U.S. students opting for science and math careers, they are sending very mixed messages.

My comments have only scratched the surface of this chapter. Arora has insightful discussions of the how the industry grew; the unintended role of government educational policies; the somewhat more intentional role of private educational institutions; and the factors like infant industry protection that did not play any role in industry growth.

CHAPTER 5

India: Past, Present, and Future

Jagdish Bhagwati, Arvind Panagariya, Ronen Sen, Arun Shourie, Frank Wisner

PART I: OPENING PANEL (EDITED TRANSCRIPTION)

Arvind Panagariya (Moderator)

Our distinguished group of commentators will focus on two issues. First, they will discuss Indian's economy: it's past performance and future prospects. In the second part, we turn to U.S.-India relations: past, present, and future. For the first part, Jagdish Bhagwati and Arun Shourie will offer remarks and Ambassadors Ronen Sen and Frank Wisner will serve as commentators.

Then, for the second part, we will reverse the rolls, with Ambassador Sen and Ambassador Wisner giving principal remarks and Professor Bhagwati and Mr. Shourie offering brief comments.

Turning to the first part of the program, economics, I note that after performing poorly for much of the three and a half decades after independence, the Indian economy has started to grow. The Indian economy's growth, on an ongoing basis, has been 6 percent per annum since the late 1980s; but in the last three years, actually, the growth rate has picked up to about 8 percent, giving some credence to the claim that India is the next emerging giant after China. Professor Bhagwati will first discuss what went wrong in the past, what has now been done right, and the lessons that India provides for sustained development of other countries around the world.

INDIA'S ECONOMIC PERFORMANCE: PAST, PRESENT, AND FUTURE

Jagdish Bhagwati

I will begin these observations by putting some of the relevant issues into perspective. There are two perspectives that can be illuminating. One is exclusively Indian; the other is across a broader range of experience with development.

INDIAN PERSPECTIVE

The Indian policy framework that had taken root by the end of the 1950s, when the Second Five Year Plan was reaching its end, was characterized by two major drawbacks: It was fearful of outward economic integration, and it preferred an inward looking trade policy and restrictions on inward foreign investment. Markets were restricted through (i) reservations for the public sector, which was to be steadily expanded beyond public utilities; and (ii) extensive Kafkaesque controls on production, composition of production, investment, and trade.

This was a policy framework guaranteed to produce slow growth; and we did get abysmally low growth rates until the reforms started. In turn, a stagnant economy failed to draw the poor into gainful employment—so poverty continued to grow. As many of us, including Professor T. N. Srinivasan, have noted repeatedly: Indian poverty grew not because the strategy of increasing growth was the wrong one but because our policy framework failed to deliver growth. Also, we have stressed, it is nonsensical to maintain that the Indian planners were not concerned with poverty reduction. I myself worked in the Planning Commission in the very early 1960s (on my return from abroad) on how to bring the bottom 30 percent of the population up to minimum living standards; and the title of Chapter 1 of my 1966 book on *The Economics of Underdeveloped Countries*, reflecting my experience, is "Poverty and Income Distribution"; it contains, years ahead of its time, a picture of a malnourished child.

The problem to stress was that slow growth rates meant that there was no direct impact on poverty through employment; and the slow growth of revenues, in a relatively stagnant economy, meant that increase in the social spending on health and education (which were also central to the

Nehru government's concerns) was handicapped by revenue constraints that kicked in alongside the other political-economy factors that need to be brought to bear in a fuller analysis. When, in the late 1960s, Professor Padma Desai and I wrote our book critiquing this lethal framework, there was palpable distress. Now celebrated, the book was decried in India at the time.

Yet, I must say that when the present Prime Minister (who had written a brilliant dissertation refuting the pessimism about India's export potential) used the 1991 payments crisis to begin the reforms, and then to sustain them, while the BJP government took them further still, we were delighted. It is clear now that the reforms have paid off. Growth has accelerated; and poverty, rural and urban, has declined. However, it is clear that, as I noted in my Radhakrishnan Lectures, published in 1993 by Clarendon Press as *India in Transition*, reforming the entire complex of bad policies is like cleaning up after a hurricane. The Prime Minister started bravely in 1991, and by now we have had a gigantic reduction in the external tariffs on manufactures. There is more flexibility in the exchange rate, so we are not plagued by overvaluation. Many of the restrictions on direct foreign investment are less bothersome than before, and the controls on domestic investment and production have largely been removed. Our growth rate has remained high in a sustained fashion, even accelerating in the last few years toward, but still stands below the two-digit figure that China has. There are a few holdouts who argue skeptically that the acceleration of the growth rate owes little to the reforms; but, against them, there are more compelling empirical studies that show the opposite.

The real challenges now are twofold. First, can the Congress Party deliver on the reforms that are stalled? In particular, can they privatize (an issue that Arun Shourie will address), and how far can we go, if at all, in the matter of labor-market reforms that would introduce some obligations and not just rights for workers and that would be more compatible with an element of flexibility? The success of the Prime Minister up until now in getting things moving in these directions appears to have been limited.

It is tempting to think that the alliance with the communists is at the heart of this problem. But the recent attempt at a minuscule privatization that was not even real privatization was sabotaged by the alliance partner, the DMK (Dravida Munnetra Kazhagam), not by the communists, showing the complexity of alliance politics. Besides, I suspect that the real problem lies within the Congress Party itself. The second President Bush made the mistake of surrounding himself with the unsatisfied hawks (led by Dick Cheney and Donald Rumsfeld) from the first President Bush's cabinet. The men who gather around Mrs. Sonia Gandhi, and detract from the reforms, appear to be the displaced socialists who went out of favor with the reforms starting in 1991.

But why are they so influential? The answer seems to lie in the assumption of the present Congress administration (which succeeded beyond its wildest dreams in the last election) that they won because the BJP had neglected the rural sector and the rural poor; and that, therefore, populist policies, rather than further reforms, will pay off politically. But this is too facile an assumption. For, as Professor Panagariya and I argued in the *Wall Street Journal*, as soon as the election results arrived, the poor had benefited from the reforms—as the decline in rural poverty demonstrated. Whereas they had suffered before from what we call the Non-Revolution of Falling Expectations—as long as bad policies produced little growth and therefore few benefits for the poor, they kept voting for the incumbents because of a spirit of fatalism—the situation changed as soon as the reforms began to deliver results for them. We now have the classic Revolution of Rising Expectations, or what we called the Revolution of Perceived Possibilities. Where Oliver Twist asked for more and got less, universal suffrage in democratic India ensured that they could now ask for more and turn the incumbents out of office.

Second, if this is true, unsustainable and occasionally corruption-prone populist "quasi-socialist" measures to win future elections is not really the answer. The aroused masses are now looking for "results"; these results have to be delivered. Thus, we must really push for the further reforms that are overdue. We must also examine whether the National Employment Rural Guarantee Act (NERGA) makes sense, and whether it is pro-poor as it appears superficially to be. And we must question whether the quotas being placed on admissions to the IITs (Indian Institutes of Technology) to reserve a large fraction of places for the backward classes will really improve the growth process and alleviate poverty.

BROADER PERSPECTIVE

In conclusion, let me say that if we manage to sustain the reforms, we are poised to reap even greater rewards than we have had so far. The broader historical experience shows that three elements make for big success in achieving sustained development:

- openness to the world economy (chiefly on trade and inward equity investment)
- economic freedom—that is, a judicious use of markets to achieve goals (e.g., the use of tradable permits to achieve environmental objectives)
- political freedom—that is, democracy (which goes beyond elections to reach out to include the underprivileged such as women and minorities).

This is a powerful developmental cocktail, made of three potent liqueurs. Countries such as the Soviet Union and North Korea, which had none of these three policies, had growth rates that were high for almost fifteen years, but then the long decline set in. India has had political freedom, but shot itself in the foot with regard to the other two elements; and her reforms have shown that the joint force of all three elements really is taking us to a new high, with no end in sight. The only regret I have is that we lost over three decades before shifting gears.

Arvind Panagariya

Arun Shourie was personally very successful at privatization and the BJP in particular in moving these reforms forward. As Bhagwati indicated, the reforms now have been a bit stalled; to the point that now they appear to be almost at a standstill. So within that context, I pose three questions. First of all, as privatization minister, what obstacles to privatization did you face? How were you so successful in nevertheless privatizing? And what do you think has been the impact of that privatization? Second, why have the reforms been stalled? Is privatization entirely shelved now? And, finally, why did the growth rate in the last three years accelerate from 6 to 8 percent in spite of a standstill on the reforms? In that context, what are the future economic prospects for India?

Arun Shourie Remarks

To begin with, I think the answer to your last question as to why the country has continued to grow even though the reforms have come to a stop was best provided by the great Indian lawyer Nani Palkhivala. He used to say that it takes a great deal of genius to keep India down, but our governments have it.

How did this all come about? In the end, the hand of government was lifted and a weak and confused political class, still caught in the cobwebs of socialism and other things, at last did the obviously right thing. Therefore, in that first two and a half years of Mr. Narasimha Rao's period and then Mr. Vajpayee's period, sufficient space has been created for Indian society to grow on its own. This is a good thing, but it also shows the potential limits that will come about since minimal functions are required and not all of society has been liberated. Even when it has been liberated, governments in India have to do a great deal.

So that Ambassador Ronen Sen does not take me to task, let me first recall that India is growing really fast. We hear, for instance, of services, but manufacturing itself has been completely reinvented on the shop floor in large part, even in the textile industry, even in Gujarat, where because of protective measures we had not done much. I feel that Indian agricultural growth is underreported, and certainly the alacrity of the Indian farmer in adopting new processes is just not looked at. For instance, when new seeds where introduced in Punjab, we used to have a black market in each new seed. People would pay bribes to the irrigation minister to get the water released in time for them. Similarly, the government for the last two years has been deliberating on what to do about Bt cotton, but the firms in agrochemicals tell me that the demand for their products is going down so rapidly that today almost 40 percent of the acreage and the cotton is in Bt cotton. In other words, society is already far ahead of the government. One of the good things that has happened is that this space has been created, so that if you were to speak to Indian industrialists, you would hear only confidence. They are growing and acquiring: in the last ten years they acquired nearly 250 firms outside of India. In Great Britain this year, India is the second largest foreign investor. Last year, the acquisitions into Britain were seventy-six firms acquired by Indian firms. This demonstrates that there is great potential and that we have just begun to scratch the surface. But this being said, there is no doubt that the momentum of reforms, as Professor Bhagwati discussed, have almost come to a standstill. In two sectors, civil aviation and railways, reform is still going ahead. In addition, there is some investment in different types of infrastructure: ports, airports, highways, although this has slowed down, it will continue. But this is not going to be enough. For instance, power-sector reforms have come to a complete standstill. They have not actually gotten off. This has already been a constraint and will become a much bigger constraint in the next three to four years.

Privatization has been completely stopped and all the feeble attempts that were made by the Prime Minister and Finance Minister have been squashed by one group or the other, and this in the face of all evidence. In the two and a half to three years that I was in charge of privatization, by selling just 1.6 percent of government equity we were able to raise $9 billion. That triggered the stock market to go from 3,000 to 13,000. People began to realize that there is this money. What has happened since then? The production in these privatized firms has increased from 30 percent to 250 percent, as in Paradip Phosphates. Profits after taxes have zoomed, therefore revenues have zoomed, therefore modernization and expansion plans have also zoomed—for example, 3,000 crores in Maruti, 5,000 crores in Belco for expansion. No one has to wait for government decisions. In the case of another captive power plant to be put up by Belco, the arguing over whether to put it up, or not to put it up, and the deciding to put it up, took seven years. Now they don't have to wait. Within two years they have set up a plant. However, in the face of all this evidence, the reforms have now stopped, in spite of the Prime Minister's and the Finance Minister's support. Three quarters of the forty-seven companies that we privatized were experiencing losses and had been experiencing losses for so many years that their networks had been completely eroded; and yet, with privatization, they were able to improve.

In the face of all that evidence, if the reforms are stopped that means that there will be no funds for infrastructure development. This means that you will not be able to unleash the productive capacity that inheres in these enterprises; you will not be able to increase the wages and allowances within these companies, because under government rules, when they are sick, you cannot revise wages. In the companies that were privatized, wages and allowances have gone up nearly 25–30 percent within the last two years. Good money will continue to be thrown after bad money, which has happened in ITI and other companies (because it was in Mrs. Sonia Gandhi's constituency)—for example, 700 crores there and another 400 crores there. This will also lead to fewer resources available for the future. In banking, in spite of the finance minister's effort, neither the consolidation of banks nor the reform of cooperative banks nor government equity being brought down to 33 percent will change this. In addition, a sudden conservativeness in allowing banks to open new branches has developed. This applies to both Indian and foreign banks; even one of the largest banks in India, ICICI, is having difficulties getting permission. I have personally been very surprised at agricultural reforms being stopped because I had thought that with Sharad Pawar (Food and Agriculture Union Minister) we would really advance. There has been a reversal in many respects. We have struggled very hard—Jaswant Singh and Yashwant Sinha as finance ministers struggled very hard to dismantle the administrative price mechanism in the petroleum sector because government was fixing prices; fixing petrol or diesel price was such a big political issue that you could not raise the prices. Now, with displaced socialists back, the prevailing opinion is that government will fix these things and the common man must be protected. The result is that last year oil companies reported a loss of 42,000 crores. This year the estimated loss will be 100,000 crores. This also leads to less for infrastructure, and therefore difficulties in growth for tomorrow.

Now, why did this happen? Everything turns on the Prime Minister. We should not merely go on the reputation of the Prime Minister as being a reformer. Academics, because of their personal friendships, are often misled by this. In the end, will a person stake everything on an issue, on a step that he or she has taken? During Prime Minister Atal Behari Vajpayee's time in office there were many times that the government could have been brought down even by RSS people, but Vajpayee forced the issue and said no, this will just be done. You want to tell your people to vote against me, then let them vote tomorrow. I was personally present on those occasions. So everything turns first on the Prime Minister.

Secondly, do not wait for consensus. The consensus in practice on these matters in India is that there is no other idea. But there will never be a consensus in words. Therefore, you cannot be too considerate. One must act in the confidence that these are the best steps for India now, and we will do them now. Five years later or even ten years later, there will be a consensus around the new configuration that will be brought about by these actions. However, since nobody knows for certain (including politicians who don't know the impact of a particular measure), everyone can be frightened.

Professor Bhagwati remarks on the question of reforms and their impact on elections. It has everything to do with the internal condition of the political parties. If neglected rural development really gave the boost to the Congress, how is it that the votes by the Congress fell by 6 percent in the election? Congress won, but their votes fell by 6 percent. If desperate rural masses were turning to the Congress, it would not fall. Additionally, in Punjab, these same reforms yielded positive results for the Akalis (Shiromani Akali Dal) and the BJP. In neighboring Haryana it wiped them out. How is it that reforms yield very good results for the BJP in Rajasthan, Madhya Pradesh, and Chhattisgarh, yet it is wiped out in Uttar Pradesh and Orissa? How is it that it does so well in Gujarat and does not do well in Maharashtra? You take one simple thing that has nothing to do with the reforms, but politicians do not realize it because they do not know that for any hypothesis, the exposed factor is *wealth*. Take the decision of the senior leaders of the government at that time not to continue the alliance with the DMK. The DMK had never given any difficulty to this coalition. Yet, that single decision meant a difference of sixty seats, because twenty-nine seats that should have gone to one coalition went to another coalition. What does that have to do with reforms? It caused this type of government to come about and not that type of coalition. The fact of the matter is that nobody knows. In India we do not have cross-verification mechanisms for information, or ways to count these hypotheses. Therefore, you believe anything and do these things that will cost the country a lot, such as the populist measures that Dr. Bhagwati discusses above.

The first obstacle to change and reform is incumbents, including existing ministers. It is their empire also. I have seen that Indian industry's core competence as developed during the License Raj was how to use the state apparatus to prevent competition from coming in. This has continued. There is a comfort level vis-à-vis the government that they don't want to change. It can be a great advantage to have a public sector unit that is inefficient in their sector; then that unit will ensure that government will continue to allow rises in prices and these industries will increase profits. The third problem really is that they have great access to several types of persons in public life. In privatization, a big member of parliament at that time—right now a very aggressive minister—produced a forged letter of the cabinet secretary. The forgery was proven on the floor of the House. But a rival, who wanted to prevent disinvestment of Air India, was able to get it past him and read it out in Parliament. It was a complete forgery, that the cabinet secretary by his signature was opposing government policy.

Then there is the problem of discourse. The nature of the discourse in India is that it has really been dumbed down to such a significant extent that it does not go beneath the slogan. So if you shout that national security is in danger, Singapore Airlines is a front for the Chinese, this is a serious proposition put in the Parliament. And the media does not help.

If, for example, Arvind Panagariya and I differ on any issue, journalists will go to Arvind and question him on a particular matter. Are you for it or against it? If he is for it, then they will go to me and ask my views in brief. I am against it. Okay, balanced story, all sides given, perfect neutrality between the arsonist and the fire fighter. Any negation can be used to stop a reform or tarnish any prospective bidder.

The least problem we had was from labor, because they knew the conditions of the enterprises, especially after the first few privatizations took place. They saw the benefits that were occurring. The difficulties that arose were because all of our national trade unions are linked to one particular party or the other. Therefore, the communists in the Congress Party in Belco and the communists in Nelco were able to organize extensive strikes that cost 200–300 crores to the new bidders. This was also compounded by, and is still true with today's reforms, a political culture in which, if I am in office, you will oppose anything I do, even if what I am doing is what you were doing before. When I go into opposition, then whatever you do, even if it is opposite of what you were doing, I will oppose it. For example, Mr. Bharenshat said in a budget speech in February that we will amend labor laws. In October, there was a discussion on the economy, so Dr. Palaniappan Chidambaram, our distinguished Finance Minister, said that this government does not know and is not clear; since it has not moved forward on its claim to amend the labor laws, no proposal has even come forward. My response was that while, at this point, the government may not be completely clear in its mind yet, but I am completely clear. So if you permit, I will now start reading these clauses in the Indian labor law that need to be amended. Please tell me by voice vote if you are for it or against it. If you are for it, then I will go with folded hands to the Prime Minister in the evening and request that he allow these agreed-upon changes, as everyone is for it. Okay, clause 5c, it reads this way, for this reason it should be this. Everyone starts shouting: "Oh no, he breaks the strike!"; "He kicks the stomach of the poor!" So, I say, okay then, not 5c, 7d—it is this way and for this reason should be this. I went through seven such clauses, and each time I was shouted down. Then I told them what I was reading, it was the Congress government party of Maharashtra's industry resolution. So when I read it for them, they shouted me down. When the poor Maharashtra government had passed the resolution, the BJP in the Vidhan Sabha stopped the Maharashtra government for two days. And we question why China is going ahead. This is a political culture which is inimical to reforms, and it is still happening today.

In conclusion, this is now our most systemic problem. The electorate has gotten completely splintered and this has meant a splintered legislature. In the Lok Sabha today we have forty-six political parties. That has meant splintered coalitions: the last coalition, this coalition, twenty-five parties—of course, two of them are the same as in the last time. The result is that everyone has the power to block everything, and nobody has enough power to push anything though. Splintering is also devastating because 98.8 percent of the legislators in the Lok Sabha have been elected on a minority vote. About 60 percent have been elected with less than 35 percent of the vote. There is a large block of legislators who have been elected with just about 15 percent of the vote. The incentive is to stop, frighten, and cajole some caste or some 15 percent of the population to get elected, and then it is a lottery. Leaders come about and yet are not very well known outside of their states. In India there are two types of leaders: some state leaders and some stateless leaders. Now everyone is a stateless leader, so now everyone can get through this lottery. This is no way to have a ruling class that is purposeful, focused, can execute things, and can sustain policies for some time. It is no way to select rulers for a billion people. Today we are getting governments of sixty to seventy ministers. I tell you, in any government not more than six or seven of them are persons you would employ as your research assistants.

Therefore, the real prospect for India to unleash its unlimited potential rests on two things. One is to continue to reduce the role of the state; but as the state has to perform certain minimal functions, it has to make great strategic choices, in economics and in other fields. So, secondly, a certain level of competence is required, and we must move toward a presidential system (which is a separate subject). This way you reduce the link between the constituent and the elected representative, between the executive and the legislature; and, in the selection of the executive, you are not confined to select from the legislature itself—a separate subject, probably unlikely at this moment. But I continue to have great faith in breakdowns. In 1991 a breakdown saw us into reforms. Judging by the way governance is evaporating in many parts of the country, I am quite confident that we will live up to the saying in psychology that "every breakdown is a breakthrough."

Ronen Sen Comments

Today's theme of "India: past, present and future" strikes me as a very useful way to understand different aspects of India, its policies, and how each aspect or facet affects the other. This goes back to our civilizational heritage, which, in a sense, is not frozen in time and place but is reflected in the way we live, the way we think, and the way we act, and also in our identity as individuals and as a nation. But, as far as the economic aspects go, it is true that, as Mr. Shourie put it so well, the ability or the genius of our governments keeps India down. What we are unleashing today is India's strength of the past. It was innovation, constant questioning, debate, and dissent. The first time privatization was called "privatization," it was also called "disinvestment," which I think we have gone back to now. You never change policy because change is very disturbing, actually downright subversive, I would say, in the view of many. So you do not change policy, you "rationalize" policy. In a sense, looking back even to the distant past, the more recent past, and the present, I agree that we should go back to the past to realize our potential for the future.

Today, what we have done is proven that democracy and development, federal democracy and development, with devolution, are inseparable. There is a social aspect to it that we must take some account of—but not sloganeering, as Mr. Shourie rightly pointed out. There is also another fact, which is that democracy and market reforms are also inseparable. And that has yet to sink in. I, of course, was a part of the system in government, not as a politician but part of the other category of permanent civil servants, which one of my good friends, Sam Pirtroda, referred to as "Draculas." I asked him why "Draculas" (I wasn't offended, because after all I am a retired "Dracula"). He said, "because you can't stand the light." I think there are less and less of those "Draculas." I have had the pleasure of hosting Mr. Shourie in different places, for example in Berlin. He would have seen in the new embassy that we have there, which is the only Indian sandstone building in all of Europe, that the business center is right in the center of that building. This is illustrative of what we have been endeavoring to do in our embassy and in all the Consulates General in this country, to try to give more of an economic ballast to our relationship with the United States. I also would like to say that if you have to do something, you might as well do it. And one thing I found was that even when we had revolving door governments—when I was in Moscow for six years we had four prime ministers in Russia and four prime ministers in India—governments came and went, but no one really went back on decisions and no one changed decisions taken. Before I came here to the United States, I found there was an aberration in this regard, which was the Enron case. That contract with Enron was before the elections in the state of Maharashtra; and then, after the elections, there was a change in the position of the new state government. One of the first things I tried to do was to get over that legacy issue and see that the contract was honored. I would say this approach is the best approach. Rather than thinking about some decisions by asking how the future will judge us, and how it will play out in certain elections, if you believe a thing is good, just get on with it; because so far, we have never reversed our past decisions.

And finally, one comment on Professor Bhagwati's remarks, which is vitally important: we must never lose sight of the fact that the most important investment, apart from infrastructure, is that of education—primary education with the focus on educating female children. Health and nutrition are also very important elements. We talk about food self-sufficiency. But malnutrition in India is on a scale witnessed in very few parts of the world, except perhaps in Sub-Saharan Africa. And we have to contend with that. Rural infrastructure, for instance, just building a road connecting every Indian village to the nearest marketplace, is important. From then on you will have Indian and foreign companies taking products to the next stage of processing. But these are areas where no private-sector company is going to invest. These are areas where we need public spending. And for that to become possible, we will have to move ourselves out from areas and sectors that we are in today. This is one of the principal reasons why I am so active in trying to promote the India-U.S. civil nuclear cooperation agreement. I emphasize *trying* to promote, as it is not successful yet. We have the nuclear technologies, but do we have the money? Do we have the money to invest in these long gestation projects which will be in operation over forty years, and will not be profitable for at least fifteen years, to put upfront those billions of dollars of investment? And at what cost? It will be at the cost of the important areas I touched upon. Therefore, we will need private-sector involvement in the commercial production of nuclear power, which the nuclear agreement would hopefully facilitate.

Frank Wisner Comments

I will not even attempt to rise to the occasion of matching the eloquence and insights into the Indian economy you have heard this evening. Rather, I will take a few minutes and think out loud with you from the perspective of American business, for we are India's largest investor and we will certainly continue to be in that fortunate position for some time to come. As a businessman it is clear to me and throughout the business community in this country, that there is a spreading realization that India is growing; the numbers are real, and it is certain that Indian growth is broadly based and that it is promising. Most importantly, growth is based on the private sector, and that private sector–driven growth and business-driven growth have been the most important factors in the last ten years in India. And I feel confident that the rate and velocity of growth will continue throughout the rest of this decade and into the next, assuming that there is no extraordinary downturn in the global economy. But will India grow at the rate of China; will we see the same level of performance in the Indian economy? I believe that we will not. India will grow at a respectable rate of growth; she will grow much at the level of nations of Southeast Asia, which is impressive. But she will not achieve Chinese rates of growth for precisely the reasons you have heard this evening. But, given the size of the Indian economy, we investors will find it promising.

Several factors are critical. The first, the Ambassador touched on in the conclusion of his comments: stability of policy. It is largely true that India has not backtracked on her economic policies. But we all have to watch assaults on established policy. The recent debate over telecommunications is something that American businessmen watch very carefully. Can government deliver on its commitments to reform? I think we have heard a very convincing argument tonight that the structure of Indian politics is going to lead to slow delivery of policy, which effects macroeconomic change. We, as businesspeople, want an environment that is competitive. Will India produce an increasingly competitive environment for domestic business and for foreigners? Here my mind turns to the financial sector, to the retail sector, to real estate, as areas that still have to be opened if they are to be competitive. And there is a way to go.

Second, infrastructure, we all know too well and have experienced it. Infrastructure growth in India will be incremental. It will be slow to produce the infrastructural basis of an economy and transportation. It will come, but it will come very slowly.

Third, the deficit. It is important to all of us as businesspeople to make certain that the money markets are not crowded with government debts.

Fourth, I cannot help but agree with the ambassador, as well, that the provision of skilled labor is a critical, important step that policy can address and has to be directed as a principally government undertaking. Wage rates are very important in India. Availability of skilled labor in critical sectors including information technology is critical, and supply is not keeping pace with demand.

And, finally, business has a stake and watches India's ability to match its words with deeds in the alleviation of poverty. Poverty alleviation is exactly what companies like my own need if we are to expand into asset management, consumer finance, savings, and the mobilization of wealth throughout the country. Poverty alleviation is good for business, it is good for foreigners and it is good for India.

PART II: INDIA–U.S. RELATIONS

Arvind Panagariya

One characterization of the relations of the 1960s, 70s, and 80s between India and the United States is that the Americans liked to lecture the Indians and Indians liked to lecture Americans, with neither side being interested in what the other had to say. That has changed. The two largest democracies in the world are now warming up to each other, and there is a lot of cooperation in a variety of different dimensions. Even a nuclear understanding is being negotiated. And so in that context, Ambassador Sen will begin by examining how this change has come about, and what the future prospects are for continued relations.

Ronen Sen Remarks

Returning to the theme of "India: past, present and future," there again I will just refer briefly to the fact that our civilizational heritage, our independence movement, very much influences our foreign policy. In fact, there is a very artificial division between foreign policy and domestic policy, because our own emphasis as diplomats is that you judge your success or failure by the extent to which you have been able to make an impact on the average living standard of our people. For instance, in 1987, when I was working with Mr. Rajiv Gandhi, it was the year of the worst drought of the century; it was the year of the pay commission increase in government salaries; the year we had our troops in Sri Lanka; and we had some Chinese incursions in Sumdorong Chu Valley. On top of that, there was the possibility that we would have AWACS aircraft supplied to Pakistan by the United States. People knew about how much the drought cost us, and what the increase in government wages cost us. But they did not know about the possible cost of the things that didn't happen. What didn't happen was much bigger. The aircraft were not supplied. Many things happen in diplomacy that are non-events but nevertheless affect our economy. The events in 1987 led us to an evaluation of a move forward. Following Rajiv Gandhi's visit to China, for instance, we had a few military movements. For instance, a brigade moving just a few miles away from the mountainous border areas; people did not realize that such movements of a few miles meant savings of hundreds of thousands, that for instance the cost of chapattis (Indian bread) at places of high altitude could cost as much as twenty to twenty-five times in rupees what it cost elsewhere at that particular time. The domestic economic implications of foreign policy initiatives are not always fully appreciated.

Talking of the past, I also want to say that there is a misconception that relations were bad during the Cold War period, and India was seen as leaning toward the Soviet Union; and then, after the end of the Cold War and the fall of the Berlin wall, everything was hunky dory, the problem had gone away, and there is no reason why these two democracies (India and the United States) could not realize the potential of their relationship. It sounds very nice, but it is not actually true. In the mid- and late-1980s, at the height of the Cold War, we had several things that happened that people didn't realize. The first supercomputer that went to any non-NATO country went to India. You had General Electric supplying engines for our light combat aircraft. You had Defense Secretaries Weinberger and Carlucci visiting India within a period of eight months. You had the first science and technology agreement permitting dual-use technologies being imported (by India). These are just some examples; I could go on. In fact, after the Cold War there was a period of "benign neglect" by both countries. This went on, I would say, until the second term of the Clinton presidency, and moved forward from there. A real watershed was the impact of President Clinton's visit to India in the last year of his second term. And then, right from the moment that President George Bush took over, the relationship changed. The relationship changed because India was no longer perceived through a distorting, blinkered, subregional perspective. It was seen in a larger context, realizing that China is our biggest neighbor, with which we have some territorial issues to be resolved, and that we had some differences on issues of nonproliferation. As a side note, I don't understand what people mean by South Asia; if one is referring to the

Indian subcontinent, then we should say so. Because if you talk of South Asia (only in the context of the Indian Subcontinent), then you ignore the fact that Srinagar is north of Lhasa. People here came close to an understanding of our region after the 2004 tsunami, realizing that Indonesia is sixty nautical miles from India, and that Central Asia is not that far. India is not just a continental country; it is also a maritime country. Some of that started filtering through in Delhi, as well, over the years.

It is from that overall perspective, after a long dialogue, where we had reached an understanding with the United States on the Next Steps in our Strategic Partnership in January 2004. This was truly a breakthrough and envisaged our cooperation in nuclear, space, high-technology issues, and missile defense. Over the past two years, we moved forward in talks of the High Technology Cooperation Group, covering cooperation in nanotechnology, biotechnology, information and communication technology, and now increasingly we are focusing on defense technology. This has been facilitated by the signing last year of the ten-year framework defense cooperation understanding. In science and technology we are moving ahead quite rapidly. In fact, most of our recent initiatives are technology-driven. You take the recently set up Bi-National Science and Technology Commission, the Science and Technology Fund, basically focusing on areas that will have industrial or commercial application. We have launched a Knowledge Initiative on Agriculture, put in about 100 million dollars for the first three years of cooperation, which should hopefully give a major boost to agricultural productivity and also promote corporate linkages. There is also our recently launched Energy Dialogue, covering not just the much-talked-about civil nuclear initiative, which is very, very important, but also several other areas of energy.

In the Economic Dialogue, and particularly the CEO's Forum, what we are stressing over here is exactly what Mr. Shourie remarked with regard to the United Kingdom. From my own experience in the United Kingdom, where I was High Commissioner, people sort of sniggered when I would say you will soon have a day—and it wouldn't be very long, maybe two to three, or at the most four to five years—when Indian investments in the United Kingdom will be equal to British investments in India. I am sure that this can also happen in the context of India and the United States. We also have a long list of things that can be done to facilitate such investments and create jobs in the United States and in India. If Indian investments in the U.S. pick up rapidly, and agreements like the one on civil nuclear cooperation continue to materialize, the implications will be much greater. It will have an impact on investments in high technology, defense cooperation, and other areas where the basic element is in terms of long-term predictability in cooperation. The CEO's Forum has been extremely useful. We have had several visits of CEOs. I keep very close track of that. I can tell you frankly that I have given that a little bit more attention to visits of CEOs than to visits by cabinet secretaries from the United States. In the last few months we have had just about six American companies, solely in the area of information technology, which have announced investments decisions in India of over $13 billion. We also got through an Open Skies Policy agreement with the United States, as Mr. Shourie acknowledged. We had discussions with U.S. airlines on their operations in India. Continental and American Airlines have started direct flights to India. I hope to have more, possibly doubling flights in the next three to four years at the maximum. In the area of air cargo, we have only about four or five cargo aircraft in India, when we should have thousands. We are trying to promote trade and also work to reduce duties. Our exporters pay on an average 25 or 30 percent more in air cargo than they should, and this issue has also to be addressed.

Finally, in all these areas we are both moving forward, and not just in the bilateral field, but in the whole and larger spirit of our relationship. It is a relationship that has changed, because of people in the United States looking at India in a global perspective. We have constant dialogue and prior consultations. There is a "no surprise" approach of what the United States is going to do in our region, whether it is in Central Asia or whether it is vis-à-vis our immediate neighbors. Even if we do not always agree, we are at least aware of what the other nation is doing. We are actively working together on many global issues; issues of environmental concern; with corporate involvement, preventing further spread of HIV and avian flu epidemics; promoting institutions of democracy; cooperation on disaster relief, and a whole heap of other areas—quite apart from our biggest national security concerns such as terrorism and prevention of proliferation of weapons of mass destruction, as well as the worst-case nightmare that we both share: a combination of the two, or nuclear terrorism.

Frank Wisner Remarks

I am delighted to join the Ambassador and other distinguished members of this panel to share a few reflections on the future of the Indian-American relationship. I am a relative neophyte; I began my own reflections in the early part of the 1990s, when President Clinton asked me to go to India and I realized I was up against a terrific challenge. I used the occasion of my nomination to call Cambridge, Massachusetts, and speak to John Kenneth Galbraith, in part because he was a long-standing friend of my family and in part because I was following in his shoes. When I finally got him on the telephone, we started talking and remembered the many times we had been together and the friendship between the two families. Then I came to the point and said, "Professor Galbraith, President Clinton has asked me to go to India and serve as the American Ambassador"—and there was a silence. I thought for a moment that something had happened or he hadn't heard me. I said, "Professor Galbraith, are you there?" And another silence. Then he said, "Frank, welcome to a life sentence." And it is true, the subject of the American-Indian relationship is so extraordinarily absorbing that I found myself, from the beginning of the 1990s to this very day, completely absorbed by it.

It is an extraordinary relationship, and I guess I only half appreciated, over a decade ago, when I joined the fray, what a roller-coaster the relationship had been on and what it would be in the years immediately ahead. I am convinced now that a dramatically important page has been turned in the relationship and it will not be turned back. But it is also worth our remembering, as Ambassador Ronen Sen did, that we do have a history that was not always obliging. We diverged, in fact, almost from the outset, despite the fact that the United States was a strong supporter of Indian independence. Our styles were different, the styles of our leadership. India made a principled commitment to state-driven growth and more socialist orientation in the economy to deal with the huge overhang of poverty. The Pakistan factor entered very quickly and clouded the relationship from the beginning. India's ties to Moscow were ones that led to disagreements: over Vietnam and Afghanistan. But by the end of the 1970s and through the 1980s, for Americans of both political parties and their leaders, there was a sense that India was reflexively opposed to the United States on most issues around the world, and that view was substantially shared by India herself. I don't dwell on this in any morbid manner. There isn't any reason to do so. But it is worthwhile to remember pages in history. When they turn, they don't always turn quickly or fully. If we are to trace the way forward, it is smart to keep a weather eye on the past, in part because nations converge or diverge because they have basic interests that bring them together. But great democracies are also hugely driven by their domestic audiences, and those domestic audiences put great demands on leadership.

Therefore I argue that as we move ahead with this relationship, we do so with sensitivity, understanding, and a degree of caution. Yes, a page turned; you can date it to the late 1980s or early 1990s, take your pick. To me, India at that time needed to expand her external options as the Soviet Union disappeared into history. India needed more mobility on the international scene, and the financial crisis at the time of the Gulf War gave additional impulse to a fresh assessment of Indian domestic and foreign policy options. Washington, in a similar manner and at exactly the same time, had begun to reflect on the troubled world that we would have to deal with after the Cold War, and to look for new allies, to think through our own options again. I am never shy at admitting that the community of Americans of Indian origin also played a huge role in focusing the two governments' attentions on what needed to be done.

The first steps in the early 1990s were wary; I witnessed them personally. They were heavily powered by economics, a sense that there was a terrific market over there with hundreds of millions of buyers of American goods, and American businesses should flock to it. Some of that optimism was also found on the Indian side. By the mid-1990s, however, some realism had settled in that India was not going to change that quickly and it wasn't going to be a snap decision for Americans to find footing. The real change came, in an ironic manner, out of an act over which we both disagreed sharply. The great black cloud over the relationship since the 1970s, the nuclear test in India, caused hostility for a brief period but then actually changed the relationship for the better. For India was newly strengthened in her own sense of her position in the world, her self-regard; and the United States realized it had run its course in trying to hold back India's nuclear capability. Therefore, the way was cleared, not blocked, to find a basis on which to move forward. Thereafter, two other events occurred quite quickly: the Kargil attacks—which gave the United States a chance to prove what it had come to conclude, that our policy toward India would be separate from our policy toward Pakistan and that our interest in India would be the dominant guidepost for United States interest in South Asia; and, second, President Bill Clinton visited. It was a measure of the estrangement that no American president had set foot in India in twenty-five years. It was even truer if you felt that President Jimmy Carter's visit was just a passing event in the evening, and President Dwight Eisenhower's visit is the standard of quality by which a presidential visit to India should be measured. Clinton opened a door that George Bush and the two successive governments in India have filled in an admirable manner. I won't go over the list of accomplishments; Ronen Sen has done that in a splendid way, tying together official policies, defense, security, and economic—the changes not only in economic policy but, most of all, the driving force of business on both sides of the ocean. Suffice it to say that at this point in time, we have seen the high-water mark, to date, but not the end of, the Indian-American relationship.

Ambassador Sen, you are absolutely right that the visit of Prime Minister Singh in July of 2005 and the President's visit to India this year focused heavily on a strategic partnership. They also focused those two visits on the issue of civil nuclear cooperation. I actually admire the work you have done and I regret the pain and suffering of American politics that you have had imposed on you. But I am an optimist. I that believe in the lame-duck session of Congress we will find an agreement in the Senate and a compromise between the bills in the Senate and in the House. We stand a very, very good chance by the end of this year to have completed civil nuclear cooperation, opening a major new chapter in American's life with India and, in my opinion, removing a major impediment to the nature of the relationship that has existed for many years. So I am an optimist. But as I look around the room at those who represent the Indian-American community, I would encourage the audience not to forget to write your representative in Congress sometime between now and early November and let them know that your next vote will matter if they vote the right way on the Indian-American civil nuclear agreement.

But today, the logic of the relationship is deep. That logic starts, in my mind, with the assumption that the shift of the power center of the world has moved from the Atlantic and Europe to Asia, and its epicenter is now in the Pacific. As global economics drag global politics, this also drives the United States in our view of where our relationships have to be. On India's side, the gathering enthusiasm about the growth and the pace means that she will need markets, technology, and finance, and the United States will be a very powerful source for these. India will keep a weather eye as well, again requiring a degree of political understanding with the United States. Again, I appear before you tonight optimistic about the relationship.

We know how to work together to save an institution that I believe is important—the World Trade Organization and the current Doha trade round. I think we can reach and take ourselves beyond the ordinary, but we are going to have to be careful and we are going to have to be patient. We are going to have to be careful with each other. We have found it easier so far to declare the Indian-American relationship as strategic, but I am not quite certain our populations and intellectuals on both sides have quite figured out what that means. We, the United States, find it hard to move forward on energy; given today that our predicaments around the world mire American diplomacy and reduce the amount of time our leaders have to think through fresh choices, to look to the edge of the horizon. Until the United States has worked its way through its Iraqi dilemma, we will remain so mired. On the Indian side, I think it is also fair to note that India has deep principles, India has interests, but has India yet worked through, in her own mind, her strategic road map, where she wants to go? Her policies to date tend to be more reflexive, waiting for the events to take place or taking leads from others. And so, it will take us a while longer; but, if we are careful, we will figure out how to do it, and this relationship will be one of those that will define where our two countries proceed, and the world's stability will be maintained through much of this century.

Jagdish Bhagwati Comments on Indo-U.S. Relations

I think there is a certain maturity in the way the two countries look at each other and handle each other. For example, when the nuclear test happened, I remember two particular instances. One, when President Clinton wrote about the sanctions to the government of India, he basically said that my wife Hillary loved India, my daughter Chelsea loved India, unfortunately I have to impose these sanctions. There was nothing of fire and brimstone about it. And the Indian government also took it in stride. It was extremely amiable. It did what it wanted to and it did not really confront. I remember Ambassador Sen's predecessor, Naresh Chandra, on the Jim Lehrer News Hour. He was asked why he didn't notify us that they were going to test them ahead of time. Instead of saying, oh you have so many nuclear weapons on your end and so on and so on—instead, he answered that that is not the sort of thing you expect us to pick up the phone and tell the State Department about, that we are about to explode a devise—and the interviewer burst out laughing. I think there was a certain maturity in the way that inevitable differences over the issue were being handled. I think, clearly the fact that India is democratic is clearly a great asset. When India and China were in competition for the world's attention, before the 1962 border invasion, at that time President Kennedy had no hesitation about sending out his support.

The sort of patience that India has shown in the past is something that we Indians have given up on. Now we are anxious for change; we want to move ahead. And the Americans now see the value of democracy a little more clearly, as in the old days, and democracy requires patience. You cannot immediately make decisions and so on. You have to negotiate minefields and carry your public opinion. I think that is another way in which the two countries are converging in their mutual understanding of how to deal with each other. So I am very optimistic.

Arun Shourie Comments on Indo-U.S. Relations

We have had two very wise presentations. Both ambassadors have enumerated several factors on account of which our relations are much better than they were before. However, being diplomats, they have not mentioned two or three other factors. I feel, for instance, that there are second thoughts about China. Earlier, during President Clinton's time, it was only seen as an opportunity, but today it is seen as an opportunity but also as a swelling challenge. Secondly, terrorism, in particular, Islamic terrorism, and what terrorism in general could do in the Malacca Straits. Forty-five percent of oil passes through these six choke points; India and the United States are collaborating for continuing protection of these straits. All these things are reasons for continued collaboration in that context.

I will just mention three things I think are important for the future. The first thing to bear in mind is that each side will pursue its own interest. Second, that it will pursue its own interest as perceived by a handful. Third, that it will pursue its own interest as perceived by a handful at that moment. This is not often realized. Let's assume that the United States correctly perceived its own interest to help arm and train the Taliban against the Soviet Union. Today it perceives its interest to be different. But we have to live with the consequences.

Similarly, as Professor Wisner reminded us, India went in for nuclear tests because it was the consistent position of the Indian government over a length of time. Your assessment was right that, at times, American interests were that, we have to stop this, this is a potential nuisance; and then, at other times, we were wrong and we should not try to contain. It is also important, as Professor Wisner also mentioned, that neither side can disregard domestic opinion. I was for one and a half years the principal negotiator on India's behalf at the WTO negotiations. Even a strong advocate like Mr. Robert Zoellick said frankly that he cannot disregard the interests of the American pharmaceutical industry. Well then, my response is, do you expect me to disregard the interests of the Indian pharmaceutical industry? As Oscar Wilde said, each of us has the courage to bear the other person's difficulties. You want us to open agricultural trade, but you will not reduce your own cotton subsidies. We have to recognize that nobody can disregard his own domestic reactions. Therefore, one of the wisest points of Ambassador Sen is that we must have multidimensional? contacts at many levels, from cargo planes to open-skies to academic institutions. Second, it is very necessary to explain incessantly. We don't do that enough in society. Third, as far possible not to let an issue become an India-versus-U.S. issue or a U.S.-government-versus-Indian-government issue. I remember when eighteen states passed legislation against outsourcing and Mr. John Kerry made strident statements. To his great credit, President Bush did not go along with that in spite of the election that he faced. Everyone in India was saying, you have to react, the government of India must react; but actually, that was not the right thing. The best course of action was nonresponse by the governments, which is what actually happened. American firms that had been benefiting from outsourcing were the ones that should speak up, not to make it a government-to-government or country-versus-country issue.

The third point that I would like to end on is about this nuclear deal. The third rule is, do not make any issue the be all and end all of a relationship. I remember Ambassador Wisner was very much a part of that delicate moment when the Dabhol power project had run into difficulties. Many of us who had seen the agreement had foreseen and pleaded not go in for this, because it will bankrupt the Maharashtra electricity board. That is what happened. The project closed. And you will remember how difficult it was to resume any dialogue on the matter. It was all, what was done was done, and Indo-U.S. relations suffered. Now I fear the same thing is happening with this civilian nuclear deal. Ambassador Sen said that this is a civil nuclear cooperation. Mr. Wisner has advised all of you to write to your congressperson. But actually, if you read those bills, they are actually not about civil nuclear cooperation at all. The declared object of both the bills of the House and the Senate is clear in terms to halt, hold back, roll back and eliminate India's nuclear development program. I can quote you the sections right now, this kind of inspection, that kind of inspection. These are much more intrusive protocols than those of the IAEA. Now you will make that the test of India-U.S. relations. To the great credit of the Indian prime minister, many of the things that were being done on behalf of the Indian population, heeding public opinion, heeding what all of us have said and documented on the floor of the Indian parliament, Dr. Manmohan Singh has brought together in an extensive statement. He has drawn what we call the *X line*, the line beyond which India cannot go. He did it to his great credit, knowing and accepting that what we were saying was going to be a deal breaker. Yet he laid down the law on each of those nine points which each of us had pinpointed. Now, if in a compromise meeting of the Senate and the House, each of those provisions are changed within the ambit of the Prime Minister, wonderful. But if you feel that now this India nuclear security issue is going to be used for other purposes, in India we will eventually have constraints on our options as a result. It will become more and more evident as years pass of the consequences and challenges of this if you have made this the central piece of Indo-U.S. relations. It will become once again the occasion for souring the relationship and will again require the intervention of such experienced diplomats as Ambassadors Sen and Wisner swooping in. In conclusion, please realize that each country will act on its own interest. The way the positions have now been defined, by the Indian prime minister and specific provisions of the bill, are incompatible. Mr. Wisner feels that it will go through and you are optimistic because you know the Senate and House better than I do. I personally tell you and such an experienced diplomat as Ronen Sen can tell you, that the Indian prime minister will not be able to dilute what he has said on the floor of the House as to his commitment on all those nine points, which are completely contradictory. So, my advice is, do not constrain the options of each other. We do not know how circumstances will be twenty years from now. We do know that we are not going to be able to constrain China. We have to live with China as a next-door neighbor. My advice is, don't make this the test, and don't write to your congressperson. If you write to your congressperson, ask him or her to read the statement of the Indian prime minister and modify the bill accordingly.

CHAPTER 6

India: An Emerging Giant

Keynote Speech by Kamal Nath, Minister of Commerce and Industry, India

It is an honor and a privilege to be in a program with Professors Bhagwati and Panagariya and such eminent people here. For the last two days, or at least today, what's been discussed is the India story. And when we talk about the India story I'm reminded of what Albert Camus once said—that great works are often born on a street corner or in a restaurant's revolving door. All good things have a ridiculous beginning. Well, fifteen years ago India embarked on reforms, and as though to prove Camus right, our reform journey started on a rather inauspicious note. In 1991 India loaded part of its gold bullion on a plane and sent it to London as mortgage to pay for its imports. So, much of India's reforms were not by design, but by default; and the challenge was to determine what kinds of reforms India should have. Today, when we talk of numbers, I recall my visit to New York and Washington in 1993, when three or four of us ministers traveled the world trying to tell everybody that India had changed. And I remember that the big firms, like Goldman Sachs, had a luncheon program to talk about India, and one of the participants remarked that he'd heard people talk about tigers and elephants from India, but he was shocked to hear about the Indian reform process.

There was some skepticism about India, which had a low growth rate and everything going wrong. The challenge before us at that time was choosing which reform process India should adopt. We had the South American model, we had the Central American model, and we had the models of some Asian countries to examine; but the complexity and the paradox that is India meant that we needed a new model. We needed to earn political consensus because in a democracy only a political consensus can sustain a reform process. That is the crucial thing. And I think that the success of our economic policies spells the success of our political policies, despite all the political colors and alliances. What have we seen in the last fifteen years? Six governments and five prime ministers, but one direction—approximately 8 percent growth, year after year. One economic policy. And I think that is the greatest thing that has happened.

Today, much has to be studied about India, and as Harvard President Lawrence Summers said, people are now studying India as a subject. I think it is one of the most exciting stories of the 21st century. What is the before and after? And what are the most visible indicators of India's success story?

Let me give you some very simple numbers. In 2005, the number of knowledge workers in the software industry had increased by more than seventeen times compared to 1992. In 2006, twice the number of people within India traveled by air compared to 2003. We see an India today railways and airlines competing with each other. I think it is one of the only countries in the world where this is happening. Never did we ever think that we would have the railways and the airlines competing with each other. Our television markets, which were worth only a half billion dollars in 2004, are now worth over three billion. With respect to passenger cars, India is the fastest growing market in the world. With respect to telecommunications, we have six million new phones in a month, but we also have 30,000 villages that have never heard the ring of a phone line. That is the great paradox of India. What else do we see happening: the emergence of mega cities. India used to be known only for its four metropolitan cities, but today other cities, like Bangalore, are on the rise. These are going to be the great cities of the next decade.

What is the most visible change that has taken place? India has moved away from state-driven growth toward private-sector growth. After being shackled for decades, India's class of talented private entrepreneurs have really been allowed to spread their wings. After some flutters in the 1990s, I think they are now showing their true worth. Many indigenous start-ups are becoming global successes. And the most important thing that is happening is the change in mindset. It is not merely that the world's perception about India is changing; our own perception about ourselves is changing. Over a period of fifteen years, more and more Indians have grown to believe that it is now within our grasp to have better prospects. India is a country where we believe that problems in life are God-ordained, but there is now a belief that there is another life. We now wish for a better life for ourselves, where we used to wish for a better life for our children and grandchildren. That is the big change that is taking place: our own perception about ourselves that in our own lifetime there is going to be a better life.

Of course we have our share of inefficiency and corruption, but the optimism lies in the growing intolerance for laziness, for shoddy products, for open corruption, for carelessness, and for the usual excuses. The point I am trying to make is about the great intangible changes that are taking place. You have seen all the figures, but intangible changes are not reflected in the figures. There is the emergence of a massive middle class. Twenty-five million people are coming into the middle class every year, and I believe that India's demographics will build a new economic architecture of the world in the 21st century.

Now having said this, many times I am asked: This is all very well, but which is the bubble that can burst, what can go wrong? I want to tell you about the challenges. One of the challenges is to have all-inclusive growth. And when I talk of this all-inclusive growth, the biggest challenge is in manufacturing. Manufacturing is just 17 percent of the economy in India, when even Malaysia has about 28 percent. The first thing we did when we came into government was set up the National Manufacturing Competitiveness Council. Why did we do that? We have to move away from our unsustainable agriculture. Six hundred and fifty million people work in agriculture, an industry that is not commercial, but rather subsistence, and often on one or one and a half acres of land.

That's where I come from. Twenty-six years of my life I spent representing a district where the challenges are like this. To move forward and sustain growth, the simple answer is manufacturing. I am happy to tell you that our manufacturing growth now is in double digits. There was a time in 1991 and years after that when our strategy focused on dollar-generating exports in trade and other areas. Now we look at employment-generating exports. We did a study on what employment is generated by our exports, and which area we should focus on for employment generation. When I say that the challenge is all-inclusive growth, I mean that if growth and development does not touch the lives of millions, if it is urban centric, then democracy and growth cannot be sustained.

When I go back to the people in 2009 for the next elections, they will ask an obvious question: Well okay, you went to New York, you went to Columbia, but what does it do for us? You went to Geneva, you talked to the WTO, but what does it do for us? And unless I have an answer for that, unless I have it, and all those who take part in the electoral process have it, the people are not going to accept us. Now aspirations have changed in India, and they are high. The biggest challenge we face in terms of all-inclusive growth is how to increase our manufacturing. The government of India today is focused entirely on this; whether it's in our textile sector, whether it's leather, whether it's in gems and jewelry, whether it's in our engineering exports.

As for services, India has made its place in services, especially in the IT sector. But even in the IT sector, we are moving away from BPOs (business process outsourcing). India is now entering the phase of the EPOs, or engineering processing outsourcing, and the KPOs, or knowledge process outsourcing. India is moving up the value chain in global competitiveness, but how does India become a manufacturing hub? Sometimes it is said that China is the factory of the world and India is the back office. I think that compliment is very back-handed, because China is a large manufacturing center and India has to become a large manufacturing center. Surely China has its own genius in mass manufacturing. But what is the kind of manufacturing that we are looking at? Today, all automation is software-embedded. Today, great synergies are apparent in many sectors, especially in pharmaceuticals, biotech, IT, and medicine. And these are the areas that we feel are going to be our success stories in the next ten years.

Until we are able to move 100 million people from agriculture into manufacturing we will not be able to make it. It is by moving 100 million people from the agriculture sector in the next decade or two that we will see a change. And I was recently asked about the disparity between rich and poor in India, which is on the rise. When I say that 25 million people are coming to the middle class, obviously those 25 million people are not coming only from urban India, they are coming from rural India also. That's a shift taking place, but is that enough? Suddenly that is not enough. And this lag in middle class growth is the biggest risk I see.

We must ask; why has there been this lag in middle class growth? Which is to say, why is there not more investment in the manufacturing sector that would generate all-inclusive growth? Certainly a major impediment has been India's labor laws. In the past, India's labor laws were based on employment protection; in no way did they serve employment generation. Now, however, they have created a competitive atmosphere between Indian states. I have governors from various U.S. states coming to Indian states looking for greater economic engagement. In India, ten years ago, this process of investment and trade was left to the Indian federal government. Our states had nothing to do with this; they looked at social issues only.

Today, we have delegations from Indian states going to New York, looking for investments in their state. Given this competitive atmosphere, one of the areas on which states must act is labor laws. At least six state governments have approached the federal government to relax their labor laws. Some part of the labor reform deals with restructuring the laws for employment protection, not for employment generation. But now the state governments are moving forward, and the federal government is going to allow states to do what they want in certain designated areas. I believe this is going to happen.

When we came into government, I thought we must have a law that attracts investment for export-oriented units. I drafted it and put it on the Internet for comments, for eight months. I asked a large number of investors, "would you bite this, if this were the law?" I spoke to manufacturers and asked, "Does this make sense?" We passed the law with complete unanimity. Nobody said it was bad. In the last two months people started asking, why do we have these? The competitive attitude of states also began to surface. We found two or three states that had everybody running there. In contrast, there were other states where no one was going, who said, "this is not fair. Why isn't anybody coming to us?"

It is up to the states to attract their own investors. I cannot drive anybody there; I cannot legislate that they must go somewhere. I would love for everybody to come to my home state, but the sad part is that no one is going there. Why? Because there is no infrastructure. I do not even have a broad-gauge railway line. It would cost $300 million, but I am going to have it, it will be built. So when I tell them that I am going to build this line, they say, "okay, build it and then we'll talk about it."

Foreign direct investment (FDI) is a force in the wheel that is moving the economy at 8.5 percent, along with manufacturing growth, exports, and domestic investment. This year I believe FDI inflow will be $12 billion. Our cumulative inflow in India of FDI since 1991 is $50 billion. How much more do we need? On a fortnightly basis I do a check on what FDI is coming in, and we have had a 49 percent growth in the last year, and a 200 percent growth last month compared to the previous period last year. Of the total, 70 percent of FDI is in the manufacturing sector. There is FDI that is replacing capital, but also FDI that is greenfield, FDI in the manufacturing sector, and I look forward to a figure of about $20 billion from next year onward. 80–90 percent of FDI is "first mile" FDI. By the first mile of investment, you know what's coming ahead to complete it.

We allow 100 percent FDI in the construction sector. This is employment generation of non-skilled labor. And most of all, it goes without saying that our infrastructure sector allows 100 percent foreign ownership, and also has tax benefits to go along with it.

An important element in promoting foreign investment is the creation of special economic zones (SEZs). As many of you know, this issue has been controversial, and has in fact received a great deal criticism from certain quarters. Some asked why investors should go to places where there is good agricultural land. We responded, of course they should not go to where there is good agricultural land. They should go to where there are wastelands. We should not be diverting agricultural land. Then commentators debated how many special economic zones we should have, and how large they should be. In China they have 150 square kilometers, but in India we have to do things the India-specific way. Where do I find 150 square kilometers of property in India? We have forest lands, we have our village lands; there is no such contiguous land. In the Indian context it cannot work.

Let us look at the scenario as it is. There are now eighteen existing special economic zones. What's happening there? They have exports of roughly $5 billion. They employ close to 150,000 people. So when somebody says the zones will not work, I say they are working. Just the other day I was challenged on this, but in India I respond by asking: have you been to an SEZ? Have you read the act? Have you read the rules? If you've done none of these three, well then why are you asking me the question?

I was asked how India engages with the global economy. A couple of years ago our engagement with the global economy was only $60 or $70 billion. We will now engage with the global economy to the extent of $500 billion in one and a half years. We are almost touching $400 billion now. What does that mean for India? And what does that mean for us in terms of engaging with the multilateral system? When we had the first round, the Uruguay Round of the WTO, India was not engaged. We were not engaged in the way we should have been engaged, but most countries were not, nobody knew. Not many countries knew we did not have civil societies and that we did not have NGOs. We did not have so much as the Internet. Today whatever we discuss in the WTO, by the time I get back to Delhi we have people who have done all kinds of research and calculations on those topics already. India, of course, does pay close attention to international issues because we have a great stake in the multilateral system, and because we are becoming more and more globally competitive.

It is not only India that is becoming more and more globally competitive. There are more than a hundred countries in the world that want to remain engaged in framing the rules of global trade. But to move forward on this we obviously need to correct one of the structural flaws. Why? That is what this round is all about. We had the Uruguay Round first, followed by the Doha Round, which is the development round. Sometimes people ask what we mean by development, and I think that the most important thing discussed in the development round is correcting structural flaws. It is here that there is a disappointing impasse, but I would like to see the two great and strongest economies, the EU and the United States, converge. It is very important for the EU and the United States to converge so that developing countries can also move forward and play their role. But it is important that we do not perpetuate in this, the structural flaws, whether they are in agriculture, whether they are in industrial goods, or even services. While we sometimes condemn the subsidies in industry, we do not condemn them in agriculture. Sometimes we talk about ad valorem duties on industrial goods, but we do not talk about ad valorem duties in agriculture. We talk of flows of merchandise trade and not enough of capital flows, but the most important thing is that the rule-based multilateral system must move forward. India remains totally committed to ensuring that and playing whatever role it can toward its success.

I am sometimes accused of being obstructionist, though I don't know why. Because though the completion of the round is very important, the content of this round is as important. Now what should the content be? Should the content be perpetuation of the structural flaws, which are not sustainable? I don't think agricultural subsidies are the answer. You have the common agricultural program in the European Union; you have the farm bill in the United States. Anyone from the Treasury in the United States could tell you how much it costs and what economic sense it makes.

I was just telling them that as a receiver, it is great for me. Look at U.S. cotton. We import $500 million in U.S. cotton, which has a subsidy of 42 percent, and we convert it to yarn and fabric and sell those textiles to the United States. But then there are the African countries who ask me, why don't you buy our cotton? And I tell them that I can't buy their cotton because the United States is so much cheaper and we get better credits from the United States. So for them it is not fair trade.

Now if there is a flip side, it is that these subsidies "distort" or create artificiality in agricultural prices. The European Union has the most unsustainable prices of sugar, and the distortions are created from the subsidies. The inability of developing countries to pay subsidies makes a difference. I can compete with the U.S. farmer, but the Indian farmer cannot compete with the U.S. Treasury. If we are going to destabilize subsistence farmers in India, it will not be sustainable, so there has to be a convergence on this, between the United States and Europe—and I am looking forward to that. In October 2006 in the EU Summit, I asked the EU, "Why don't you go to the United States, sit down with them and arrive at convergence?" Once the United States and EU have converged, I think there will be movement forward.

India's cooperation will not be lacking, because we have a great stake in the multilateral system. The next ten years will not be about tariffs but about the global trading system, and that is what all countries are concerned about. So I believe that once this happens we will move forward where industrial goods are concerned. In India, our applied tariffs on U.S. imports are low. Leaving aside wines and spirits, textiles, and automobiles, tariffs are low; the issue will be on services. Of course the United States wants further liberalization on services. We will try to move forward, but we have certain demands.

Our demands on liberalization in the United States are perceived as immigration. We understand that immigration is sensitive—we needn't be told that. So I look at the United States only on the nonimmigration aspects of services. Let's be practical. India and the United States chaired the WTO group on services, and we will find convergence there. And I wonder why there is this impression that India, or I, was obstructionist. The intention is to see that there is convergence, but by India accepting something, convergence does not happen. The WTO is not a treaty; the WTO is a contractual agreement between states. So you are going to have the major players, the Africa group, the Caribbean, Southeast Asia, and East Asian countries agree on these things, and when India sits on the G6, I represent many other countries. They have to accept it, too. But I am confident that this is going to happen.

Where comparisons sometimes are made between India and China, I only want to say this: that India and China have their own genius. Sometimes I am told that India's infrastructure is bad. Yes, of course India's infrastructure is disappointing, but it is not only a problem, it is also an opportunity. We must recognize that in the last fifteen years, an important difference between India and China is that in India our investment was in rural employment generation and in building up our rural infrastructure. I come from a poor district with one million people living on less than one dollar a day. It took twenty-six years of my life to extricate 400,000 or 450,000 people from living below one dollar a day, and that could happen only because of the investments which were made in rural India. So India's pattern was in creating rural employment and rural infrastructure, and all the programs of India were directed toward rural employment generation programs. On the other hand China's investment was in the urban sector, and their great urban employment generation programs, which were very successful. That's why you see a lot of urban pressure in China. In India, there is urban pressure, but it is not that substantial.

Another point on which we all need to reflect is that while China's foreign direct investment is ten times greater than India's, with four times more exports, China's and India's growth rates are similar. Some economists have said that this represents more efficient capital usage in India, because India has maintained its growth figures with a much lower FDI flow and much less exports. But, again, India's difference with China is that India's growth pattern is domestic demand–driven, whereas China's is export market–driven. I do not know whether a study on this has been done, but India today remains an unbeatable combination of an ancient civilization embracing economic globalization in a context that is open and democratic, and that is what really makes India the emerging giant that it has become.

Of the challenges we have before us, both economic and political, the biggest is employment generation. India is a young country with 60 percent of our population under twenty-five years old, and some figures say that India is becoming even younger. Therefore, the challenge that India has is different from the challenges of most developed countries, which have large aging populations. How does India continue with a politically workable transformation, when we call ourselves the fastest-growing free-market economy in the world?

Sometimes I'm told that our reforms are not fast enough. I was told in 1993 that our reforms would never work. But we have reached political consensus and have succeeded. Even in the last two years, the reform process that we have worked on, whether in intellectual property or the liberalization of our FDI regulatory framework, has succeeded. Of course there is much more to do, but in India today, the biggest changes are a change of perception and a change in government. Today, in government, there is a consciousness as never before, a consciousness of the expectations of the people of India and of the expectations of the world toward India, to which India must respond.

CONTRIBUTORS

Ashish Arora is professor of economics and public policy at the Heinz School of Public Policy and Management, Carnegie Mellon University. He served as codirector of the Software Industry Center at Carnegie Mellon until 2006. Arora sits on the editorial board of six academic journals, and has served on a number of committees for bodies such as the National Academy of Sciences and the Association of Computing Machinery. His research focuses on the economics of technology and technical change, and he has studied technology-intensive industries such as software, biotechnology, and chemicals; the role of patents and licensing in promoting technology start-ups; and the economics of information technology. His most recent book (edited with Alfonso Gambardella) is *From Underdogs to Tigers? The Rise and Growth of the Software Industry in Brazil, China, India, Ireland, and Israel* (Oxford, 2005).

Jagdish Bhagwati is Arthur Lehman Professor of Economics and a Professor of Political Science at Columbia University. A prolific researcher, Bhagwati has published more than 300 articles and 40 volumes, while also writing extensively in leading newspapers and magazines. Widely regarded as the preeminent international trade economist today, Bhagwati has also made contributions to public finance, immigration, and the new theory of political economy. His works include *Protectionism* (MIT, 1988) and *A Stream of Windows: Unsettling Reflections on Trade, Immigration and Democracy* (MIT, 1998). His book *India: Planning for Industrialization* (Oxford, 1970), coauthored with Columbia economics professor Padma Desai, provided the intellectual case for the economic reforms now under way in India. He has received several awards, including the

Freedom Prize (Switzerland) and the Seidman Distinguished Award in Political Economy (United States).

Barry Bosworth has been senior fellow in the Economic Studies Program, Robert V. Roosa Chair in International Economics, at the Brookings Institution in Washington, D.C., since 1979. His research has involved work on the determinants of economic growth in developing countries, saving, capital formation, and productivity growth. In addition, his current projects include a study of the economic consequences of population aging, productivity growth in U.S. services-producing industries, and a study of policies to promote economic growth in Puerto Rico. Recent publications include *Productivity in the U.S. Services Sector: New Sources of Economic Growth* (with Jack Triplett; Brookings, 2004); "The Empirics of Growth: An Update," *Brookings Papers on Economic Activity* 2:2003 (with Susan Collins); "Increased Life Expectancy: A Global Perspective" (with Benjamin Keys), in Henry Aaron and William Schwartz (eds.), *Coping With Methuselah* (Brookings, 2003); and *Aging Societies: the Global Dimension* (Brookings, 1998). He has coedited, with Gary Burtless, *Coming Together? Mexico-U.S. Relations* (Brookings, 1997); and, with Susan M. Collins and Nora Lustig, "Valuing the Renminbi," *Tokyo Club Papers, 2004*.

Charles W. Calomiris is Henry Kaufman Professor of Financial Institutions at Columbia Business School and a professor at Columbia University's School of International and Public Affairs. Professor Calomiris codirects the Project on Financial Deregulation at the American Enterprise Institute. He is a member of the Shadow Financial Regulatory Committee, is a Research Associate of the National Bureau of Economic Research, and was a Senior Fellow at the Council on Foreign Relations. Calomiris served on the International Financial Institution Advisory Commission, a Congressional commission to advise the U.S. government on the reform of the IMF, the World Bank, the regional development banks, and the WTO. His most recent publication is the edited volume *China's Financial Transition at a Crossroads.*

Mihir A. Desai is Rock Center Associate Professor of Finance and Entrepreneurial Management and the MBA Class of 1961 Fellow at Harvard Business School. Desai's research focuses on international corporate and public finance. Within international corporate finance, he has investigated how the globalization of firms provides a laboratory for financial decision making and how multinational firms make critical investment and financing decisions. Within public finance, his research has emphasized the effects of taxation on the export, financing, organizational form, and investment decisions of firms facing multiple tax regimes. His research has also developed the links between capital taxation and corporate governance, the real consequences of earnings manipulation, and the policy options for countries facing losses of talent. Desai is a faculty research fellow in the National Bureau of Economic Research's (NBER's) Public Economics and Corporate Finance Programs, is the codirector of the NBER's India program, and his research has been cited in *The Economist*, *BusinessWeek*, *The New York Times*, and other noted publications. His academic publications have appeared in leading economics and finance journals, and he is the author of *International Finance: A Casebook* (Wiley, 2006), which features his many case studies on international corporate finance. In 1994, he was a Fulbright Scholar to India. His professional experiences include working at CS First Boston, McKinsey & Co., and advising a number of firms and governmental organizations.

Frank Levy is a Daniel Rose Professor of Urban Economics in the MIT Department of Urban Studies and Planning. His research examines the ways that computer technology and offshoring are reshaping opportunities in the labor market. He has written numerous papers on the impact of computers on worker skills and has published, with Richard Murnane, *The New Division of Labor: How Computers are Creating the Next Job Market* (Princeton, 2005). Also, he has done research on U.S. income inequality, living standards, and the economics of education. *The New Dollars and Dreams* (Russell Sage, 1999) recounts the history of U.S. incomes and income distribution from the close of World War II to the present. *Teaching the New Basic Skills*, with Richard Murnane (Free Press, 1996), examines the growing mismatch between what K–12 schools teach and what employers require and presents case studies of schools that have worked to close the gap.

Kamal Nath is Minister for Commerce and Industry (India) with cabinet rank. He is a member of the Congress Party, which leads India's current United Progressive Alliance (UPA) government. Nath took over as Union Minister of Commerce and Industry in May 2004. In that capacity he leads the Indian delegation to the Doha Round, where India has emerged as one of the six key players that include the United States, the

European Union, Brazil, Japan, and Australia. Mr. Nath has played an important role in advancing developing-country interests through his leadership role in the developing-country grouping G-20. Under his leadership, India played an active and constructive role in the conclusion of the WTO Framework Agreement of July 2004 and hosted the G-20 meeting in New Delhi consolidating the G-20 alliance. Nath's tenure as the Commerce and Industry Minister has witnessed major trade policy initiatives. For the first time, a comprehensive Foreign Trade Policy (2004–09) has been announced laying out a coherent roadmap with a twin focus on exports as well as employment. Major bilateral trade initiatives have been taken with countries like China and Pakistan and there has been significant progress in the area of regional trade agreements. In the past, Nath has served with distinction as the Minister of Environment and Forests and as the Minister for Textiles. He has a keen interest in welfare issues, particularly tribal upliftment and rural development. He is also President of the Board of Governors of the Institute of Management Technology, Ghaziabad; Chairman of the Madhya Pradesh Child Development Council; and Patron of Bharat Yuvak Samaj.

Arvind Panagariya is Jagdish Bhagwati Professor of Indian Political Economy in the Department of International and Public Affairs and of Economics at Columbia University. He has advised the World Bank, IMF, WTO, and UNCTAD in various capacities. Panagariya has written or edited more than a half dozen books, including *The Economics of Preferential Trade Agreements*, with Jagdish Bhagwati (AEI, 1996); *The Global Trading System and Developing Asia*, with M. G. Quibria and N. Rao (Oxford, 1997); and *Lectures on International Trade*, with J. Bhagwati and T. N. Srinivasan (MIT, 1998). Panagariya is the founding editor of the *Journal of Policy Reform*, which he edited with Dani Rodrik from 1996 to 2001. His technical papers have appeared in the *American Economic Review*, *Quarterly Journal of Economics*, and *Review of Economic Studies*. Panagariya writes a monthly column in the *Economic Times*, India's top financial daily. He has also written guest columns in the *Financial Times*, *Wall Street Journal*, *India Today*, and *Outlook*. He has appeared on the Jim Lehrer Newshour (United States), CNN (Asia), CNBC (Asia), CNBC (India), Reuters TV (Asia), Bloomberg TV (Asia), NDTV (India), Aaj Tak (India), Doordarshan (National-India), Chicago Public Radio, Minnesota Public Radio, and BBC Radio.

M. Govinda Rao is director of the National Institute of Public Finance and Policy in New Delhi, India. He is a member of the Economic Advisory Council to the Prime Minister. His past positions include director of the Institute for Social and Economic Change in Bangalore (1998–2002) and fellow in the Research School of Pacific and Asian Studies at Australian National University (1995–98). Rao has a number of additional advisory roles. These include member of the International Advisory Panel on Governance, chairman of the UNDP regional office, chairman of the Expert Group on Taxation of Services, and chairman of the Technical Experts Committee on Value-Added Tax. Rao's research interests include public finance, fiscal policy, fiscal federalism, and state and local finance. He has published technical articles in a number of journals besides twelve books and monographs on various aspects of public finance. His recent books include *Political Economy of Federalism in India* (Oxford, 2005); *Sustainable Fiscal Policy for India: An International Perspective,* edited with Peter Heller (Oxford, 2005); and *Poverty, Development and Fiscal Policy* (Oxford, 2002).

Ronen Sen has been Ambassador of India to the United States since August 2004. Prior to this position, he served as India's ambassador to Mexico (September 1991 to August 1992), to the Russian Federation (October 1992 to October 1998), and to Germany (October 1998 to May 2002), and as High Commissioner to the United Kingdom (May 2002 to April 2004). Sen participated in summit meetings in the United Nations, Commonwealth, Non-Aligned Movement, Six Nation Five Continent Peace Initiative, South Asian Association for Regional Cooperation, IAEA, G-15 and other forums and also in over 160 bilateral summit meetings. He held several assignments as Special Envoy of the Prime Minister of India for meetings with heads of state.

Arun Shourie is a Member of Parliament and belongs to the Bharatiya Janata Party. He held the offices of Minister of Disinvestment and Minister of Communication and Information Technology in the Atal Bihari Vajpayee cabinet. As disinvestment minister he led the sale of several public-sector companies, including Maruti, VSNL, BALCO, the Computer Maintenance Corporation (CMC), and Hindustan Zinc. In a poll of India's top one hundred CEOs in February 2004, Shourie was ranked the most outstanding minister of the Vajpayee government. He is an acclaimed author and journalist. ASA Publications recently published his twentieth book, *Falling Over Backwards: An Essay Against Reservations and Against Judicial Activism* (2006). His previous book, *Governance* (Rupa, 2004), has been described as essential reading for those interested in India. Shourie has won many national and international awards including Padma Bhushan, the Magsaysay Award, the Dadabhai Naoroji Award, the Astor Award, the K.S. Hegde Award, and the International Editor of the Year Award. The Federation of Indian Publishers conferred the Freedom to Publish Award on him. To mark its fiftieth anniversary, the International Press Institute, Vienna, honored Shourie as one of fifty "World Press Freedom Heroes" whose work over the previous half century has helped sustain press freedom across the world.

T. N. Srinivasan is Samuel C. Park, Jr. Professor of Economics at Yale University. Formerly a professor, and later a research professor, at the Indian Statistical Institute, Delhi (1964–1977), he has taught at numerous universities in the United States. His research interests include international trade, development, agricultural economics and microeconomic theory. Srinivasan recently authored, with Jessica Wallack, *Federalism and Economic Reform: International Perspectives* (Cambridge, 2006); as well as, with Suresh Tendulkar, *Reintegrating India with the World Economy* (Institute for International Economics, 2003). He edited, with Timothy Kehoe and John Whalley, *Frontiers in Applied General Equilibrium Modeling: Essays in Honor of Herbert Scarf* (Cambridge, 2005), and was editor of *Trade, Finance and Investment in South Asia* (Social Science Press, 2001). He is also the author of *Developing Countries and the Multilateral Trading System* (Westview Press, 1998).

Frank G. Wisner is Vice Chairman, External Affairs, of American International Group (AIG), the leading U.S.-based international insurance organization. Prior to joining AIG, he was the U.S. ambassador to India from July 1994 through July 1997. He retired from the U.S. government with the rank of career ambassador, the highest grade in the Foreign Service. Wisner joined the State Department as a Foreign Service officer in 1961 and served in a variety of overseas and Washington positions during his thirty-six-year career. Among his other positions, Wisner served successively as U.S. ambassador to Zambia, Egypt, and the Philippines. Before being named U.S. ambassador to India, his most recent assignment was as

Under Secretary of Defense for Policy. Prior to that position he was Under Secretary of State for International Security Affairs.

Jessica Seddon Wallack is assistant professor of political economy at the School of International Relations and Pacific Studies (IR/PS), University of California—San Diego. Her research and teaching focuses on the factors that create successful interaction between entrepreneurs, NGOs, corporations, and governments in creating and implementing public policy. Wallack's current academic projects include work on the politics and economics of private participation in India's infrastructure development and the effect of federalism on economic reform and investment risk. In addition to a variety of articles in scholarly journals, Wallack recently published, with T. N. Srinivasan, the book *Federalism and Economic Reform* (Cambridge, 2006). She is working on a second book based on her research on India's infrastructure markets. Prior to coming to IR/PS, Wallack held consulting positions at the World Bank, Inter-American Development Bank, and Asian Development Bank. She also serves on the advisory board of the Wilderhill Global Energy Innovation Index.

Frank Wolak is professor of economics at Stanford University. His fields of research are industrial organization and empirical economic analysis. He specializes in the study of privatization, competition, and regulation in network industries such as electricity, telecommunications, water supply, natural gas, and postal delivery services. He is the author of numerous academic articles on these topics. He has studied the design and performance of the competitive electricity markets internationally and domestically. He has also worked on the restructuring and privatization process in network industries around the world. Wolak is a research associate of the National Bureau of Economic Research (NBER) and an associate of the University of California Energy Institute in Berkeley. He has served as a consultant to the California and U.S. Departments of Justice on market power issues in the telecommunications, electricity, and natural gas markets. He has also served as a consultant to the Federal Communications Commission and the Postal Rate Commission on issues relating to competition in network industries. He is the chairman of the Market Surveillance Committee for the Independent System Operator of the California Electricity Supply Industry.

Index

[Note: Page numbers followed by *f* or *t* indicate figures and tables.]